CONSTITUTIONS IN A NONCONSTITUTIONAL WORLD

SUNY series in Middle Eastern Studies
Edited by Shahrough Akhavi

and

SUNY series in Near Eastern Studies
Edited by Said Amir Arjomand

CONSTITUTIONS IN A
NONCONSTITUTIONAL WORLD

*Arab Basic Laws and the
Prospects for Accountable Government*

Nathan J. Brown

STATE UNIVERSITY OF NEW YORK PRESS

Published by
State University of New York Press, Albany

Printed in the United States of America

For information, address State University of New York Press,
90 State Street, Suite 700, Albany, NY 12207

Cover photo: Reproduced courtesy of the Kuwait Information Office.

Library of Congress Cataloging in Publication Data

Brown, Nathan J.
    Constitutions in a nonconstitutional world : Arab basic laws and the prospects for
accountable government / Nathan J. Brown.
    p. cm. — (SUNY series in Middle Eastern studies) (SUNY series in Near Eastern
studies)
    Includes bibliographical references and index.
    ISBN 0-7914-5157-7 (alk. paper) — ISBN 0-7914-5158-5 (pbk. : alk. paper)
    1. Constitutional law—Arab countries. I. Title. II. Series. III. SUNY series in Middle
Eastern studies.

KMC524 .B76 2001
342'.02'09174927—dc21

                                                                00-054790

10   9   8   7   6   5   4   3   2   1

To Aaron and Ruby Kohn

CONTENTS

Foreword

Many potential readers of this book might regard its topic as either too narrow or too broad. Both criticisms have some merit, so it might be best to begin by explaining how I chose it.

It is my colleagues in political science who might find the book too narrow, or, more precisely, marginal and old-fashioned. As I discuss more fully in the introduction, disciplinary interest in constitutions and constitutionalism began to dry up about four decades ago, based on the conviction that many constitutional texts were not closely related to broader political dynamics. It is true that interest in constitutions has recently revived, but thus far it has been those countries aspiring to some form of liberal democracy (especially in central and eastern Europe) that have drawn attention. I have tried to keep abreast of this scholarship and in a small way contribute to it.

Still, it is not my colleagues who have led me to the topic of Arab constitutionalism. Instead, my interest stems from conversations and readings in the Arab world. In the course of conducting earlier research on Arab legal institutions, I was surprised to find a set of rich constitutional traditions. Arab constitutional documents are not always liberal, as will be clear, but they are often carefully crafted and based on sophisticated political visions. And in recent decades, as many Arab intellectuals have become increasingly troubled by the authoritarianism that their constitutions have often enabled, regional interest in liberal and Islamic variants of constitutionalism has grown. While my own attention was attracted by these regional concerns, I have tried to cast the arguments in this book to make them of wider interest: I believe that the Arab constitutional experience can shed light on broader issues regarding constitutions, constitutionalism, and politics.

In contrast to my colleagues in political science, scholars of the law (and historians as well) will likely regard this book as brash and excessively ambitious.

ix

I have tried not simply to cover most of the Arab world (with only a few countries excluded); I have also insisted that one non-Arab case (Iran) be included in the analysis. I have cast my net so widely for three reasons.

First, there is an Arab constitutional tradition (and even a broader Middle Eastern one)—constitutional architects in most Arab countries, for instance, have relied extensively on Ottoman and often on Egyptian documents. Second, commonalties extend beyond texts to broader political contexts: much of the constitutional engineering in the region has occurred in a variety of authoritarian contexts. Third, even where dissimilarities exist, viewing Arab countries together is helpful in illuminating alternatives and unrealized possibilities. It is also for these reasons that the Ottoman constitution (the starting point for much twentieth-century constitution writing in the Arab world) is included. And two Iranian constitutional experiments are included as well: the first (in the early twentieth century) because of the strong parallels to contemporary Arab developments; the second (the Islamic Republic of the late twentieth century) because it helps illuminate the implications of some current arguments about Islam and constitutionalism in the Arab world.

This ambitious scope carries undeniable costs. I have done extensive primary research on several constitutional traditions in the Arab world (the Egyptian, Kuwaiti, and Palestinian) and less extensive primary research on some others (chiefly Jordan and Iraq). For North Africa and Iran, I am almost wholly dependent on the work of other scholars. To exclude these countries from the analysis would have been a mistake, because of the light they shed on the countries I am more familiar with. Modesty has led me to keep the sections on North Africa shorter; I have also consulted with those who have deeper knowledge than I do about the political systems in Iran and North Africa. In this regard, I wish to thank Said Arjomand for assistance on Iran and Emad Shahin for guidance on North Africa. My gratitude should not implicate them in my conclusions: both scholars have their own works which readers should consult for more expert coverage of these cases.

I have enjoyed able research assistance from several individuals, all of whom deserve thanks: Hakim al-Samawi, Halla Abudaff, Shannon Laughlin, Kevin Kreutner, Carrie Gerkey, Maha Juweied, and Jessica Lieberman. I have also benefited from discussions with students in a variety of seminars at The George Washington University. Three former teachers—Roger Bass, Dean Brink, and Carl Brown—helped me in ways that they have likely long forgotten. Scholarly dialogue with a variety of colleagues has been quite helpful. Special mention must be made in this regard to those whose greater expertise in a subject related to this book has helped guide me: Awad El-Morr, Adel

Omar Sharif, Keith Lewinstein, Armando Salvatore, Karim Mezran, Ingrid Creppel, Bruce Rutherford, and Frank Vogel. The anonymous readers of the manuscript were unusually helpful and constructive in their suggestions. The Middle East Institute hosted me as scholar-in-residence while this project was in the very final stages. On several occasions, I have been able to present some of my ideas to scholars and practitioners; the United States Information Agency (now the Department of State's Bureau of Education and Cultural Affairs) made possible a tour of Egypt, the West Bank, Gaza, Jordan, and Tunisia where I could share some ideas with experts in the Arab world. On two occasions Egypt's Supreme Constitutional Court and the British Council have jointly sponsored conferences in Cairo, which enabled me to meet a wide variety of scholars with similar interests to exchange ideas. At SUNY Press, I owe thanks to Michael Rinella, Cathleen Collins, and Donna Plesser. The Kuwait Information Office supplied the cover photograph.

Several members of my family deserve special mention. I did not design the study in order to have my parents host me in Kuwait, but it had that happy effect. Judy, my wife, read the manuscript quite carefully, contributing editorial suggestions and her own insights based on her regional expertise. Our children, Ariel and Eran, have accepted my absences (though I should confess that I selected a topic that could be based partly on textual studies to avoid making these absences any longer).

This book is dedicated to my wife's parents, Aaron and Ruby Kohn. It is unusual to cite one's in-laws in a dedication, but those who know them will not be overly surprised. They are, of course, kind and generous parents, grandparents, and in-laws. Yet it is not such qualities that deserve mention in this context: instead it is their boundless intellectual curiosity, a virtue that I not only admire but also work to pass on to their grandchildren.

INTRODUCTION

A RECENT RENAISSANCE of constitution writing, particularly in newly democratizing countries, has led to a revived interest in constitutions and constitutional design—a field that political science abandoned more than a generation ago. Scholars stopped studying constitutions because they increasingly seemed quixotic: if political authority was to be constrained, it would not be done with mere pieces of paper. Constitutional authors and scholars came to be seen as well intentioned but naive. Despite the recently renewed interest in constitution writing (far more pronounced among practitioners than scholars), such a view still prevails in the academy.

The purpose of this work is to show that an interest in constitutions (and constitutionalism) is not necessarily well intentioned nor is it always naive. More specifically:

1. *Constitutions have generally been written to augment political authority; liberal constitutionalism (aimed at restraining political authority) has generally been at most a secondary goal.* Thus, constitutions are not only of interest when they serve liberal ends. Many constitutional authors have been far from quixotic; they are often even more cynical than those scholars who have ignored or dismissed their efforts.

2. *Even though constitutionalism has been a secondary goal, its prospects are often brighter—and far less related to democracy—than initially appear.* The Arab world, the focus of this study, is often viewed as particularly hostile to constitutionalist values. Accountable and limited government seems alien to the area. While the record of Arab authoritarianism is real, so too are the prospects for movement toward constitutional government. It is not naive to see constitutionalist seeds in Arab political practice. To do so, however, we need to study constitutions as they operate over time, turning away from the standard emphasis only on the moment of composition. What is especially

remarkable about the Arab experience is that many of the possibilities for constitutionalist practice lie in divorcing constitutionalism from democracy. Arab constitutionalism is far more likely to emerge from institutional balancing and elite bargains than it is from any authentic form of popular sovereignty.

Over the past century and a half, the Arab world has grown rich in constitutions—documents that spell out the basic legal framework for governing—without growing richer in constitutionalism—limited and accountable government. Basic laws have proliferated but few Arab governments have been restricted in their authority by them.

The structure of this study is designed to answer two questions. First, why are constitutions written in the Arab world? Arab constitutional architects, like their counterparts in many nondemocratic societies, have been far less hypocritical, and their texts far less desecrated, than is often believed. What purposes are they designed to serve? Part One addresses these questions, presenting the view that constitutions have been designed primarily to render the political authority of the state more effective and secondarily to underscore state sovereignty and establish general ideological orientations.

Second, what are the prospects for Arab constitutionalism? In other words, can a document written to serve the purposes of a generally authoritarian regime metamorphize into the legal basis for limiting and regularizing state authority? Part Two addresses these questions, presenting real but limited possibilities for the development of accountability in Arab governance. Oddly, such possibilities seem only loosely linked—and sometimes in tension with—any movements toward democracy.

The Arab experience is far from unique. Most states in the world now have written constitutions; the number of states without such documents has decreased to a mere handful. Yet if constitutions have become the norm, constitutionalist practices have not. Most political scientists lost interest in constitutions a generation ago because constitutions did not seem to reflect political reality. Political philosophy continued to take constitutionalism quite seriously, but other parts of the discipline of political science focused on other issues and approaches.

A renewed interest in constitutions and constitutionalism has begun to emerge among scholars. As in the past, political scientists have reacted to the world around them. The collapse of authoritarian regimes in the former Soviet bloc and Latin America was accompanied by a new bout of constitution writing. Scholars have explored questions of constitutional design and the process of constitution writing. And the resurgence of liberalism and democracy has led some to see new constitutions and providing (or benefiting from) new opportunities to build constitutionalist practices.

This book represents an attempt to contribute to the renewed effort to understand constitutions and constitutionalism in two major ways. First, it explores the consequences of separating constitutions from constitutionalism: why are constitutions adopted in the absence of any desire for constitutionalism? Understanding the various (and not merely constitutionalist) purposes of constitutional documents is vital to understanding their appeal. In addition, it will prevent us from dismissing nonconstitutionalist constitutions as liberal facades irrelevant to the actual practice of politics. Second, the book explores how constitutional structures built for nonconstitutionalist ends might still serve as a basis for the emergence of constitutionalist practices.

In undertaking these tasks, we must recognize that some of the conceptual framework we have used to understand constitutions and constitutionalism is inadequate—or, more accurately, some of the most appropriate concepts have been lost or confused, partly as a result of our prolonged disinterest in the subject. This work will therefore appear old-fashioned to some, focusing on subject matter and concepts that have been relegated to political philosophy. It should not appear old-fashioned to political practitioners—especially those in the Arab world—however, because the issues it explores are very much the material of daily political struggles in the region.

PART ONE

The Purposes of
Arab Constitutions

INTRODUCTION

Constitutions in a Nonconstitutional World

WHY ARE CONSTITUTIONS issued in parts of the world where constitutionalism has never been established? This section presents various nonconstitutionalist motives for writing constitutions.

Arab politics joined the global trend toward writing constitutions very early. During the late nineteenth century that part of the Arab world under direct Ottoman rule became subject, albeit briefly, to the Ottoman constitution of 1876. Constitutional documents were also written in Tunisia and Egypt, though their effects were only slightly less fleeting. In the twentieth century, constitutional documents have multiplied, some countries rewriting theirs approximately every generation. Even some longtime recalcitrant states—such as Saudi Arabia and Oman—have recently adopted "basic laws." Palestinians began drafting such a document even before any other attributes of statehood were assured. Yet these documents do not seem to have successfully established constitutionalism, especially in practice. The idea that state authority should be regulated and limited by law has found adherents but has yet to establish itself firmly in institutional form.

Constitutions in a Nonconstitutional World

Why do constitutions continue to proliferate in the Arab world, an area largely bereft of constitutionalist practices? A deep cynicism pervades the region: many political activists and ordinary citizens remain convinced that constitutional texts remain worthless papers written to hide the reality of despotic, even

3

tyrannical rule. Constitutions are generally viewed as elegant but insincere expressions of aspirations that rulers issue in an effort to obscure the unrestrained nature of their authority. Constitutions are written not to limit authority, according to this view, but to mask it; it would be naive to take them seriously.

This cynicism is shared not only by residents of the area but by scholars of the Arab world (and of the nondemocratic world more broadly). Indeed, it was precisely the expansion in scope of American political science to encompass newly independent states in the postwar decades that led scholars to abandon any serious focus on constitutional structures. Political scientists in the 1960s and 1970s favored a variety of other approaches to politics, including modernization, political culture, and dependency. More than a generation has passed since constitutional analysis has occupied a central part of the effort to understand politics in other countries. Even a renewed interest in political institutions that began in the 1980s has largely bypassed constitutions, except in a few very specific areas. Fleeting attention has been given to electoral rules and the attributes of presidential and parliamentary systems, but greater attention to constitutional texts has been avoided by those trained to dismiss "formal legalism" or "the old institutionalism."[1]

Scholarly cynicism about constitutions is thus hardly restricted to the Arab world. In fact, the cynical attitude toward constitutional texts emerged long before specialists in comparative politics abandoned constitutional analysis. Its roots can be traced back to the formal legalists themselves in their efforts to understand Soviet and Nazi politics. Constitutional structures and written documents hardly seemed to be the appropriate focus of study of such systems. The carefully designed Weimar constitution was insufficient to prevent the Nazis from coming to power through constitutional methods. The Soviet Union was similarly unrestrained by its constitutional documents. The Soviet constitution was viewed just as Arab constitutional documents are today: an insincere promise of rights, freedoms, and democratic processes meant to fool both citizens and foreign observers by obscuring the untrammeled authority of the rulers. Stalinism was hardly restricted by vague statements of rights incorporated in Soviet constitutional documents; the promises contained in the Soviet constitution were never meant to be honored.

Formal legalists were far less naive than later generations of scholars have treated them: they summarily dismissed such constitutions. Constitutions either served constitutionalist goals or were described as "paper" or "facade" constitutions. Herbert Spiro wrote that constitutions might not be "wanted as a device for helping the system deal with its substantive problems, but as a facade behind which anticonstitutionalist rulers can hide."[2] Karl Loewenstein, like Spiro one of the last political scientists to specialize in comparative constitutional analysis, wrote: "Mussolini, Goebbels, Peron, Ngo Dinh Diem, Naser and *tutti quanit* are modern men and no fools. They cannot believe in what their constitutions proclaim and their elections produce."[3] Scholars justified their continued interest in such constitutions by seemingly grasping at straws: perhaps some day constitutional provisions would come to life; in the meantime nonconstitutionalist rulers could be denounced as hypocrites.

This cynicism that constitutions are often hypocritical documents whose provisions are ignored in practice is deeply unsatisfying, however, precisely because it is so widespread. If everybody knows that constitutions do not limit authority, then why bother to promulgate them? Why bother to speak what everybody knows to be a lie? Why have constitutions become ubiquitous in a world where constitutionalist values have been so difficult to establish?

In fact, constitutions are often far more frank than cynics claim. Karl Loewenstein was incorrect when he wrote that such documents hid reality so that "The proverbial man from Mars, when confronted with these documents, would not imagine that behind the structural and often verbal identity of these provisions is hidden a vast differentiation of the actual power dynamism."[4] This view is misleading for two reasons. First, nonconstitutionalist and constitutionalist orders both leave key features of the political system outside of the constitutional text. In some areas nonconstitutionalist documents are actually more accurate and complete. The most frequent and obvious example is the party and electoral system. Generally such matters are referred to only briefly in a constitutional document, yet they can work profound effects on the nature of the political system. Strong party discipline and a two-party system, for instance, can gut the practical importance of a parliament in a so-called parliamentary system, converting it into a mere electoral college for the prime minister and a debating forum for the opposition. Similarly, many of the democratic constitutions of sub-Saharan Africa were turned to authoritarian purposes not by violating the constitutional text but by creating a one-party system that robbed constitutional mechanisms of their viability.[5] Nonconstitutionalist constitutions are far more likely to include detailed language on the party system, often by establishing a single political party. All constitutional texts—and not just authoritarian or so-called "facade" ones—can work in a wide variety of ways and admit a panoply of structures.

More fundamentally, the cynical view of constitutions in nonconstitutional orders is misleading because such constitutions often are far less hypocritical than claimed. So-called "facade" constitutional documents often present the political system with as much candor and comprehensiveness as their supposedly authentic counterparts. Perhaps the most cited example of a country with a "facade" constitution was the Soviet Union. But Soviet constitutions were far too honest and clear to be simply disingenuous facades. The first such constitution—that of the 1918 Russian Socialist Federal Soviet Republic—proclaimed that its fundamental aim was "to establish (in the form of a powerful All-Russian Soviet Government) the dictatorship of the urban and rural workers, combined with the poorer peasantry, in order to secure the complete crushing of the bourgeoisie, the abolition of the exploitation of man by man, and the establishment of Socialism, under which neither class divisions nor state coercion arising therefrom will any longer exist." Lest the implications of this be lost to Loewenstein's "proverbial man from Mars," the document explicitly stated: "In the interest of the working class as a whole, the Russian Socialist Federal Soviet Republic shall deprive individuals and sections of the community of any rights used by them to the detriment of the interests of the Socialist revolution."[6] Subsequent Soviet constitutions were less brutally frank, but they were equally clear; the final, 1977 version included a clause that one observer described as abolishing "not only the rest of its text, but the rest of legislation also":

> The leading and guiding force of Soviet society and the nucleus of its political system, of all state organization and public organizations, is the Communist Party of the Soviet Union. The CPSU exists for the people and serves the people. The Communist Party, armed with Marxism-Leninism, determines the general perspectives of the development of society and the course of home and foreign policy of the USSR, directs the great constructive work of the Soviet people, and imparts a planned, systemic and theoretically substantiated character to their struggle for the victory of communism. All party organizations shall function within the framework of the Constitution of the USSR.[7]

Thus a one-party dictatorship was not hidden behind a constitutional facade but directly and unambiguously required by the constitutional text. Any other system would have been a violation of the constitution. Other constitutions establish the basis for nonconstitutionalist government in a variety of ways: unchecked executive authority; extensive and poorly supervised provisions for emergency rule; and rights provisions that fail to establish real protections.[8]

If we define facade constitutions as those that provide only an incomplete description of the political order, then all extant constitutions are facades.

If we define them more realistically as texts that are routinely and incontrovertibly violated, then there are a surprisingly small number of such documents. As will become clear in later chapters, it can be argued that there are no facade constitutions in the Arab world. The Saudi basic law, to give one example, is largely followed; no reader would take it to aim at establishing a constitutionalist democracy. A close reading of Arab constitutions reveals that they are rarely blatantly violated; problems stem from the content of their clauses and more portentously from their silences. On most occasions, regimes have interpreted existing constitutional texts in plausible (though often authoritarian) terms.[9] When constitutions become inconvenient, it is rare for governments to run roughshod over their provisions; instead they completely abolish them, issuing a new constitutional text.

The discovery that constitutional texts are not routinely violated makes our task of explaining their emergence more difficult. If Arab constitutions are not ignored, then why are they written? If they do not restrict state authority, what is their true purpose? (The answers to these questions, the focus of Part One, will lead us to a further question, to occupy our attention in Part Two: once written, can Arab constitutions serve as the basis for building constitutionalist government, even if they are designed to serve other purposes?)

Recovering a Language for Understanding Constitutions and Constitutionalism

Our ability to enunciate basic concepts has atrophied through prolonged scholarly disinterest in constitutions and constitutionalism. Distinctions that long ago seemed vital in educated political discourse have been lost to all but a narrow group of specialists. Until a couple generations ago, the distinction between tyranny and despotism was widely understood; now we speak more vaguely about authoritarianism. Only specialists in political theory attach much importance to the distinction between republican and democratic government. Constitutionalism and democracy were viewed until fairly recently as operating in tension; now we have trouble envisioning nonconstitutionalist democracies or nondemocratic constitutionalist systems. The global spread of an interest in "human rights" has detached the substance of rights from their source; sharp debates even within the liberal tradition about the origin and nature of rights have been forgotten except among scholars, as has the traditional liberal view that democracy represents one of the greatest threats to such rights. Thus, during Newt Gingrich's tenure as Speaker of the House in the 1990s, nobody found it anomalous when he routinely recommended reading of the *Federalist Papers*, a set of writings centrally concerned with justifying precisely what Gingrich purported to oppose: an increase in federal power and limitation of the influence of popularly elected legislatures.[10]

The shifts in thinking and vocabulary are not products of mere ignorance. General understandings of politics have also been informed by the political experience of the twentieth century, in which limited, constitutionalist democratic government has come to be seen as the major alternative to a wide variety of unlimited, unconstitutional, and undemocratic systems. Yet the new muddiness has costs. A recent series of dramatic political changes that seemingly transcends regional boundaries has exposed the conceptual imprecision that has guided attempts to understand various systems of governing. Regime changes (and sometimes revolutions) in Latin America, East Asia, and the former Soviet bloc were initially referred to as "transitions," a term that focused attention on the process of change while leaving the beginning and especially the end points murky. Others talked of "democratization" although political change has hardly been restricted to the construction of democratic institutions and process.

In seeking to analyze these changes, scholars have finally been forced to revive seemingly archaic vocabulary. The distinction between republicanism and democracy emerges in Robert Putnam's influential *Making Democracy Work*; the distinction between constitutionalism and democracy is at the center of a recent collection of essays by leading scholars; understanding the complex relationship between democratization and economic liberalization is the task of some recent widely read scholarly works.[11]

While interest in older distinctions and vocabulary has begun to widen in scholarly circles, more general political discourse still reflects amnesia about these distinctions. It is not simply in the United States that respect for human rights, constitutionalism, democracy, the rule of law, and the market economy are seen as so mutually reinforcing as to be virtually a single phenomenon; such an assumption has spread to many areas of the world with very different histories.

Thus it is especially important that terms be clearly defined at the beginning of this inquiry into Arab constitutions and constitutionalism. Definitions used here will reflect older usage for the most part (though even within the older vocabulary precise meanings changed over time). The term *constitution* here will indicate the basic legal framework for governing. The term *constitutionalism* will refer to ideologies and institutional arrangements that promote the limitation and definition of means of exercising state authority.[12]

It is as important to note what these definitions exclude as what they include. There is no necessary definitional relationship, for instance, between either constitutions or constitutionalism on the one hand and democracy on the other. This usage might seem slightly anachronistic, because democracy is currently defined in ways that virtually require it to be constitutionalist. Older views of democracy focused on the rule of the people (or the majority); constitutionalism was understood as an ideology that sought to place limits on the government, especially government by popular will.[13] Recent scholars have introduced a subtle change by advancing a procedural view of democracy that inevitably involves some fundamental (and constitutional) legal limits and guarantees. Adam Przeworski, for instance, distinguishes democratic from authoritarian rule not in terms of popular sovereignty but in terms of institutionalized uncertainty in political outcomes: "Hence the crucial moment in any passage from authoritarianism to democratic rule is not necessarily the withdrawal of the army into the barracks or the opening of the elected parliament but the crossing of the threshold beyond which no one can intervene to reverse outcomes of the formal democratic process."[14] Przeworski's alternative to democracy—authoritarianism—is explicitly defined as well in procedural terms: authoritarianism exists if there exists "some power apparatus capable of overturning the outcomes of the institutionalized political process."[15] More abstractly, Stephen Holmes pursues a constitutionalist view of democracy when he defines it as "government by public discussion, not simply the enforcement of the will of the majority."[16] Such discussion requires precisely the sorts of limitations, protections, and guarantees that constitutionalism seeks to provide.

It may be true, as these authors imply, that democracy needs constitutionalism. But the reverse is not true. We must admit the possibility—and historical reality—of some nondemocratic constitutionalist governments. Many constitutionalist systems of the nineteenth century—such as Britain, Germany, and pre-Jacksonian America—operated in accordance with constitutionalist principles while excluding the majority (even of the male citizenry) from a meaningful role in the political process. We need not accept the older view that democracy and constitutionalism operate antagonistically, but we must concede that the two can be, and have been, separated.

Just as there is no necessary requirement that constitutions or constitutionalism be democratic, there is no requirement that they provide for basic individual rights. Such relationships might (and often do) exist in practice, but these are links to be explored empirically rather than decreed by definition. The American constitution was drafted to contain all sorts of procedural and even some substantive limitations on government. Only after the initial drafting was the Bill of Rights, enumerating individual rights, added. The Bill of Rights made the American political system more liberal but it did not make it more constitutional. Nineteenth-century European constitutions generally contained weak rights provisions (or none at all), even as they placed definite limitations on how state authority would operate. Twentieth-century constitutions tend to have more extensive rights provisions, though a close reading of the language used will reveal that guarantees are often weak and easy to circumvent. One can write a constitution that contains no mention of individual rights; one can limit government without necessarily providing individuals with strong guarantees.

Perhaps most important for present purposes, there is no necessary relationship between constitutions and constitutionalism. The existence of constitutions that serve nonconstitutionalist ends is not only theoretically possible; it is empirically quite common.

The Purposes of Nonconstitutional Constitutions

What ends do constitutions serve if they are not meant to limit government? What is the purpose of nonconstitutionalist constitutions? Several possibilities may be cited. First, constitutions have become so common as to be considered a natural accouterment of sovereignty. A country proclaims its independence (or a revolutionary regime proclaims its triumph) by writing a constitution, just as it designs a new flag, national anthem, and postage stamps. And while such things may be accurate expressions of national feeling, none is intended to define or limit authority. Karl Loewenstein wrote: "Sovereignty of the people and the written constitution have become ideologically and practically synonymous. . . . It is safe to say that the written constitution has become the most common and universally accepted phenomenon of the contemporary state organization. So deeply implanted is the conviction that even modern autocracies feel compelled to pay tribute to the democratic legitimacy inherent in the constitution."[17]

If Arab constitutions are issued as an expression of national sovereignty, we should expect that to be reflected in their timing and their content. They should be issued upon independence (and after revolutionary—or purported revolutionary—change), and whatever the reality of their authorship, they should present themselves as expressions of the national will.

Second, constitutions may serve the purpose of proclaiming basic ideology. It has often been observed that constitution writers have become progressively more verbose. Among the chief reasons has been the insertion of lengthy sections describing the basic goals, ideology, or program of the state. Such proclamations may be sincere when issued but are too vaguely worded to bear much legal weight; they are not designed to limit the government. Instead they serve notice that an ideological orientation represents not a transient policy direction but a defining feature of the state. The intended audience may be internal to the society; indeed, it might even be internal to the state, as the senior political leadership might use a constitution to signal its orientation to the bureaucracy. Said Arjomand writes that constitutions are "important as transcendental justifications of political order."[18] In the wake of the Soviet constitution of 1918, Arjomand asserts "we witness the advent of a new genre, the ideological constitution, whose central goal is not the limitation of government but the transformation of society according to a revolutionary ideology."[19] In a sense, most constitutions have ideological elements in that they define the nature of the political community and the identity of its members.[20] What makes an "ideological constitution" distinctive is that its ideological and programmatic nature overwhelms its substantive and procedural content.

If Arab constitutions fall in this category, we would expect them to contain lengthy and elaborate preambles or ideological statements and poorly developed provisions for the definition and operation of political authority.

Finally, a constitution may serve to make lines of authority clear without restricting the actions of senior leaders. In this sense, a constitution might be designed to define state authority but not limit it. Just as most regimes cannot rule without some use of law, few can rule without some clear delineation of basic structures and chains of command. Constitutional rules can serve not to limit but to express the will of the rulers. Power might be made to operate in a more organized and efficient manner without being limited in any way observable by the citizenry.

Indeed, even liberal constitutionalists have sought not simply to limit political authority but also to render it more effective and efficient. Montesquieu himself, for instance, noted that the problem of political succession could disrupt despotic, nonconstitutionalist states:

> In countries where there are no fundamental laws, the succession to the emperor cannot be fixt. The crown is then elective by the

prince either in his own or in some other family. In vain would it be to establish here the succession of the eldest son; the prince might always chuse another. The successor is declared by the prince himself, or by a civil war. Hence a despotic state is, upon another account, more liable than a monarchical government to dissolution.

As every prince of the royal family has an equal capacity to be chosen, hence it follows that the prince who ascends the throne, strangles immediately his brothers, as in Turkey; or puts out their eyes, as in Persia; or bereaves them of their understanding, as in the Mogul's country, the vacancy of the throne is always attended with a horrid civil war.[21]

In the nineteenth century, liberals insisted on inserting emergency provisions that would also have the effect of defending the society against revolution and civil war, this time with the object of giving the government the necessary tools to defend itself against reactionaries and monarchists.[22] And, as is explored more fully in Part Two, it is possible to limit and enhance governmental power simultaneously.

Thus, constitutionalists join others in seeking to render government more stable and effective. They do not stop there, of course, but the constitutional tools they have developed can be borrowed by those with nonliberal purposes.[23] Montesquieu's observation that fundamental laws help regulate succession is of contemporary relevance; nonconstitutionalist regimes might use constitutions simply to regulate relations among the ruling group.[24] Provisions for emergency rule and states of siege can turn from exceptional measures in constitutionalist systems to normal modes of operation in nonconstitutionalist ones.

Nonconstitutionalist constitutions therefore might serve the primary purpose of organizing power without limiting it. Such constitutions should be easily recognizable. Loewenstein adduces Germany's 1871 constitution as an example; he characterizes it as a simple set of bylaws: "the ideological inspiration equals that of a telephone directory; any reference to fundamental rights, always alien to German tradition, is conspicuously absent. But the absence of programmatic embroidery suggests to the constitutional sociologist its intrinsically authoritarian *telos* and character."[25] Hans Kelsen also described telltale features of an autocratic constitution:

That no State organ can act without positive authorization from the legal order does not, as one might think, hold true only for democratic States. It is true also of an autocratic State, for instance, an absolute monarchy. The constitution—the absolute monarchy, too, has a constitution, because every State has a constitution—here gives the monarch an almost unlimited authority to issue, not only general, but also individual norms and to perform coercive acts, so that every act of the monarch or of an organ authorized by him appears as an act of the State if it presents itself as such. The constitution of the absolute monarchy is chiefly characterized by this extensive competence of the executive power vested in the person of the monarch.[26]

Unchecked executive authority, poorly developed rights provisions, succession mechanisms that fail to make the leadership in any sense accountable, and escape hatches to allow rulers to violate their own rules should be the hallmark of a constitution meant to organize power without limiting it.

The remainder of Part One focuses on the question of why constitutions have been written in the Arab world. If not intended to define and limit state authority, which of these three other purposes—symbolic, ideological, and enabling—have they been designed to serve?

ONE

EARLY CONSTITUTIONAL DOCUMENTS IN THE MIDDLE EAST

In THE NINETEENTH CENTURY, a remarkably similar sequence of events occurred in several Middle Eastern polities. Autocratic rulers, operating under severe fiscal and foreign pressures, issued constitutional documents containing limited promises of constitutional government, representative assemblies, and individual rights. While these documents might appear to a current-day audience to be incomplete and circumscribed, they proved to be the object of intense political struggle. All were abandoned—at least in part—within a short period after they were promulgated.

In this chapter, we will try to uncover why these documents were issued, what impact they had, and why their viable lives were so short. The focus is not on the Arab world alone, because the Arab experience in this period shows little difference from the broader Middle Eastern experience; indeed, much of the Arab world was governed by the Ottoman Empire (and thus by the Ottoman constitution). The three nineteenth century constitutions that will draw attention are the Tunisian, Ottoman, and Egyptian. Two twentieth-century constitutions that followed a similar pattern, the Iranian and Kuwaiti, are also considered. In addition to considering the origins, workings, and fate of these constitutions, we also examine the political systems that eschewed any constitutional documents in order to test and refine our explanation of the motivations for and meanings of constitutional texts.

The experiences of the countries presented in this chapter will show that the origins of Arab constitutions lie in attempts to build political systems that were more efficient, fiscally responsible, and better ordered. While often dismissed as alien implants, these constitutions were far more likely to be designed to shore up the state from the inside than satisfy European audiences. For some architects of these documents, constitutionalism (but not democracy) was an additional goal. However, the more that constitutionalism was present as a motive, the more likely it was to prove fatal the effort to write a basic law.

Tunisia

The *qanun al-dawla al-tunisiyya* [law of the Tunisian state or dynasty] of 1861 was the first written constitution in the Arab world.[1] The document was issued in the midst of a period of political changes introduced by an ambitious centralizing administration at a time of increased European influence.[2] At the time, Tunisia formed a virtually independent province within the Ottoman Empire; the reform program followed by the country's rulers loosely followed the Ottoman *tanzimat* (nineteenth-century political reform program) in content and vocabulary. It involved an assertion of central control over loosely administered outlying areas and construction of a more powerful military. The program was pursued unevenly at best, encountering difficulties because of the rudimentary administrative structure as well as fiscal constraints. Growing European (especially French and British) interest in Tunisia affected the course of political reform: an outbreak of Muslim-Jewish tension in Tunis led the European powers to demand that the Tunisian *bey* (hereditary governor) adopt some of the reforms recently promulgated in the Ottoman Empire.[3] Thus, in 1857, the *bey* issued the *'ahd al-iman* [Charter of Faith], which promised protection of persons and property, regularization of taxation, military service, and justice, and concessions to non-Muslims in the adjudication of disputes.[4]

Shortly after the issuance of the *'ahd al-iman*, the *bey* formed a commission of Tunisian officials to study the application of Ottoman legal reforms and draft a constitution. The group worked for close to three years before producing a draft.[5] However, the *bey* waited until he could present the document to Napoleon III before promulgating it.[6] While there was much European interest in the document, the Tunisian constitution of 1861 actually reflects European structure and practice less than almost any other Middle Eastern constitutional text (only the laconic Kuwaiti constitutional document of 1938 and perhaps the constitution of the Hijaz appear to be less European in style and content). The Tunisian constitution is rooted partly in Islamic terminology (members of the Grand Council, for instance, are referred to as *ahl al-hall wa-l-'aqd*, literally, the people who loosen and bind; the population was generally referred to as *ra'ayana*, literally, our flock), though some European usage is also adopted (the ruler is referred to as the king—*al-malik*—rather than *bey*—perhaps an implicit assertion of Tunisian sovereignty).

The constitution consists of thirteen sections. The first two deal with the king and the ruling family and not only require the king to act through his ministers but also absolves the community of loyalty to him if he violates the law. The third section established a Grand Council; other councils were also established for administration and adjudication. While the mixture of these two functions violated emerging European conceptions of the separation of powers, it was quite standard for Middle Eastern governments in the nineteenth century to blend judicial and administrative functions. The Tunisian constitution steered these bodies to acting on the basis of written law. Members of these councils were to be dismissed only for cause and then only by the council itself.

The fourth section of the constitution designated some state income directly for the king and another portion for the family of the king; the rest was to be the responsibility of the bureaucracy. The fifth section covered the ministries, dividing the authority of the minister among those things that he was authorized to do by himself, those things that required the king's agreement, and those things that required the Grand Council's agreement. While ministers were responsible to the king, they were also responsible for his actions to the Grand Council. Only written communications between the king and the ministries and councils were accorded validity.

The sixth and seventh sections concerned the Grand Council itself. One third consisted of ministers and officials; the others were notables initially selected by the king with the approval of his ministers. New members of the Grand Council were to be selected from a list drawn up by the Council with the king's approval. A section of the Grand Council functioned as a standing executive committee. The Council was charged generally with protecting the rights of the people and equality among them; more specifically, its assent was required for all laws and changes in expenditures. The Council was given some limited judicial and investigatory authority and was allowed to review the annual accounting of the ministers.

The following three sections dealt with state employees, budgets, revenues, and ranks of government service; employees could not be dismissed without cause. The twelfth section covered the rights and duties of Tunisians, and affirmed the guarantees of the *'ahd al-iman* for legal equality regardless of residence, social position, and religion. Very few of the economic and civil rights customarily mentioned in twentieth-century constitutions appeared in the Tunisian constitution: there was no mention of freedom of expression or association, for instance. Yet the right to security of person, honor, and fortune were guaranteed; Tunisian subjects could not be forced to do anything against their will except for military service in accordance with the law. Taxation must be established according to law as well. The thirteenth and final section dealt with residents of Tunisia who were subjects of friendly states, granting them many of the same rights and guarantees.

The Tunisian constitution of 1861 was in force for only three years. During that period, the Grand Council operated as intended; that is, as a body combining legislative, administrative, fiscal, and judicial functions. A recent study of the work of the Council reveals both the extent of its activities and the serious nature of some of its debates.[7] Yet foreign support for the constitution and the political reforms fell victim to British-French rivalry.[8] More important, the growing ambitions of the Tunisian state had led to an increasingly onerous tax burden; this was aggravated by foreign loans, which, when they came due, increased already heavy taxation. The reform program—including the constitution—became an issue in a rebellion that compelled the political leadership of Tunisia to beat a hasty retreat.[9] In April 1864 the *bey* rescinded both a tax increase and the constitution. The rebellion was still not suppressed until the summer, however, after the *bey* accepted help from the Ottoman government.

The constitution's short life span and the foreign involvement led to its frequent characterization as either inappropriate to Tunisian conditions or as a facade. L. Carl Brown, for instance, likens the constitution to a "hothouse plant" and writes that it was composed:

> more to curry favor and suppress criticism from abroad than to regularize the actual balance of political forces within Tunisia. Moreover, those immediately in charge—and Tunisia was still very much in the hands of Mustafa Khaznadar and his entourage—had little interest in it beyond exploiting the facade of modern, Western constitutionalism and continuing governmental operations along the old lines of private enrichment in the absence of accountability.[10]

Brown's observation that the constitution was partly designed to obtain European support is difficult to question, because of both the circumstances surrounding its adoption and the guarantees for foreign subjects contained in the document itself. Similarly, it is clear that the constitution was designed to serve the political elite, given the self-perpetuating nature of political authority envisioned in the document. But designating the Tunisian constitution as a "facade" seems to judge it by twentieth-century constitutionalist and democratic standards unsupported by the document itself. A reading of the Tunisian constitution reveals that it promises no democracy and that authority is to be held accountable only to the existing political elite. It supports the rule of law but not of the people.

The structure and content of the Tunisian constitution suggests that its authors had specific concerns. Most fundamental was the rationalization of the administration of the country. Much attention is given to chains of command, definitions of responsibilities, and proper procedure. The constitution is especially detailed on fiscal practices, displaying a probable concern by its authors with accountable and clear procedures for use of public funds. While the Grand Council was clearly conceived as representing the Tunisian population, it was not to do so through any recognizably democratic procedures; it was an appointed and partly self-perpetuating body. Its clear purposes involved consultation and some measure of accountability; popular sovereignty was not even considered. The Tunisian constitution seems to have been designed to serve constitutionalist ends in limited but real ways: political authority was to be rendered more accountable and effective. Constitutionalism was not blended with any democratic elements.

This understanding of the purposes of the constitution is based simply on extrapolation from the text itself. But it can be measured against the writings of a leading Tunisian politician of the period. Khayr al-Din al-Tunisi was a minister and the president of the Grand Council during the constitutional period until his falling out with his father-in-law, Mustafa Khaznadar, the bey's chief minister. Khayr al-Din later replaced Khaznadar and also briefly served as the grand wazir of the Ottoman Empire. Khayr al-Din was therefore involved in the writing and operation of the constitution but not in its abrogation. A few years after the end of the Tunisian constitutional experiment he wrote an extended treatise on government. While he did not mention the Tunisian constitution, he provided a thorough ideological justification for its structure and content. The treatise advances a powerful argument for a constitutionalist polity, and locates constitutionalism not only in European practice but also in the Islamic tradition. While his vocabulary was Islamic, his argument was reminiscent of the *Federalist Papers*: human beings need government to restrain them, but those who exercise power are themselves human and need to be restrained.

> [S]ome form of restraint is essential for the maintenance of the human species, but if the person exercising this restraint were left to do as he pleases and rule as he sees fit the fruits to be expected from

> this need to have a restrainer would not appear to the *umma* [community], and the original state of neglect would remain unheeded. It is essential that the restrainer should have *his* restrainer to check him either in the form of a heavenly *shari'a* or a policy based on reason, but neither of these can defend its rights if they be violated. For this reason it is incumbent upon the *'ulama* [Islamic scholars] and the notables of the *umma* to resist evil. The Europeans have established councils and have given freedom to the printing presses. In the Islamic *umma* the kings fear those who resist evil just as the kings of Europe fear the councils and the opinions of the masses that proceed from them and form the freedom of the press. The aim of the two [i.e., European and Muslim] is the same—to demand an accounting from the state in order that its conduct may be upright, even if the roads leading to this end may differ.[11]

Khayr al-Din therefore argued for a political system in which rulers would be required to account for their actions to the *ahl al-hall wa-l-'aqd* (the people who loosen and bind; the identical phrase was used in the Tunisian constitution for the members of the Grand Council). For Khayr al-Din, such people would include both notables and the *'ulama*. From his writings it is clear that he viewed the rulers as merely one obstacle to the construction of such a system; the *'ulama* themselves were little trained to play such a role and suspicious of a seeming European import. Khayr al-Din argued that such accountability served Europe well and was thoroughly in keeping with traditional Islamic conceptions of the role for the *shari'a* (Islamic law) and the *'ulama*. The *umma* could prosper only if it rediscovered such practices.

Viewed in light of Khayr al-Din's writings, the Tunisian constitution appears to be an attempt to develop a constitutionalist system that is Islamic but not democratic. The point is to render authority accountable to the *shari'a* and to an elite that keeps the interests of the community in mind. The argument for an Islamic constitutionalism hardly died with Khayr al-Din, as will become clear in Chapter Six. Yet the attempt to put such a constitutionalism into practice proved abortive not only in Tunisia but elsewhere.

Ottoman Empire

The Ottoman constitution of 1876 was issued in circumstances quite similar to those surrounding the Tunisian constitution of 1861.[12] Its fate initially seemed quite similar as well, because it was suspended after only a short period of operation. In the longer term, however, not only was it eventually revived for the Ottoman Empire in its final decade; it also served as the basis for most Arab constitution writing in the twentieth century.

The Ottoman Empire faced a profound crisis in the mid-1870s. Like Tunisia, it had embarked on a program of administrative centralization and rationalization coupled with an attempt to build a powerful standing military force. The Ottoman program was far more extensive and sustained than its Tunisian counterpart (indeed, the Tunisian program was partly modeled on the Ottoman), but by 1875 the Ottoman government faced a series of related problems. Internally, several provinces in the Balkans were in open revolt. The political and military program had been expensive, leading the government to borrow so extensively that it could not avoid bankruptcy. Externally, the military position of the Empire had so eroded that it could not resist European encroachment without diplomatic maneuvering designed to solicit European support and play European powers off against each other.

In this environment, a group among the political elite of the Empire evinced increasing interest in constitutional government as the key to political and fiscal rationalization and reform. The idea was controversial, partly because a constitution had the potential to encroach on the prerogatives of powerful individuals and groups. Not only might it restrict the authority of the sultan; it might also further the legal equality between Muslims and non-Muslims and diminish the role for *shari'a*-based law in the administration of justice.

A group of senior officials, military leaders, and *'ulama* was appointed to draft a constitution; they considered a number of drafts and proposals. The draft they finally submitted to the sultan most closely resembled the Belgian constitution of 1831; others noted parallels with the Prussian constitution, itself a more royalist version of the Belgian model. The sultan submitted the draft to the cabinet, which made some changes before promulgation.

As finally adopted, the Ottoman constitution of 1876 had twelve sections. The first defined the nature of the state and of the sultan, designating him as caliph and enumerating his prerogatives (without limiting his authority to those designated in the constitution). The second section granted Ottoman subjects rights and equality under the law. The third and fourth sections dealt with the cabinet and public officials. The fifth, sixth, and seventh sections established an elected parliament and an appointed senate. The eighth and ninth sections dealt with the judiciary, guaranteeing the irremovability of judges and establishing a high court for offenses involving ministers, judges, and treason.

The final three sections established the necessity for a budget, provincial government, and emergency and amendment provisions.

The procedure for drafting the constitution, coupled with its content, made clear that many key issues related to constitutionalism were left ambiguous. On the one hand, the Ottoman constitution seemed to mimic constitutional forms while avoiding constitutionalist substance. It was drafted by a narrow group and issued by the sultan. Thus, the constitution would seem to draw authority from—rather than grant authority to—the sultan and the political elite. While the constitution did create an elected parliament, deputies had very limited rights to initiate legislation; for the most part its legislative authority was restricted to reviewing drafts submitted by the ministers. The constitution also failed to specify that only legislation approved by parliament was valid; the authors, relying on European constitutional tradition, took this for granted (with the exception that the constitution expressly gave the sultan and the cabinet such a right when parliament was not in session so long as the laws were presented to parliament at its next meeting). The sultan, however, exploited the silence to claim the authority to issue decrees with the force of law regardless of the parliament, arguing in effect that the authority that issued the constitution could hardly be bound by that document. The sultan's claim would have seemed highly dubious in a nineteenth-century European context (and indeed hearkened back to some early modern European political debates), but it was authoritative in the Ottoman Empire.

Under the constitution, ministers were politically responsible to the sultan; their responsibility to the parliament was limited. The constitution did contain some provisions for individual rights, but it followed the European practice that generally allows such rights to be defined by statute. Only torture was absolutely prohibited; all other rights depended on legislation that could be in practice quite limiting. And the sultan was granted a virtually unlimited right to order exile; the first victim of this provision was Midhat, the politician most influential in securing the adoption of the constitution.

On the other hand, the constitution was not without concessions to parliamentary prerogative and constitutional government. While ministers were politically responsible to the sultan, the parliament was granted some authority over them. The parliament could try ministers for criminal offenses with the sultan's permission. It could also direct questions to them and force their resignation by rejecting their legislative initiatives. While the text of the constitution seemed at first glance to render parliament quite weak, it must be borne in mind that ministerial responsibility to parliament was generally secured in nineteenth-century Europe by political practice rather than constitutional text (see Part Two). The Ottoman constitution did give the parliament some tools if it wished to pursue such a goal. The constitution gave the parliament some genuine (though hardly absolute) control over the budget; it also insisted that taxation be carried out on a legal and equitable basis. Finally, the constitution allowed judges to be removed only if condemned by their colleagues. Special courts were prohibited, robbing a would-be authoritarian government of an important instrument.

The Ottoman constitution thus left much to be determined by law and practice. While it allowed many avenues for avoiding its provisions and left the parliament only a few crude ways of enforcing limits on executive authority, an assertive parliament did have the potential to obstruct government action (if not determine policy), question ministers, and call them to account. Indeed, it was precisely the attempt of some parliamentarians to realize the constitutionalist potential of the 1876 constitution that led to the suspension of the document.[13]

Given the crises faced by the Ottoman government—bankruptcy, military weakness, internal rebellion, and European diplomatic pressure—it was natural that the newly created parliament would take its oversight responsibilities fairly seriously. This soon led to a clash between the cabinet (and implicitly the sultan) and the parliament. The clash began when some deputies succeeded in inserting veiled criticisms of the government into the parliamentary reply to the speech from the throne. It became more serious in a dispute over essential legislation mandated by the constitution. In its first session, the parliament passed three laws related to the press, provincial administration, and provisions for a state of siege. Rather than approve the laws, the cabinet revised them and resubmitted them to parliament. The parliament indicated its displeasure by not acting on the resubmitted drafts. The confrontation reached its peak when the parliament prepared to vote no confidence in five ministers and request the trial of a former grand *wazir* (the highest official under the sultan), citing the military defeats.[14] The sultan reacted by appointing a new cabinet, but the parliament still asked that the constitutional provisions to try ministers for criminal offenses be activated against the former grand *wazir*. When the sultan moved to transform the position of grand wazir into a prime ministership (as will be seen, this was a key part of the program of the constitutionalists), deputies objected, pointing out that this violated explicit constitutional provisions for the appointment of a grand *wazir*.

In short, the Ottoman parliament had begun to turn fairly weak constitutional provisions into real mechanisms of accountability; it even seemed to be moving toward forcing ministerial responsibility to the parliament. Rather than accept the parliamentary effort to transform the constitution into the basis for a constitutionalist system, the sultan disbanded the parliament, ordering all deputies to leave the city. Parliament was not reconvened for three decades.

The Ottoman constitution thus had a far more contentious history than its equally short-lived Tunisian predecessor. It was written to conform to conflicting visions of the proper political order; some of the nature of this conflict can be discovered by an examination of the matters that provoked the greatest controversy in the writing of the document. Four issues proved especially divisive in the process of drafting the Ottoman constitution of 1876. First, some members of the *'ulama* so bitterly and publicly opposed the entrance of non-Muslims into the Parliament that they were exiled. Yet while these opponents lost the battle over the constitutional text, the victors were far from secularists. The final draft clearly established Islam as the state religion in various institutional and symbolic ways. The authors of the constitution most likely sought to further legitimate positive legislation alongside the Islamic *shari'a*; they also probably wished to wean non-Muslims away from separatist hopes. (Indeed, an earlier proposal had been based on federalizing the government of the Empire.)

The other controversies focused directly or indirectly on attempts to restrict and regularize the authority of the sultan and the government. Most directly, the precise nature of ministerial responsibility was debated. While the final draft provided for ministers to be appointed by and responsible to the sultan, not all elements of parliamentary authority over ministers were removed, as was made clear in practice. The sultan also insisted that he be granted the authority to order the exile of persons deemed dangerous, a claim unsuccessfully but bitterly resisted by leading constitutionalist political leaders. A dispute over the position of the grand *wazir* was more subtle: the sultan successfully resisted attempts to replace the grand *wazir* with a prime minister. This step would have introduced real cabinet government by having ministers report to the sultan through the prime minister; it might have brought about a stronger measure of collective responsibility and diminished the role of the sultan in day-to-day governance.

Equally interesting is the lack of controversy over two seemingly essential innovations. The rights provisions of the constitution occasioned less debate because they deferred the most critical issues to subsequent legislation. And the demand for regularization and legalization of taxation and fiscal affairs provoked little dissent.

The nature of these debates—and the short history of the constitution itself—suggest that the Ottoman political elite was badly divided in the 1870s.

The constitution served only to focus these divisions rather than resolve them. On the one hand stood constitutionalist politicians. While they were anxious to establish an assembly, the goal was less to provide for an element of democracy in Ottoman governance than it was to provide for a measure of accountability. The authority of state actors was not to be diminished, but it was to operate on a more legal and rationalized basis. Accountability, fiscal reform, and rationalization would serve as tools to strengthen the Empire and enable it to face its formidable domestic and international challenges. Robert Devereux writes:

> As crisis followed crisis the liberals became convinced that the safety, if not the very existence, of the Empire lay in a radical reshaping of its faulty government structure. Above all they perceived a need to end the absolute rule of the sultan and to substitute a constitutional form of government. Although they viewed non-Muslim co-operation and participation as an essential element of the new regime, they were by no means advocates of abandonment of Turkish-Muslim supremacy. They appear to have been constitutionalists not because they desired a constitution as an end in itself but because they saw in a constitution the best hope for the regeneration of the Empire. Comparing the strength and vigor of the Western European states and impressed by the form without fully understanding its basis, they appear to have become imbued with the idea that the creation in Turkey of a regime patterned on those of Europe would *ipso facto* restore to their country its vanished strength and vigor.[15]

Devereux's description of the motivations of the constitutionalists is accurate, though it considerably exaggerates their naivete. More to the point, however, his description of this group as "liberals" needs to be qualified: the Ottoman constitutionalists were very much members of the political elite. By trying to regularize the authority of the sultan and introduce a measure of accountability they were, in a sense, attempting only to render their own positions more effective and efficient. The precarious international and domestic position of the government allowed them to negotiate an ambiguous document that secured some of their ends. The constitution that resulted did not emanate from the population of the Empire nor did it really empower any group other than elements of the existing political leadership. When the ambiguous structures and procedures established by the constitution seemed to be leading to real constitutional government, its opponents were powerless to prevent its suspension.

While the Ottoman constitution was suspended after less than two years of operation, it was not forgotten. In 1908, a group of army officers allied themselves with some reform-minded political leaders and compelled the sultan to reinstate the constitution.[16] One year later, they forced the anticonstitutionalist sultan to abdicate and secured several constitutional amendments that seemed to resolve many of the ambiguities of the earlier text in the parliament's favor. It required the sultan to swear an oath to the *shari'a*, constitution, homeland, and nation. Ministers were now responsible to the parliament, both individually and collectively. Parliament also was accorded the right to initiate legislation and could pass legislation over the sultan's veto by a supermajority.

The revised constitution theoretically remained in effect until the collapse of the Ottoman Empire after the First World War, but it ran into early difficulty. On an international level, the new government proved no more able to resist European armies in either Libya or the Balkans; internally, the opposition to the new leadership showed surprising electoral strength. The new government was forced to rely on heavy suppression of the opposition and electoral manipulation to retain control of the parliament that it had brought back into being.

Despite its imperfect record, the reinstatement of the Ottoman constitution had permanent effects, especially on Arab constitutional history. The text provided a starting point for most of the attempts to draft constitutions in the former Ottoman provinces. Its attempt to balance parliamentary authority with a monarchy provided the basis for similar efforts in Syria in 1920, Egypt in 1923, Jordan and Iraq under their British mandates, and Kuwait in 1962.

Egypt

The final constitution promulgated in the Middle East during the nineteenth century was the Egyptian constitution of 1882. It was issued in the midst of the same sort of crises that afflicted Tunisia and the Ottoman Empire during their experiments with constitutions. The country was bankrupt and operating under a degree of European financial control, and there was rising anti-European agitation, military discontent, and an increasingly assertive assembly. Politics in Egypt was even more contentious during the brief constitutional interlude, so much so that the country was occupied and the constitution rendered irrelevant within months of its passage.[17]

The first attempt to implement an Egyptian constitution came in 1879. The Consultative Council of Delegates, first convened in 1866, exhibited increasing resentfulness toward European financial control and the political influence that came with it. Egyptian bankruptcy had led to the introduction of a French and a British minister into the Egyptian cabinet; these ministers angered the Council of Delegates by refusing to answer questions directed to them. While the Council had little formal power, its members joined with some leading members of the religious and political elites to pressure the government to resist European financial initiatives (particularly those that would have resulted in higher taxation for the notables and landowners who dominated the Council). The Khedive [hereditary governor] Isma'il, effective ruler of the country, responded favorably to the pressure, most likely delighted to develop a counterweight to European pressure. Isma'il appointed a new government in which European ministers and non-Europeans deemed excessively accommodationist were excluded. The prime minister, Sharif, prepared a draft constitution with the aim of introducing a measure of parliamentarism, accountability, and limits on the khedive's authority. The balance between royal prerogatives and parliamentary powers was not altogether different from that in the Ottoman constitution of 1876: the khedive would have retained predominant influence over the cabinet and legislative process, but the parliament did have some tools at its disposal.[18] Isma'il was deposed, however, and the Council was adjourned before any action could be taken on the draft.

Two years later a military resentful of European influence, discrimination against ethnically Egyptian officers, and arrears in pay demonstrated at 'Abdin palace where Tawfiq, Isma'il's successor as khedive, resided. Under this pressure, Tawfiq agreed to elections for a reconvened Council; he also recalled Sharif to the premiership. Sharif resurrected his draft, which was submitted to the newly elected Council. The Council, anxious to reduce foreign financial control, sought to increase its control over the budget. Sharif insisted that the matter be referred to the European powers, probably not only out of deference to Egypt's creditors but also in recognition that a greater role for the Council in public finance would further alienate European powers already suspicious of nationalist and anti-European sentiments in Egyptian politics. Angry parliamentarians brought the matter to Tawfiq, insisting that Sharif be dismissed and the draft constitution approved. Tawfiq acceded to both demands. The Council obtained not only a constitution; it also secured the potentially important precedent that a prime minister without the confidence of the parliament was in an untenable position.[19]

By twentieth-century standards, the 1882 constitution (termed the Fundamental Ordinance, or *al-la'iha al-asasiyya*) was fairly brief, focusing almost all of its fifty-two articles on the Council. An elected body, the Council was given an extensive role in legislation and in oversight of public finances. Ministers were invited to attend the Council sessions; they could also be summoned. While the constitution stipulated that ministers were responsible to the Council, it also mandated new elections if a difference between the cabinet and the Council could not be resolved. If a newly elected Council insisted on the position of the former Council, its opinion was binding. The few rights provisions were directly related to the Council, covering issues such as petitioning the Council or the immunity of Council members.[20]

The Egyptian constitution of 1882 may have provided a sounder basis for constitutionalism than the Tunisian constitution of 1861 or the Ottoman constitution of 1876. The difference lay not so much in the text of the document as in the political circumstances surrounding its adoption. All three documents contained tenuous and ambiguous limits on royal authority; the Egyptian constitution was distinctive in that the parliament not only asserted an ambitious interpretation of its prerogatives but did so successfully (and with the backing of the military). Yet shortly after having secured this triumph the parliament went into recess, never to reconvene. Under foreign threats, the political elite of the country split into two hostile camps; Tawfiq fled to the protection of the British fleet. In the summer of 1882, Great Britain occupied Egypt, restored Tawfiq, and allowed the constitution to be forgotten.

The Egyptian constitution of 1882 can thus be seen as a more ambitious effort than its Tunisian and Ottoman counterparts. Nevertheless, it did not start out that way. Juan Cole accurately characterizes Sharif, the political leader most responsible for drafting the constitution and pursuing adoption of the text: "His constitutionalism was of an elitist variety aimed at shifting some power away from the khedive and the Europeans to the nobles."[21] The agenda of the Council was more ambitious—which is why it successfully demanded Sharif's resignation when he balked at their demands for a stronger role in supervising the budget. But even the constitutional agenda of the members of the Council should not be exaggerated; Alexander Scholch notes:

> The delegates thus did not have in mind at all the establishment of a system of 'parliamentary government'. They wanted to control that half of the budget which was at their disposal, to subject fiscal policy to their will, and to shut the door on any further economic and political progress by the Europeans in Egypt.[22]

Egyptian constitutionalists therefore should not be seen as fundamentally different in their aims than their Tunisian and Ottoman counterparts. They came from the political elite and saw a constitution as a way of rendering government more efficient and fiscally responsible. Their aim was not to end all khedival prerogatives—nor did their draft even contain them all within constitutional channels—but to diminish the khedive's discretion and allow him to be as responsive to domestic as to foreign concerns. Once again, democracy was hardly an issue: the Council, though elected, was essentially a way to ensure representation primarily of the provincial notability.

Other Early Constitutional Experiments in the Middle East: Iran and Kuwait

In the early twentieth century, changes in Middle Eastern politics often took the form, at least in part, of constitutional changes. For instance, the collapse of Ottoman rule in the Arab provinces motivated the composition of short-lived and little-remembered constitutional documents in areas that eventually became part of Transjordan and Libya.[23] Two other constitutional experiments bear examination in this analysis of early Middle Eastern experiences with constitutions: the Iranian constitution of 1906 and the Kuwaiti constitution of 1938. In Iran, a constitution was written in 1906 and 1907 under circumstances quite like those in Egypt, Tunisia, and the Ottoman Empire. Such similarities suggest the usefulness of a consideration of the origins of the Iranian constitutional experiment. Despite strong common political and textual origins, however, the Iranian constitution did not prove tremendously influential in the Arab world, so this brief discussion will focus only on the motivations behind the promulgation of the constitution. It is worth noting, however, that the Iranian constitution was in some ways more successful than the experiments analyzed in this chapter. It remained in effect—officially, if only rarely in spirit—until the Islamic revolution of 1979.[24]

The same combination of fiscal crisis (verging on bankruptcy) and foreign pressure that provoked crises in Egypt and the Ottoman Empire operated in Iran with increasing severity in the late nineteenth century. By the early twentieth century they had provoked sufficient popular unrest that the shah finally allowed a parliament to be convened. A committee was entrusted with drafting a constitution, which the shah approved in 1906; the following year the parliament passed (and the shah ratified) a supplementary text. As with its Egyptian and Ottoman counterparts, the Iranian parliament was especially anxious to secure some control over state finances, treaties, and concessions. The issue of ministerial responsibility was resolved ambiguously, though more favorably to the parliament than in the Ottoman Empire and Egypt: the authority to appoint ministers clearly lay with the shah, but the parliament could withdraw confidence. Equality and individual rights were provided for, though their precise meaning often depended on implementing legislation. The constitution introduced a potentially important innovation in the attempt to reconcile positive law with the Islamic *shari'a*: a council of *'ulama* was to be established to review matters proposed in the parliament with the power to strike down any proposal not in accordance with the *shari'a*. This provision of the constitution was effectively ignored throughout most of the history of the Iranian constitution.

Despite this attempt to establish its compatibility with Islam, the Iranian constitution soon came under attack from some members of the *'ulama* as an attempt to marginalize the Islamic *shari'a* and replace it with positive law. Iranian monarchs also strained at some of the constitutional limits placed on their authority. While the constitution continued in force, its viability depended on a strong and independent parliament. In the few years after the constitutional revolution, and again in the late 1940s and early 1950s, such a parliament emerged. It might seem ironic that a constitution that was designed to establish a fairly strong parliament instead depended on that parliament for support, but this has not been an unusual pattern in Middle Eastern constitutional history.

The Kuwaiti constitution of 1938 was a brief document with a brief history.[25] Like all the other documents, the Kuwaiti constitution was engendered partly by fiscal difficulties, but of a quite different sort. Far from bankrupt, the Kuwaiti government had to deal with the influx of revenues stemming from an oil concession signed with a British company. By later standards, the revenues were modest indeed, but they caused a dispute both within the ruling Al Sabah family and with leading merchants over the division of royalties among the amir, the Al Sabah, and the population. A group of leading merchants allied themselves with a dissident faction of the Al Sabah family and compelled the amir to accept an assembly; that assembly adopted a basic law that was designed to serve as a provisional constitution.

The Kuwaiti constitution of 1938 contained just five articles. The first designated the nation [*umma*] as the source of authority as represented by the assembly. The second listed a series of laws that the assembly should pass. The third article mandated the assembly's responsibility for treaties, concessions, and agreements, banning those that did not obtain the assembly's consent and oversight. The fourth article designated the assembly as a temporary appeals court until an independent court could be formed; the final article designated the assembly's president as the executive authority in the country.[26] The amir resisted the draft but ultimately acceded to it. When the assembly attempted to assert increasing control over revenue, the amir dissolved it and arranged for new elections. He attempted to have the new assembly approve a constitution he found more appropriate but failed. Accusing members of the new assembly of looking to outside powers (especially Iraq) for support, the amir abandoned the experiment altogether.

As with its nineteenth-century predecessors, the Kuwaiti constitution of 1938 was an elitist affair. Only leading merchant families and dissident members of the royal family were included. Far shorter than the earlier documents, the Kuwaiti constitution contained the same ambiguous hints of parliamentary government and foundered when ambitious members of the assembly tried to make those hints the basis for political (and fiscal) authority in the country.

Nineteenth-Century Constitution Writing

Nineteenth-century constitutions were almost always so short-lived that they appear quixotic in retrospect. What were their authors attempting to achieve? And why did they not succeed?

Three possible nonconstitutional motives were suggested in the introduction, related to sovereignty, ideology, and enhancement of state authority. The first of these, sovereignty, implicitly holds that the major audience for a constitution may be external. The international context was critical to all of the efforts examined in this chapter. Despite their short-lived nature, however, nineteenth-century Middle Eastern constitutions cannot be dismissed as mere window-dressing, designed primarily for foreign consumption. In some of the cases, most notably Egypt and Iran, the constitutions were issued in the face of a hostile international environment. In Egypt, the constitution's life was terminated by foreign occupation. Only in the Tunisian case was there clear European support for the constitution. Nineteenth-century constitutions were generally written primarily for local, rather than foreign, consumption (though in the Tunisian and Ottoman cases, some clearly hoped that European powers would be favorably impressed by the local efforts). Nor can the constitutions be seen merely as accouterments of sovereignty; in several of the cases (Tunisia, Egypt, and Kuwait) the political systems involved had not yet clearly established their own sovereign natures, despite the proclamations of constitutional texts. Nevertheless, the constitutions were designed to establish sovereignty (or something close to it), but not in a merely symbolic way. The constitutions were to be more than the equivalent of flags or postage stamps: in all cases except the Kuwaiti, the constitution was designed to support a state more able to resist foreign penetration. Constitutions were designed to establish the autonomy of the state in the international arena.

The second, ideological motive suggested in the introduction does not seem to fit the nineteenth-century Middle Eastern experience: the constitutions did little to proclaim new ideological orientations. It would be difficult to deny that there was a real ideological ferment involving issues of Islam, nationalism, and constitutionalism. But the constitutions analyzed here seemed better designed to hide innovations rather than proclaim them. As opposed to more recent constitutions, there is little in these documents of a direct or explicit ideological nature: there is no statement of basic principles, no declaration of policy direction, and no programmatic content. Instead the constitutions are phrased in preexisting ideological terms. They generally present themselves as the will of the ruler rather than the people or the nation. There is explicit (and genuine) obeisance to Islamic vocabulary of governance. This takes several forms: reference to the *shari'a*; the official establishment of Islam; provision for Islamic institutions; and the use of Islamic terminology. Nineteenth-century constitutions did not seem to serve the purpose of proclaiming new principles; they generally dressed in the guise of old ones.[27]

Finally, a striking similarity in political circumstances surrounding these attempts at writing constitutions suggests that the fundamental purpose was to reform state authority in an attempt to make it more effective. First, almost all constitutions were issued during a period of fiscal crisis and devoted much language to establishing clear procedures for determining the budget. And nineteenth-century constitutions seemed far more focused on taxation than any of the traditional liberal rights: subjects were generally given surer guarantees against any tax not imposed by law than they were given to freedom of expression or association. Coming in the wake of fiscal crisis, bankruptcy, and pressure to grant economic concessions, such constitutions are best conceived— at least in part—as attempts to put the fiscal house in order. Autocracy had led to fiscal irresponsibility; clear legal procedures for fiscal matters could help the state operate on a sounder basis.

Second, all the constitutions discussed here (with the partial exception of the Iranian) originated very much within the governing elite. They were not composed by constituent assemblies seeking to define the nature of the political community but by individuals or small groups of politicians who generally occupied very senior positions. Often little public discussion surrounded their composition, even when they occasioned sharp private debate within the elite. And they were promulgated by rulers who made clear—though not always explicitly—that they could be taken away in the same manner that they were given. That is, the ruler or governing elite granted legitimacy to—rather than drew legitimacy from—the constitutional document.

In short, nineteenth-century Middle Eastern constitutions represented attempts by some members of the governing elite to find a formula for more accountable, regularized, and effective government. The goal was to strengthen the authority of the state in the face of internal rebellion, fiscal crisis, and external penetration. Nineteenth-century constitutions were not always designed to strengthen the authority of the ruler, but they were uniformly designed to strengthen and order the state apparatus.

This purpose becomes even more clear if we consider the areas of the Middle East that completely avoided any constitutional document. Despite the fleeting lives of nineteenth-century constitutions, their geographic reach was wide indeed. Only two regions escaped any attempt at issuing a constitution: Morocco and the Arabian peninsula (the only exceptions for the Arabian peninsula were Kuwait, discussed above, and the Hijaz, which briefly had a constitution in the 1920s).

Not coincidentally, these regions managed to avoid the acute crisis of governance that afflicted Tunisia, the Ottoman Empire, Egypt, and Iran. This is not to say that they avoided political problems altogether, only that they lacked the existence of a political elite fending off a simultaneous internal and external challenge, linked to and compounded by fiscal crisis. The Arabian peninsula lacked the bureaucratic state that existed in the other cases, and while its rulers were certainly poor they were not caught between the requirement to repay foreign loans and resistance to rising tax rates. For the most part, their fiscal appetites were more limited.

Morocco was less exceptional. The country certainly attracted European attention (and eventually French rule). But for a long time Morocco's rulers managed to avoid the pattern of rising debt, taxation, and discontent that led their counterparts elsewhere in the Middle East to the desperate measure of a constitution. Moroccan exceptionalism did not survive the nineteenth century, however, and by the early twentieth century it had begun to follow the pattern so familiar in Tunisia, Egypt, the Ottoman Empire, and Iran. It should therefore be no surprise that it was precisely at such a period that the idea of a written constitution was first mooted in Morocco. In the first decade of the twentieth century, a series of draft plans was developed, and in 1908 a complete constitution was drafted by some intellectuals and published. Their draft followed the Ottoman model in broad outline. The effort to establish some sort of constitution was given a boost by the decision of the 'ulama to condition their pledge of obedience [bay'a] to the new sultan, 'Abd al-Hafiz, on his defending the kingdom and consulting the population.[28] Given the experience of other Middle Eastern countries, it may be surmised that a Moroccan constitution was forestalled by the coming of the French protectorate.

Why were the constitutional experiments of the period so short-lived? The principal problem was that the documents served not only the nonconstitutionalist motives described thus far; they also could serve constitutionalist ends. Generally, constitutionalists focused their attentions on the new assemblies, hoping they would hold government accountable. Indeed, it was precisely on this point that nineteenth-century constitutionalism tended to break down. The documents described here did not determine all issues related to political structure; indeed, they generally set off new battles. The new constitutions were clearly designed to render state authority more effective, but were they also designed to restrict the authority of the ruler and allow him to act only through constitutional channels? Some would-be constitutionalists worked precisely for this end. Constitutionalism—and not simply writing a constitution—was very much on the agenda of some Tunisian, Egyptian, Ottoman, and Iranian reformers. Yet the constitutions that were promulgated were uncertain instruments even in the hands of the constitutionalists. In cases where they began to serve constitutionalist ends, they often provoked severe political crises; the constitutions themselves were often the victims. Given that the attempts to write constitutions were often connected with struggles to ward off European penetration, the constitutionalists often found that they had powerful enemies both inside and outside the countries. Thus, even where the constitutions survived—in Iran and the Ottoman Empire—the effective period of constitutionalist government can be numbered in months.

TWO

CONSTITUTIONS AND ARAB MONARCHIES

In the nineteenth century, Middle Eastern states desperately experimented with constitutional texts in the face of both international and domestic challenges. This pattern continued into the twentieth century, even in monarchies, which seem unlikely locations. Indeed, it is initially puzzling why constitutional documents and basic laws were promulgated in any monarchical states in the Arab world. Constitutions were rarely forced on Arab kings from abroad or from below. In fact, they were often issued in the face of colonial suspicions or in the waning days of colonial influence; and the monarchs issuing them were very suspicious of popular forces and elected assemblies. Arab monarchies would seem to be some of the least likely sources of constitutions, yet by the late twentieth century all Arab monarchies had issued them.

The first wave of constitution writing in Arab monarchies came in the wake of nominal independence in the interwar era. Egypt, Iraq, and Jordan all issued constitutions while under some degree of British oversight. The second wave came after other Arab states obtained independence in the 1960s and early 1970s (Morocco, Kuwait, Bahrain, Qatar, and the UAE). Finally, Oman and Saudi Arabia, long resistant to constitutional texts, issued basic laws in the 1990s.

This chapter demonstrates that monarchical constitutions can largely be explained in similar terms to those of the nineteenth century, though there are some significant differences in emphasis. The primary motivation for issuing constitutions in twentieth-century monarchies should be understood in terms of the support such documents lent to the cause of national independence; this explains much about their timing and content. Ideological aspects seem to have been less significant. Constitutions in Arab monarchies have

35

served to delineate political structures without limiting rulers in most locations. While the motivation of organizing state authority has been apparent in most monarchies, it has generally been of secondary importance except concerning one critical issue: succession. In addition to these motivations, constitutionalist values have sometimes emerged in Arab monarchies, but rarely have they found effective institutional expression.

Egypt

The British occupation of Egypt in 1882 reversed any movement Egypt may have been making in a constitutionalist direction. The draft document of 1882 (discussed in the previous chapter) clearly had no place under British rule. The occupation left the country's status extremely ambiguous—autonomous for close to a century, Egypt was now occupied by a European power that shied from severing links with the technically sovereign Ottoman sultan. With the khedive restored to the throne, and the British neither annexing the country to their empire nor withdrawing, it became difficult to locate the formal source of authority. The British deliberately decided to maintain that ambiguity, making any comprehensive constitutional document virtually impossible. In 1914, a journalist described the approach, which was designed to make British influence paramount even as it operated outside of institutional channels:

> We fell back on a compromise. We did not annex and we did not retire. The Anglo-Saxon, says Lord Cromer [the British consul-general], asserted his native genius 'by working a system which, according to every canon of political thought, was unworkable.' And the line he took was that he would do all that was necessary for Egypt without accepting the responsibility of incorporating it with his own dominions. 'He would not interfere with the liberty of action of the Khedival Government, but in practice he would insist on the Khedive and the Egyptian Ministers conforming to his views.'[1]

The British therefore resisted any formal limitation on the authority of the khedive, either domestic (from an elected assembly) or international (from the Ottoman Empire or the European creditors). On an informal level, British policy was firm: the khedive and his ministers must consult the British and accept their advice on all major matters. In 1883, an "organic law" established a purely consultative assembly; in 1913 the law was revised to give the council some very limited fiscal authority. This expansion in authority was short-lived: the council was suspended in 1915.[2]

At the outset of the First World War, the British finally determined to resolve the question of Egypt's international status, declaring a protectorate over the country and severing the link with the Ottoman Empire. While various options (including annexation to the British empire) were discussed, final decisions were postponed until the end of the war. Britain did use the opportunity to depose the khedive (deemed insufficiently cooperative). His successor was named *sultan* (a title that emphasized the break from the sovereignty of the Ottoman sultan).

At the end of the war, the British encountered a new obstacle: a strong nationalist movement arose that insisted that Egypt's contributions to the war effort were sufficient to earn a seat at the peace negotiations. The British responded by arresting the movement's leaders, sparking a nationalist uprising that rapidly spread from the cities to most provinces in the country. The British managed to reassert authority, but any hope of annexation was dashed. Instead, the British resolved to negotiate an agreement that would grant Egypt autonomy (and even formal independence) so long as Britain could protect its interests inside the country and maintain its strong voice in foreign and security policy.

The nationalist movement eventually organized itself as a political party, the *Wafd* [delegation, referring to the origins of the movement in the demand to represent Egypt in postwar peace negotiations]; the new party's appeal was based largely on its demand for complete independence. After several years, Britain found that it could not come to an agreement with the Wafd. Other political forces might be more pliant but lacked the Wafd's standing and therefore could not negotiate a viable agreement. Frustrated, the British finally took unilateral action, declaring the country independent while reserving broad areas (such as protection of foreigners and security policy) for their own oversight. The Egyptian sultan assumed the new title of king [*malik*].

Egyptians, though their independence remained limited, were confronted with the need to define a political structure. The king appointed a committee to draft a constitution, but the committee was forced to work in difficult circumstances. The British had greatly reduced but not eliminated their role in matters of internal governance. The Wafd rejected the British reservations on independence and demanded that a constitution be written by a popularly elected constituent assembly. Many leading politicians, legal figures, and jurists were willing to participate in the committee despite the Wafd's suspicions, but it was not clear how much constitutionalism the king would tolerate.

While the committee worked in a difficult political atmosphere, it was able to draw on European and Ottoman precedents, as well as Egyptian experience. The minutes of the drafting committee, later published, show its members to be very conversant in matters of constitutional law and design.[3] While they worked predominantly from Ottoman and continental European constitutional models, they showed particular interest in writing a document that would help the country assert its independence and establish a measure of parliamentarism.[4]

To secure independence, the drafting committee prepared a draft proclaiming the country's monarch "King of Egypt and Sudan." The step angered the British who had not fully accepted Egyptian sovereignty, much less inclusion of the Sudan. More subtly, the drafters included an article that implicitly recognized the capitulations, which granted extraterritorial status to foreigners, as a way of undermining the British claim of responsibility for protecting foreign interests and communities in Egypt.[5]

Debate on royal prerogatives and democratic elements was especially extensive. Strong elitist arguments were introduced, justifying indirect electoral systems and literacy requirements for voting.[6] Ultimately, those with more democratic inclinations prevailed, and the constitution, though issued in the name of the king, proclaimed the principle of popular sovereignty without reservation. In addition, a list of political and civil rights and freedoms were to be guaranteed or defined by law. Such phrasing made rights less than absolute, since they depended on implementing legislation to give them meaning (and potentially limits), a feature that was not lost on the constitutional drafters.[7]

Much more attention was given to extremely practical concerns, especially those relating to the prerogatives of the parliament and the king. Here the advocates of strong parliamentary rule and limited royal prerogatives won a qualified victory. Ministers were to be responsible to parliament and the king was to rule through them. Royal powers to dissolve parliament and take emergency measures were recognized but circumscribed and limited. The king did retain substantial powers of appointment (especially over the upper house of parliament), but many members of the drafting committee familiar with European constitutional practice clearly expected that such appointments would be exercised through the king's ministers, as the constitutional text seemed to indicate.

The draft came under attack from many sources. The British successfully insisted that the matter of the king's title be deferred. The Wafd denounced the nature of the committee's work in very harsh terms, insisting that only a constitution composed by an elected constituent assembly would be legitimate.

For all their severity, however, the Wafd's criticisms focused on the composition of the document rather than its content; the constitutional draft would offer the party opportunities for exercising authority after parliamentary elections. The king displayed clear disappointment that the committee had inclined toward a parliamentary system, and successfully obtained some changes (chiefly in increasing his authority over appointments).

The constitution was therefore promulgated in 1923, after the British and the king had obtained the changes they deemed most essential. In its first decade, the constitution worked quite differently than anticipated. The Wafd quickly showed its ability to muster impressive parliamentary majorities whenever allowed, leading to clashes with both the British and the king. Having denounced the process of writing the constitution, the Wafd became the document's staunchest defender. Yet neither the king nor the British would allow the constitutional system to work as designed. The British intervened extraconstitutionally to force political changes on several occasions. In 1924, following the assassination of Lee Stack, the British commander of the Egyptian army, Great Britain demanded an apology and compensation and threatened military force if its demands were not accepted. The Wafdist government then in power resigned rather than comply with the ultimatum.[8] Most notoriously, in February 1942, the British ambassador forced the king at gunpoint to appoint a Wafdist government. While generally hostile to the Wafd, the British wished Egypt to have a stable government at a time when their energies were entirely focused on World War Two.

The king proved to be an even more consistent enemy of constitutionalism than the British. King Fu'ad had reluctantly accepted the constitution of 1923, but he refused to accept any limits, either explicit or implicit in the constitutional text. Most royal violations centered on the status of the parliament, especially because the Wafd dominated any free election.

On an explicit level, the constitution of 1923 was fundamentally violated three times in its first seven years of operation.[9] The violations were increasingly egregious. The first royal violation occurred in 1925. Following the assassination of Lee Stack and the resignation of the Wafdist government in 1924, a new government acceded to the British demands; shortly thereafter the parliament was dissolved and new elections were held. When these elections resulted in a Wafdist victory, the new parliament was dissolved at its first meeting. Complaining that this was a violation of the letter and spirit of the constitution (by dissolving parliament twice for the same reason and, in effect, refusing to accept the results of the election), a majority of deputies clung to the view that the dissolution was void and attempted to hold a parliamentary session in a hotel. The standoff was eventually ended with new elections in which the Wafd obtained a majority once again.

In 1928 the constitution was attacked more directly: the king dismissed a Wafdist government and asked Muhammad Mahmud, a member of the Liberal Constitutional party (backed by many of those who had written the 1923 constitution) to form a government. Mahmud not only dismissed the parliament but also announced that the parliamentary system itself was suspended.

In 1929, the constitution was reinstituted, but within a year a government led by Isma'il Sidqi abolished the 1923 constitution, substituting a new document. While the 1930 constitution followed most of the text of the earlier document, it strengthened royal prerogatives, especially over appointments and financial matters. In addition, an indirect electoral system was instituted that effectively allowed the rural administrative structure—under control of the government—greater ability to influence electoral outcomes.[10] With a few minor changes in the constitution, Egyptian constitutionalism was effectively suspended. Shortly before his death in 1936, King Fu'ad restored the 1923 constitution, which then continued in operation until the monarchy was overthrown in the aftermath of the 1952 Free Officers' coup.

King Faruq was far less inclined than his father to violate the explicit provisions of the 1923 constitution, but he followed his father's example in ignoring implicit constitutional arrangements or taking steps that robbed constitutional structures and procedures of their meaning.[11] Much of royal effort to circumvent the constitution focused on the electoral process. Two separate attempts were made under Fu'ad to establish palace parties; they only realized success when the Wafd boycotted elections. Under both Fu'ad and Faruq the palace was also often charged with manipulating elections in order to provoke a boycott by the Wafd or prevent a Wafdist majority. This was generally done through appointing a cabinet to administer elections using procedures or structures unfavorable to the Wafd (often through conversion of the rural administrative apparatus into an electoral machine).[12]

More subtly, however, the palace conception of the meaning of the key constitutional provisions deviated sharply from what the drafting committee had anticipated. This was particularly the case on the relationship between the king and the ministers. Versed in European constitutional tradition, the drafting committee expected the king to rule through his ministers who would be responsible to parliament; in short, the drafters saw themselves as establishing a constitutional monarchy. Such a conception was probably naive, because nineteenth-century Middle Eastern efforts at constitutionalism had foundered on precisely this issue: ministers effectively remained responsible to the ruler rather than the parliament. Moreover, the European tradition of a constitutional monarchy had emerged slowly, unevenly, and uncertainly throughout the nineteenth century; when it did emerge it was often not inscribed in any constitutional text. Thus the drafting committee appropriated language that had admitted nonconstitutionalist interpretations in Europe and would almost certainly do so in Egypt.

Two particular issues emerged in this regard. First, the king insisted on exercising his appointment authority (in the senate, the army, and elsewhere) directly rather than through his ministers. The constitution had granted him such authority, of course, but its drafters had anticipated that he would act according to the advice of his ministers. Second, the king proved far more active in appointing and dismissing governments than was anticipated. Of course, such governments could only serve if they enjoyed a parliamentary majority (except during the periods when parliament was suspended). Yet the king did not restrict his selection of the prime minister to the leader of the majority party; and on some occasions the Wafd felt compelled to accept the situation. The king had the constitutional authority to dissolve parliament and call for new elections. He used this authority on several occasions to dismiss a government that enjoyed a strong parliamentary majority; he failed to restrict himself to instances in which the government wished to hold new elections or feared the loss of its majority. In effect, the king refused to accept the anticipated limits of a constitutional monarchy and exercised the full range of his constitutional authorities directly.

Some Egyptian constitutionalists found these actions contrary to the spirit of the 1923 constitution and to constitutional traditions more generally. Indeed, the palace successfully transformed the structures and procedures of the 1923 constitution into a system that was at best vaguely constitutionalist. And the constitutionalists had no mechanisms in the constitution in which to enforce their vision of a constitutional monarchy. In effect, the 1923 constitution placed far weaker checks on royal and executive prerogatives than anticipated. Blatant violations of the 1923 constitution ceased after 1935 (with the notable exception of the British coup of 1942), but precedents were established that made such violations less necessary. The palace was allowed to pursue a plausible but hardly restrictive interpretation of key constitutional provisions. The 1923 constitution survived only after some of its constitutionalist spirit was removed. The palace's ability to enforce its interpretation of the constitution was never directly challenged; judicial review of the constitutionality of legislation and executive actions was only beginning to emerge at the time that the constitution was totally repudiated (as seen in chapter 5).

Iraq

Great Britain had begun to occupy Iraq during the First World War, but the basis of its presence in the country was not formalized until the granting of a mandate by the League of Nations. After suppressing a rebellion, Britain moved to construct an independent Iraqi government; in 1921 Faysal (from Hijaz), recently ousted by the French from Syria, was brought in as king. Before formally assuming the throne, the British arranged for a measure of popular legitimacy: the Iraqi Council of Ministers endorsed a resolution supporting Faysal's assumption of the throne provided that his government be "constitutional, representative and democratic" as well as "limited by law."[13] A process was then carried out in which residents of the country were asked whether or not they supported the resolution. While this process was presented externally as a referendum (answered by an overwhelming majority in favor), it would have appeared internally as a loyalty oath.[14]

The British then set to work drawing up a constitution for Iraq. The document was originally drawn up by British officials in Baghdad, who based their work primarily on the Ottoman constitution, though other constitutions were consulted. The Egyptian constitution, then being drafted, was influential, especially concerning the rights provisions.[15] They submitted the draft to the Colonial Office in London and to King Faysal shortly after he took the throne.[16] The original draft was sufficiently a British product that it was initially drafted in English.[17]

While working from the Ottoman model, the Iraqi constitution introduced potentially important modifications. Not only did it proclaim the principle of popular sovereignty, it also introduced some institutional departures from the Ottoman constitution of 1876. First, ministerial responsibility was clearly given to the parliament. The king was authorized to select a prime minister (an office that had been purposely omitted from the 1876 Ottoman constitution); the other ministers were appointed by the king on the advice of the prime minister. Yet the ministers could only continue to serve with the confidence of the Chamber of Deputies, the lower house of parliament. The Chamber could remove confidence from either an individual minister or the entire cabinet. Many of the ambiguities concerning ministerial responsibility contained in earlier constitutional texts seemed to have been avoided in the Iraqi case, and the prospects for a fully constitutional monarchy seemed quite real.

Second, provision was made for a special "High Court" composed of judges and members of the Senate, the upper house of parliament. The Ottoman constitution had provided for a similar court, borrowing from European constitutional designers anxious to ensure that ministers and high officials were criminally responsible (even in countries where the question of political responsibility remained undetermined). What was innovative about the Iraqi court was the explicit provision that the Court could, when called, interpret the constitution even to the extent of striking down legislation deemed unconstitutional.

Third, the rights provisions of the constitution were expanded, generally along lines that rapidly became standard in most Arab constitutional texts. Personal liberty, resort to the courts, and freedom of expression, meeting, association, and religion (extending to the freedom of religious minorities to operate their own schools) were all guaranteed. All rights were to be defined or regulated by law, except equality before the law and freedom from torture, deportation, forced labor, and uncompensated confiscations, which were absolute.

The Iraqi constitution seemed to provide a real basis for constitutionalist politics. State authority was to be exercised in accordance with the law; the constitution provided real checks on the actions of high officials; and the king and the executive branch operated within constitutional bounds. Yet the order introduced by the British contained some subtle but deliberate and extremely important limitations on constitutionalist practice, as British officials noted frankly at the time. As long as the mandate continued, it was clear that the British and not the king, the parliament, or the constitution had ultimate authority in the country. The British designed a constitution and a treaty that originally were to operate within the context of the mandate (despite strong Iraqi pressures that they replace the mandate immediately). Yet from the beginning the end of the mandate was anticipated. Accordingly, the constitution stipulated the continuing validity of all laws and regulations issued since the British had asserted control (along with pre-war Ottoman law) until and unless they were declared unconstitutional or repealed. Court judgments (including those from military courts) issued under British rule and the mandate were constitutionally endorsed without qualification. Thus it became impossible to contest any action that the British had taken.

Most subtly, the British-drafted constitution placed not only the mandate but also the entire relationship between Iraq and Britain outside the constitutional order as much as possible. An oil concession, for instance, was negotiated and presented to the cabinet one week before the constitution came into effect (so that it would not have to be presented to the parliament).[18] Article 26 of the Iraqi constitution allowed the king to take emergency measures in the absence of parliament, provided only that he obtain cabinet approval. The king was required to submit all such measures—with the explicit exception of those taken in fulfillment of treaties—to parliament at its next sitting for approval. The effect of this exception was to allow the king—at his own initiative or under British pressure—to move completely outside constitutional structures and procedures by dissolving parliament and taking whatever actions the Anglo-Iraqi treaty was deemed to require.

The constitution was thus carefully written to restrict the Iraqi state domestically but not to render it independent from the British. The practical effect of the document depended on the provisions of the Anglo-Iraqi treaty. And the first such treaty—drafted alongside the constitution—clearly provided for ultimate, if indirect, British control. For instance, the first treaty required that the king must consult the British high commissioner on all fiscal matters; this, in conjunction with a constitutional requirement that proposals for public expenditures could be introduced only by ministers (and not by parliamentary deputies) ensured that, in the words of a contemporary observer, "Iraqi finance is completely under British control insofar as that power chooses to exercise it."[19] The Anglo-Iraqi treaty provided for a number of subsidiary agreements that required the Iraqis to appoint British officials to key posts and defer to British wishes in matters including military forces and the legal position of foreigners.[20]

While the British clearly drafted both the constitution and the treaty to their liking, they required the assent of the Iraqi authorities to endorse them and make them work. Accordingly a Constituent Assembly was elected in 1924. The Iraqi cabinet proved reluctant to support a treaty that codified rather than replaced the mandate. Accordingly the British pledged to support eventual Iraqi entrance to the League of Nations (an implicit sign of independence) and to renegotiate the treaty after only four years. The cabinet also insisted that the treaty be submitted to the Constituent Assembly for final approval. That step led some Shi'i leaders to call for a boycott of the elections, arguing that the Constituent Assembly was effectively a body that would only sanction British occupation.[21]

When the Constituent Assembly met, it understandably focused most of its attention on the Anglo-Iraqi treaty. After months of bitter criticisms and debate, the Assembly had not acted, leading the British to issue a deadline for ratification. The Assembly finally approved the treaty by narrowly passing a resolution that criticized the text but indicated acceptance conditional upon effective British support for the inclusion of Mosul in the Iraqi state.[22]

The Assembly then turned its attention to the constitution itself, introducing a small number of revisions. Tribal leaders successfully insisted on striking a requirement that members of parliament be literate. The Assembly also modified the requirement for a parliamentary vote of no confidence, replacing the necessity for a two-thirds vote with a simple majority to bring down an individual minister or the entire cabinet. In almost all other respects, however, the British draft was accepted.[23]

As soon as it was adopted, the imperfections in the draft became quite clear. The constitution went into effect in March 1925, but the parliament was not to be convened until November 1. Without parliament, there was no constitutional mechanism to approve the budget in time. The constitutional drafters had neglected to provide for special sessions. A special session of parliament had to be convened in order to amend the constitution allowing for special sessions. And when that amendment was passed, the amended clause inadvertently dropped the provision allowing the parliament to recess.[24]

Yet the real changes in Iraq's constitution came not through amendment of the text but through renegotiation of the treaty relationship with Britain. In 1930 a new treaty was finally negotiated that made possible the termination of the mandate and Iraq's admission to the League of Nations in 1932. The new treaty removed some, though not all, of Britain's ability to move outside the constitutional structure. By retaining some special (especially military) privileges, Britain was still in a good position to insist on enforcement of treaty obligations without reference to parliament.

By 1932, therefore, Iraq appeared to be a pioneer in the Arab world with a fully constitutional monarchy. On paper, Iraq's parliament was as powerful as any that has existed in the Arab world. Yet on no occasion did a single government, or even a single minister, fall because of a parliamentary vote of no confidence.[25] In the late 1930s, a series of coups effectively established the military as the ultimate arbiter of the political system: civilian governments had to retain the confidence of the shifting military leadership rather than the parliament. In 1941, a division in the governing elite led to the flight of many civilian leaders, as well as the young king and the regent; they were returned after a brief war between the Iraqi government and the British. Despite this political instability, the Iraqi constitution remained in force. Even if not particularly relevant to political life, the constitution remained not only intact but also largely unviolated.

It was not until 1958 that the constitution was finally abandoned. Early in the year, a hastily arranged union between Iraq and Jordan (a Hashimite answer to the republican Syrian-Egyptian union) resulted in a new constitution for the new federal state. In July, a military coup overthrew the existing government, abolished the monarchy, suspended the constitution, and disbanded the parliament. A three-member Council of Sovereignty was established with complete authority in the country. The constitutional order of Iraq has grown more complex, but it has not changed in essence since that step was taken (see Chapter Three).

Jordan

Constitutional development in Jordan generally followed that of Iraq up to 1958, though at a fairly torpid pace. It took some time for the territory to establish a separate identity of any sort. After some uncertainty, it was attached to the Palestine mandate, though the British sought and obtained sanction from the League of Nations to exempt it from the provisions of the Balfour declaration (which had been incorporated into the mandate for Palestine). As part of the process of mollifying the Hashimite family, Faysal's brother 'Abd Allah was designated amir in 1921; the British then set about working to establish an independent administration in the territory—now designated as Transjordan—under 'Abd Allah. The British followed a similar policy to that which they adopted for Iraq, though with considerably less alacrity. In 1922, they declared their goal of constitutional government in the context of the mandate (and a British-Transjordanian agreement recognizing Britain's position as mandatory power). Early British dissatisfaction with 'Abd Allah led to heightened demands for constitutionalism for Transjordan. Yet what the British meant by constitutionalism centered on rendering the amir's finances accountable and limited; they considered his practices irresponsible and profligate. Britain went so far as to cut a financial subsidy to his government and was on the brink of deposing him before he finally consented to a greater measure of financial control.[26]

While establishing control over the Transjordanian government, British officials also worked on drafting a constitution and a bilateral agreement. The matter proceeded quite slowly until 1927, when British officials finally came to an agreement with 'Abd Allah over the draft.[27] The final product was based on an adaptation of the Iraqi constitution, in turn based on the earlier Ottoman text. Most of the constitutional innovations in the Iraqi constitution were deleted, however, leaving the Transjordanian constitution a weak basis even for a limited constitutionalist experiment. The constitution created a unicameral legislative council with elected membership; the cabinet was termed the "Executive Council;" its members sat in the Legislative Council (even if they were not elected) but were not responsible to it. Not only did the draft avoid the Iraqi introduction of judicial review; it made no provisions for a High

Court at all. Indeed, British officials even neglected some of the practical lessons of the Iraqi experience: it was 'Abd Allah who thought to request that the draft be modified to allow the Legislative Council to meet in special session after the constitution was adopted to allow it to adopt the budget.

The British also followed the policy of moving their position entirely outside of the constitutional framework. The strategy followed was similar to that devised for Iraq, though in practice the British proved even more intrusive. The constitution was coupled with an agreement that required 'Abd Allah and his government to be guided by British advice in some essential areas (especially finance). Because the power of the Legislative Assembly was more limited than that of the Iraqi parliament (especially concerning ministerial responsibility), this put the British in a position to determine Transjordanian policy and legislation virtually at will. British officials recognized this; the senior British representative in Amman reasoned on the eve of the completion of the constitution:

> There can be no doubt that it would be to the advantage of the people of Trans-Jordan that its legislation should be subjected to the expert control of the Colonial Office and indeed the Mandatory cannot fulfil its international obligations unless it has that control in certain directions, nor can the Agreement on which the independence of Trans-Jordan depends be considered as anything but worthless unless it makes provision for the retention of that control.
>
> Independence with such a proviso would be anything but independence but without such a proviso His Majesty's Government would certainly be faced with the need to protest against measures which had been taken in opposition to the Agreement.[28]

In order to ensure that their control would not be subject to constitutional limitations, the British consciously rejected the idea that some British officials should serve as Jordanian ministers, mindful that they could then be subject to parliamentary questioning. Instead, Britain maintained the same system of a network of advisers in key ministries devised for Egypt and Iraq. The chief British resident also routinely communicated advice directly to Transjordanian ministers and made his feelings known on suitable candidates for ministerial positions.

The British constitutional proposals were not warmly greeted. Indeed, the considerable delay in drawing up a constitution and an agreement was greeted by some Transjordanian leaders as an opportunity to put forward their own ideas concerning a constitutional order. 'Abd Allah seems to have lent some support to these efforts at times, motivated by a desire not to limit his own authority but to limit the British.[29] In 1923, an official Transjordanian committee drafted a constitution that resembled the eventual draft in its provisions for the authority of the assembly and ministerial responsibility, but without the clauses the British designed to ensure the supremacy of the agreement over the constitution.[30] Other Transjordanians pressed for a fuller parliamentary system, with clear ministerial responsibility to an elected assembly.[31] When 'Abd Allah issued the constitution drafted by the British in 1928, a group of Transjordanians formed to write a "National Pact" repudiating the mandate (accepting only "honest technical assistance" from Britain). The document called for a political system headed by 'Abd Allah but with ministers responsible to a fully representative assembly. Elections for any other kind of body were denounced.[32] While neither the British nor 'Abd Allah heeded the call of the authors of the National Pact, the issues raised in the document were not dropped but recurred over the next generation in Jordanian politics.

The Legislative Assembly was elected but made its consent to the bilateral agreement contingent on the Transjordanian government pursuing modifications. 'Abd Allah did pursue such amendments over the next decade and a half, but had secured only minor modifications by the end of the Second World War. Over the same period, some leading Jordanian politicians called for a fully constitutional monarchy, but were even less successful. Indeed, when the first Assembly proved too lively it was dissolved and a more pliable body elected.[33]

In 1946, Britain finally recognized the end of the mandate and negotiated a treaty with Transjordan similar to the Anglo-Iraqi treaty of 1930. While retaining strong vestiges of the former relationship, Transjordan was now far freer to arrange its internal affairs. The constitution was amended to change 'Abd Allah's title from amir to king, but the demands of the constitutionalists for a move toward parliamentarism went unanswered. The following year the constitution was amended again to provide for a Senate with its members appointed by the king. While the king rejected calls for ministerial responsibility to parliament, the creation of the Senate was probably designed to provide a check on the parliament in preparation for granting it more extensive powers.

After the Arab-Israeli war of 1948, 'Abd Allah moved to annex the West Bank of the Jordan River (and change the country's name to Jordan). In order to obtain parliamentary support on the East Bank and assuage West Bank fears about Hashimite autocracy, the king promised constitutional revision. The constitutionalists, strengthened by the addition of West Bank deputies into the parliament, pressed the issue. While they had no control over the cabinet, they used the few crude tools at their disposal by refusing to pass any legislation, including the budget. 'Abd Allah seemed determined not to give into the demands and dissolved the parliament, calling for new elections. But 'Abd Allah's assassination in 1951 left the matter completely open. When Talal, 'Abd Allah's son, took the throne, his mental instability prevented him from playing an active role in governing the country. Leading Jordanian associates of 'Abd Allah were now left controlling the country, and some of them were strong backers of constitutional revision. Their position was strengthened by the realization that they would have to find an alternative to a strong monarch, whether Talal remained on the throne or was deposed in favor of his teenage son, Husayn. The newly elected parliament proved to be as insistent on strengthening its position as the body 'Abd Allah had dissolved. Thus the Jordanian cabinet finally drew up proposals for constitutional revision and submitted them to the parliament in 1951.[34]

The government's proposals were criticized by the constitutionalists in parliament as not going far enough. While the revisions would allow the parliament to bring down the government, a two-thirds majority was required to withdraw confidence. The proposals also did not strengthen the rights provisions of the constitution sufficiently for the opposition. In particular, there was no provision preventing detention without a court order. (The importance of this issue was made clear when the following year prime minister had two lawyers arrested after they challenged the constitutionality of the regency council set up after the deposition of Talal). Others observed that following the Arab constitutional practice of allowing freedoms to be defined by law provided an insufficient basis for a constitutionalist order. The amendments finally adopted reflected a compromise between the government and the parliament. The two-thirds requirement for a vote of no confidence was eventually changed to a simple majority. Some deputies, noting Syrian constitutional changes introducing the idea of social and economic rights, succeeded in introducing a right to work. A High Court and limited provisions for judicial review were introduced. More extensive changes in rights provisions—including rendering them absolute rather than defined by law—failed, however.

The resulting Jordanian constitution went into force in 1952. For five years, it seemed to provide a firm basis for Jordanian constitutionalism. Constitutional provisions for deposition of the king were followed when the parliament unanimously voted to remove Talal. In 1957, however, rising Arab nationalism led to a confrontation between an increasingly bold opposition and the king. A failed coup attempt and an increasingly nationalist parliament led King Husayn to have opposition deputies expelled from parliament and parties disbanded. These changes, which ended the Jordanian constitutionalist experience, were carried out with only minor modifications to the constitutional text. The amendments adopted in 1952, while they remained in effect, proved unable to protect constitutionalism. When a new parliament was elected in 1961, the effectiveness of the authoritarian period became clear: constitutional institutions were restored but robbed of their former vitality. Jordan lost control of the West Bank in the 1967 war; by 1974 the Palestine Liberation Organization had successfully obtained Arab League (though not yet Jordanian) recognition of its claim to the territory. King Husayn reacted by replacing the elected parliament with an appointed consultative body.

In the late 1980s, a second, more limited Jordanian experiment with constitutionalism began. King Husayn finally renounced all claims to the West Bank of the Jordan and an elected parliament was restored in 1989. Two years later, Jordanian political leaders and parties produced a document calling for a series of political reforms in Jordan, including a specialized constitutional court and greater parliamentary control over states of emergency. Despite the wide consensus in support of these reforms, no concrete actions were taken. Indeed, the Jordanian government continued to use its ability to move outside of regular constitutional channels. Most importantly, the constitution grants the cabinet the authority to issue decree-laws in "matters which admit of no delay" when the parliament was not in session. These decree-laws require the king's approval and must be submitted to parliament at its next session. Such provisions are not unusual in constitutional texts, but the Jordanian constitution strengthens the hand of the government in a subtle way: instead of requiring parliamentary assent for the decree-law to remain valid, the Jordanian constitution requires that the parliament repeal the law. Parliamentary inaction constitutes acquiescence. In effect, such decree-laws have a status little different from ordinary legislation. And the Jordanian government has displayed an inclination to discover the need for revisions in critical legislation (such as the electoral and press laws) only when parliament is not in session. Arguing that such matters admit of no delay, laws have been issued by decree that the government would have had difficulty coaxing out of an assertive but divided parliament. The recent resurgence of constitutional practices in Jordan thus has had clear limits, with the king and the government unwilling to subject their authority on all matters to constitutional safeguards.

Morocco

A combination of imperial opposition and royal reluctance made Morocco the second to last Arab state outside of the Arabian peninsula to receive a constitution (the last was Algeria). While it did receive a constitution in 1962, shortly after independence, the country has witnessed more constitutional discontinuity than far more unstable states. In 1996, the country's sixth constitution was adopted in a popular referendum.

Despite Morocco's late entry into the ranks of states with constitutional documents, pressure for a constitution occurred intermittently, beginning even before the full assertion of French control.[35] A consultative council was established by the Moroccan sultan and quickly became a source of opposition to growing French influence. In 1906, a group of intellectuals proposed a constitution that would have established a mixed judicial-legislative body as well as a measure of administrative reform. Shortly after, a group of Moroccan 'ulama made their obedience to the sultan contingent on several conditions connected with defending the country against European encroachment. This step, combined with the temporary triumphs of Ottoman and Iranian constitutionalism, encouraged a more extensive effort at drawing up a constitutional document. In 1908, a group of intellectuals published a draft constitution that focused on several diverse issues: independence from foreign encroachment, separation of powers, an elected parliament, political freedoms, and administrative reform. The French protectorate prevented any such proposals from being adopted, though the idea of a written constitution did not die. A rebellion in the 1920s attempted to establish a constitutional government, and the Istiqlal, a nationalist political movement, also raised a constitutionalist banner.

The prospect of independence forced the issue of a written constitution back on the political agenda, and in 1958 the Moroccan king issued a pledge that democracy and the separation of powers would be instituted in stages.[36] The king moved uncertainly toward honoring his pledge. On the one hand, he issued a charter of public freedoms in 1958 and promised in 1960 to have a constitution within two years. On the other hand, he disbanded an increasingly assertive consultative assembly and refused calls for an elected constituent assembly. An appointed group attempted to draft a constitution, but it soon foundered. King Hasan II came to the throne in 1961 and immediately proclaimed a set of constitutional principles and pledged to honor his father's commitment to have a full constitution by the end of 1962. Rather than convening an elected or even an appointed assembly, he worked privately with a small group of advisers to draft a document. Relying heavily on the constitution of the French Fifth Republic (but also on some Arab, especially Tunisian, experience), the king's draft was published in November 1962 for approval in a referendum twenty days later.

As with the 1923 Egyptian constitution, some political forces in Morocco objected to the procedure by which the constitution had been adopted. One leftist political party called for a boycott of the referendum and even obtained support from a leading religious official who denounced the provisions for allowing positive legislation and thus (in his mind) implicitly challenging the Islamic *shari'a*. (As is seen in Chapter Six, this is an argument that is increasingly out of favor, even with conservative religious scholars.) Yet most Moroccan political forces viewed the constitutional draft, notwithstanding its procedural and substantive problems, as a step toward constitutional and democratic rule.[37]

The Moroccan constitution of 1962 was a fairly royalist document. The king headed the cabinet, and could name and dismiss ministers, veto legislation, and make the most important appointments. An elected lower house could bring down the government by withholding its confidence at the time of appointment or, no more than once a year, mustering an absolute majority. An upper house, drawn from local government and professional associations, joined the lower house in the parliament. One observer described the constitution as separating powers without balancing them.[38] The description was apt but perhaps too flattering: the king hardly separated himself from legislative and judicial functions. He had the authority to refer legislation to referendum or issue it by decree during time of emergency. Since he headed the council responsible for judicial assignments, the king effectively presided over the judiciary as well.

The constitution thus allowed the king dominance over the executive and the administration, and strong authority over the legislative and judicial functions of the state. There was a significant concession to popular sovereignty contained in the establishment of an elected parliament, but even that concession soon proved too much for the Moroccan monarchy to tolerate. After a year and a half of operation, the king proclaimed a state of emergency and suspended the parliament. The parliament had not been a serious threat to royal prerogatives but it was increasingly annoying: it delayed adopting legislation; directed embarrassing questions at the government; proposed legislation that the king would have preferred not to have to consider; and debated a censure of the government. One Moroccan constitutional scholar wryly observed that the motion of censure effectively ended the life not of the government but of the parliament. A quarter century passed before another Moroccan parliament summoned the nerve (and the necessary deputies) to debate a motion of censure.[39]

Morocco thus lived in a "state of exception," provided for by the constitution, until 1970. Yet rather than declare an end to the state of exception and amend the older constitution, the Moroccan monarchy chose to write a new document and submit it to a popular referendum. Amending rather than abrogating the constitution would have required reconvening the parliament whose independence had so offended the monarchy. The 1970 constitution closely resembled the 1962 document, though some changes were introduced to address the sources of the monarchy's annoyance. Parliamentary immunity no longer protected deputies who challenged Islam or the monarchical system. The number of deputies required to introduce a motion of censure was raised; the upper house of the parliament was folded into the lower house (because, it was argued, parliament had been inefficient); and the regulatory authority of the king was increased. Yet before full constitutional life could be restored, two coup attempts led the monarchy to hesitate. In 1972, a third constitution was introduced (with very minor changes from the 1970 document). While constitutional life had thus resumed by the mid-1970s, a fourth document was issued in 1980 strengthening provisions for a regency in the event of the succession of a youthful king and lengthening the term of the parliament. Steady criticism from opposition parties and constitutionally minded leaders led to a series of minor reforms being introduced by the king in the form of a fifth constitution in 1992. The prime minister was strengthened (though the king retained his predominance over the cabinet), stronger language was used to guarantee rights, and a constitutional council was established. The constitution's preamble included a vague but bold acknowledgment of "human rights as they are universally recognized." While none of these changes presaged a transformation in Moroccan governance, they did hint at the potential for more systematic albeit controlled political liberalization.[40]

That potential was gradually realized in the remainder of the decade. Tolerance of dissent increased, human-rights concerns were taken more seriously, and opposition voices in parliament began to grow stronger. In 1996, the king introduced yet another constitutional draft and submitted it for approval in a popular referendum. Changes were again fairly minor, though the document did reestablish an indirectly elected upper house. This sixth constitution seemed designed to make further liberalization safe for the monarchy: as the lower house gained independence, an upper house would form a potential counterbalance (upper houses are often features introduced in Arab constitutions to check directly elected lower houses).

Moroccan political liberalization was signaled, and, in a limited way, enabled by this series of constitutional changes, although most observers focused greater attention on changes in personnel than those in constitutional text. After the constitutional changes had taken effect, a widely respected jurist was appointed minister of justice, an opposition politician gained the premiership,

King Hasan was succeeded by his son, and a long-serving and much feared minister of interior was replaced. The changes in constitutional text were generally small, but they had served as important symbols during this process and they ensured that a measure of oversight and control remained in royal hands.

Moroccan constitutions have consistently described the authority of the monarch more than they have limited it. While popularly elected parliaments have been allowed, constitutional mechanisms still allow the king to bypass or ignore it on almost all occasions. Most remarkably, perhaps, has been that the king has retained effective authority over the constitutional text itself: rather than use constitutional procedures to amend the text or allow constituent assemblies to draft new documents, the king has issued all drafts himself and submitted them directly for approval in popular referenda. While observing the form of popular sovereignty, the Moroccan monarchy has essentially treated constitutions as emanations of its own will. Recent political liberalization have obscured but not eliminated the basis for this non-constitutional vision.

Kuwait and the Arabian Peninsula

The polities of the Arabian peninsula show a surprising range of constitutional experiences. On the one hand, Saudi Arabia and Oman were among the last Arab states to adopt written basic laws. And the constitutions that have been adopted generally do not even take the guise of restricting the authority of the ruler. On the other hand, one peninsular state, Kuwait, has a constitution that has survived for close to four decades that was composed with popular participation and has emerged at the center of debates about the nature of the country's political system. The Kuwaiti exception stands as a little discussed but much noted alternative for other peninsular societies.

Kuwait's brief experience with an elected assembly and constitution in 1938 (see chapter 1) left no institutional traces but very strong memories. 'Abd Allah Salim, the Kuwaiti amir upon independence in 1961, had been an active participant in the 1938 assembly. Many leading merchants continued to support the idea of constitutional rule, as did some returning graduates from foreign education. At the end of 1961, elections were held for Kuwait's Founding Assembly [al-majlis al-ta'sisi], which was to serve as a constituent assembly and provisional parliament. The amir worked with some Egyptian constitutional experts to present a draft to the Assembly. A special committee of the Assembly revised the draft and then submitted it to the entire body for approval.[41]

The content and context of the Kuwaiti constitution give strong indications of 'Abd Allah Salim's motives. Externally, Kuwait's newly independent status was challenged by Iraq. The experience of writing a constitution would assert Kuwaiti sovereignty and cultivate a sense of Kuwaiti nationality. It would also have the effect of sharply distinguishing between Kuwaitis and non-Kuwaiti Arab residents of the country, thus limiting any potential internal support for merging Kuwait with Iraq or other Arab states (including Egypt).[42]

Beyond affirming Kuwaiti sovereignty, the constitution served to assist the process of building Kuwaiti political institutions. The decade before the writing of the constitution saw the foundation of the Kuwaiti state as a bureaucratic apparatus: ministries, a cabinet, and specialized agencies and councils were created. The constitution created a framework for this effort.

More subtly, the constitution also created a framework for the internal and external relations of the ruling family. First, it created an elected parliament; no members of the ruling Al Sabah family have ever run for election to that body. The exclusion of the Al Sabah from the parliament is not stipulated in the constitution but it is obliquely recognized: ministers need not be one of the fifty elected members of the Assembly; if not, they are granted Assembly seats by virtue of their ministerial status. The number of ministers may not exceed one third of the Assembly. Members of the Al Sabah have occupied senior administrative positions and often monopolized key ministries. The effect of this system has been to ensure that there has been little challenge to the ruling family as a whole (though individual members have come under severe criticism, as will be seen) while giving some role to popular oversight of government policy and implementation. Further, the parliament was given the task of ratifying the amir's choice of an heir apparent. While no Kuwaiti parliament has ever questioned the choice of the amir, this procedure makes succession crises far less likely and bestows a level of popular legitimacy on the ruler. Given the divisive struggles and rivalries that have occurred within the Al Sabah, these constitutional mechanisms seemed designed to unify the family partly by defining its role and partly by making clear the amir's dominance (most critically in the matter of succession). As is explored more fully in chapter 4, on two occasions when parliamentary criticisms seemed to divide rather than unite the ruling family, full constitutional life has been suspended.

Nonroyal participants in the Founding Assembly had their own set of motives that generally complemented those of the amir.[43] In general, they seemed motivated by a firmly constitutionalist vision of Kuwaiti politics. Surviving members insist to this day that the constitution is best viewed not as a unilateral grant from the amir (which presumably could be retracted in the same manner as it was given) but as a contract between the amir and the Kuwaiti citizenry about how the country should be governed. While previous experiments in elected assemblies might have seemed at best abortive, they continue to be cited as evidence that the absolute rule by the Al Sabah family was never accepted. The project of the Founding Assembly, in that sense, was to give new and formal articulation to previously accepted constitutional practices. Al Sabah predominance and the emirate were accepted but only on condition that constitutional and parliamentary life be given firm expression.

This constitutionalist understanding of the central bargain underlying the Kuwait polity, whatever its historical accuracy, was entrenched in the text produced by the Founding Assembly. Article 175 provides the best example in the unusual way it limits amendments: "The provisions relating to the Amiri System in Kuwait and the principles of liberty and equality, provided for in this Constitution, may not be proposed for revision except in relation to the title of the Emirate or to increase the guarantees of liberty and equality."

Kuwait's constitution of 1962 follows the Ottoman constitution of 1876 in much of its form, though it is modified in light of Kuwaiti and other (especially Egyptian) experience and practice. The constitution opens with a series of general provisions describing the nature of the Kuwaiti state and broad political principles. The second article introduces mention of the Islamic *shari'a* into an Arab constitutional text, providing for it as "a main source of legislation" (the phrasing was borrowed by the authors of the Egyptian constitution of 1971, as is seen in chapter 6). Sovereignty is proclaimed to reside in the people, "the source of all powers," and the political system is decreed to be democratic (Article 6). Socialism, an influential ideology in the Arab world at the time the Kuwaiti constitution was written, is reflected in frequent citations of the need to be guided by social justice in economic and political affairs and the assignment of tasks to the state (including education, public health, encouraging co-operative activities, and—critical in Kuwait—ownership of natural resources). Yet mindful perhaps of the nationalizations that were being enacted in Egypt at the time the Kuwaiti constitution was written, "confiscation of the property of any person" was prohibited (Article 19).

The Kuwaiti constitution contained a list of public freedoms and guarantees, including work, education, and the petitioning of officials. Many key political freedoms, however, were left to legislation to define: freedom of the press, communication, and association were all guaranteed in manners to be specified by law. One standard freedom—the inviolability of personal residences—did take on special meaning in a Kuwaiti context. Since many Kuwaiti homes have a special hall for regular meetings of visitors and guests (*diwaniyya*), the constitutional protection of domicile offered opportunities to potentially political gatherings beyond the normal freedom of assembly. (This potential was actualized during the constitutional movement of 1989–90, when much of the agitation for a full restoration of constitutional life took place within the *diwaniyyas*.)

The Kuwaiti constitution betrays the strongest tensions between its monarchical context and its democratic pretensions in the matter of ministerial responsibility. On the one hand, the amir was to govern through his ministers, and the ministers were responsible to him. On the other hand, the parliament could question individual ministers and withdraw confidence from them, forcing their resignation. Further, ministers who were not elected to the parliament, though ex officio members of parliament, were specifically enjoined from voting on a no-confidence motion. The parliament could not withdraw confidence from the prime minister (since the prime minister has always been the crown prince, such a vote would be a grave step indeed), but it could declare itself unable to cooperate with the prime minister, leaving the amir with the option of dissolving the cabinet or the parliament.

The parliamentary role in legislation is paramount. All proposed laws (including the budget and several kinds of treaties) must be passed by the parliament to become valid. The amir may either promulgate a law passed by parliament or return it for reconsideration; in the latter case, the parliament can still pass the bill into law over the amir's veto by approving it with a supermajority at the same session or a regular majority at the next session. And while the amir is granted some emergency powers, these generally require parliamentary approval to become valid.

The viability of the Kuwaiti constitution was put to the test almost immediately. In 1964, the prime minister composed a cabinet containing several leading merchants. Some parliamentarians strenuously objected that the cabinet composition clearly violated Article 131, which forbid ministers from practicing "even indirectly, any profession or undertake any industrial, commercial or financial business." The amir, then on vacation in India, returned home to handle the confrontation by forming a new cabinet without the controversial members.

While 'Abd Allah Salim thus showed acceptance of the document written largely at his instigation, his successors displayed more suspicion of constitutional mechanisms. On two separate occasions, amirs have suspended key provisions of the constitution and moved in the direction of revision of the entire document. First, in 1976, the amir disbanded the parliament and transferred its authority to the cabinet. This required suspending parts of the constitution without the consent of parliament, something specifically forbidden by the constitution. The decree suspending parts of the constitution did contain a vague pledge to revise the document. No clear reasons were given for the suspension, but most speculation centered on the increasingly assertive nature of the parliament. The amir's claim of authority to take such actions displayed a sharply anti-constitutionalist perspective: only if the constitution were regarded as based solely on the amir's authority and will could one reasonably argue that it could be suspended and amended by decree.[44] Having staked out an extreme anticonstitutionalist position, the Al Sabah gradually retreated from it. The amir eventually agreed to restore the constitution but coupled this with the appointment of a committee to revise the text. The partial retreat became total when the parliament reconvened in 1981: not only did the new parliament fail to pass any constitutional amendments; it also cited the provision of the constitution regarding emergency legislation (Article 71) to argue that legislation issued by decree during the suspension would be retroactively invalid unless specifically approved by the restored parliament. In essence, the parliament argued that the constitution had been violated but never suspended. This position has been contested by the ruling family. Kuwait's courts have generally either evaded the issue or hinted at a rejection of the parliament's argument. But Kuwaiti cabinets have generally not forced the issue and refrained from enforcing decree-laws issued by the amir but not approved by the parliament.

The newfound tolerance for full constitutional and parliamentary life was short-lived. In 1986, the parliament again showed a willingness to use its prerogatives (especially related to removing confidence from ministers) that the amir found excessive. Once again parts of the constitution were suspended and the parliament's legislative authority assigned to the cabinet. When a strong constitutionalist movement arose in 1989 and 1990, led by many former parliamentarians, the amir offered a much more guarded compromise. Rather than restore the old constitutional provisions, he convened a new body that would serve as a substitute for the parliament and oversee the revision of the constitution. The opposition demanded a full restoration of constitutional life and boycotted elections for the new assembly. The Iraqi invasion of 1990 interrupted the confrontation.

Meeting in exile, the Kuwaiti government and leading political figures hammered out a compromise: the opposition would pledge total loyalty to both the amir and the constitution. The outcome was widely regarded as a concession by the amir and the government to restore constitutional life fully upon restoration of Kuwait.[45] The pledge was fulfilled in 1992 and the constitution has remained fully in force since that time. To be sure, Kuwaiti parliaments continue to confront the government and have not shied away from confrontation with leading members of the ruling family. Parliamentarians have even taken sides in disputes internal to the Al Sabah. Kuwaiti newspapers have carried accounts (even transcripts) of MPs lecturing the crown prince about the need to respect the constitution his father promulgated or the failure of the ruling family to protect the country against Iraq in 1990.[46] And while such moves have provoked royal ire and threats to dissolve parliament, the constitution remains in force. In 1999, when the threat to dissolve parliament was actually carried out, the step was taken in accordance with constitutional provisions. It is true that the amir used the opportunity to issue a series of decrees in the absence of parliament (most notably granting women the right to vote) but he also remained faithful to the constitution by submitting these decrees to the newly elected parliament (which rejected nearly all of them, partly because the amir's authority to issue such decrees was intended for national emergencies admitting of no delay).

The unusual nature of the Kuwaiti experience is clear when the constitutional experience of its peninsular neighbors is considered. Saudi Arabia, the United Arab Emirates, Oman, Bahrain, and Qatar share similar constitutional features, though there are significant variations in their constitutional texts. All documents provide for assemblies with sharply limited consultative roles. All are also issued by monarchs and do little to limit the authority of the monarch in any institutional way. In these ways, the constitutions are not simply nonconstitutional; they do not even clearly qualify as constitutions according to the definition employed here. They provide only the barest of basic legal frameworks for their countries' governance.

The only country among this group with any older constitutional document is Saudi Arabia. When the Saudis conquered the Hijaz region, they issued a law that loosely provided for a governmental structure. There was to be an appointed consultative council and a council of ministers, but all political authority was to be exercised by the king or those appointed by him. The king himself was to rule in accordance with the Islamic *shari'a*. One Arab constitutional scholar dismissed the document and other procedural laws for bodies such as the council of ministers as not being a constitution "in the modern sense, because it is the king who issues them and changes them at will."[47] In 1932, the various areas ruled by the Saudis were brought together to form the Kingdom of Saudi Arabia, and a constitution was promised. That constitution was not issued for sixty years. When finally promulgated by royal decree, the

Saudi "Basic Law" served to strengthen the position of the king. Not only was the king granted almost unlimited authority in his lifetime, he was also allowed to appoint his successor. The king was constitutionally empowered not simply to appoint and dismiss ministers but to chair the Council of Ministers—essentially combining the throne and the premiership.

Even by the standards of Arab constitutional documents, constitutional provisions for rights and freedoms were very weak. Taxes could only be imposed by law, but since laws were simply issued by decree this required only that the government clearly establish its own rules. The state was charged with providing for education, health care, and employment. The document also provided for the existence of a consultative council and a budget, but provided little guidance on how these were to be implemented. (A consultative council was indeed appointed.) The constitution did contain numerous references not simply to Islam but to the Islamic *shari'a*; if there were any limitations on political authority implied in the document, they could only be found there.

While their constitutional history is newer, the other Gulf states generally have constitutional documents with more detailed political structures. All except Oman's were issued at the time of independence, and all were issued by decree. The need for constitutional documents was not always completely clear: Britain had not governed internal affairs in any of the newly independent states of the Gulf, so that there was no imperial political order to replace upon independence.

The constitutions are not without substantive content. The Qatari and Bahraini constitutions provide for elective assemblies with very little authority. Qatari elections have never been held (the assembly thus filled by appointment), though in the late 1990s, a new amir seemed to be moving toward allowing popular participation in government and issued vague pledges of a new constitution. The elected Bahraini parliament was disbanded in 1975 and replaced by an appointed assembly. In 1994, a political movement arose in Bahrain (chiefly among the Shi'a) demanding without success that the elected parliament be reconvened. Only after the movement had subsided and the ruling amir replaced by his son did Bahrain move toward the resumption of constitutional life. In 2000, a fulsome but vague "national charter" was prepared and then passed in a plebiscite in 2001. In Qatar, the constitution was amended by decree in order to transfer some authority from the prime minister to the amir.[48] Perhaps more significantly, the Qatari amir promised in 1999 to have a new constitution written; he appointed a thirty-member council and gave them three years to compose a draft. Initial work, however, proceeded quite slowly.

The United Arab Emirates has the most complex constitutional structure of the Gulf states because of its federal nature. The creation of the federal structure was negotiated in an interim document in 1971 among the leaders of the separate emirates and reflects a level of collegiality among them. The amirs of the seven-member emirates form the Supreme Council; they also appoint members to the consultative Federal Council. The Federal Council meets more often to handle routine matters, but ultimate authority lies in the Supreme Council. In 1996, the emirates agreed to turn the temporary constitution into a permanent one. While some members of the Federal Council expressed an interest in some changes (such as turning the Federal Council into a real legislative body, allowing some of its members to be elected, and strengthening the federal government in some fields), the only change actually made was to designate Abu Dhabi the permanent capital.[49]

The last peninsular state to promulgate a constitution was Oman. In 1991, the sultan decreed the establishment of the Consultative Assembly; its members were appointed by provincial leaders. Five years later, a constitution was suddenly issued by decree. It changed little in the governing structure, though it did codify the existence of the Consultative Assembly and the council of ministers. It did contain extensive rights provisions, though almost all of the rights were to be defined by law.[50]

Arab Monarchical Constitutions

In the introduction, a distinction was drawn between constitutions and constitutionalism. Three possible purposes were adduced for those constitutions not designed to serve constitutionalist ends. Do these provide adequate explanations for the emergence of constitutional texts in Arab monarchies?

First, constitutions might serve to express national sovereignty and independence. It was observed in the first chapter that such purposes would be indicated by the timing of the promulgation (after independence or revolutionary change); such constitutions would also likely present themselves as expressions of the national will. Indeed, the constitutions of the Arab monarchies examined in this chapter betray both features: in virtually all cases, independence (or sometimes the prospect of independence) occasioned the writing of a constitution. In most cases, the constitution issued at independence was eventually modified, replaced, or suspended, but in general the basic framework and most of the text survived as long as the monarchy did. Two Arab monarchies that did not need to assert their independence from European control—Yemen (covered more fully in chapter 3) and Saudi Arabia—long resisted the regional trend towards constitution writing, further underscoring the link between independence and constitutional documents. Further, the motive of establishing sovereignty and independence helps explain the initially puzzling assertion of popular sovereignty in some monarchical constitutional documents. Arab monarchies anxious to assert their independence in a world of nation-states resorted to the declaration (though hardly the practice) of popular sovereignty as evidence of their full membership in the society of nations and their monopoly of authority internally.

Yet if monarchical constitutions served to assert national independence in a public sense, they had a far more complex relationship with independence in an institutional sense. In particular, monarchical constitutions were often written at a time when a new relationship was being constructed with an imperial power, and they often betrayed those origins in some subtle ways. In some instances (such as Kuwait and Morocco), constitutions served to proclaim a firm break with European control. In other instances (most notably Egypt but also Iraq) the constitution served to proclaim such a break while still showing some signs of concessions to continued European oversight. While the authors of the Egyptian constitution of 1923 sought to minimize British control, they were forced to acknowledge it; and British intervention did affect Egyptian constitutional development, especially during the 1920s.

Most ominously for the forces of constitutionalism, European imperialism generally worked to move important political issues outside of the constitutional framework. This was the case in Egypt: until the British unilaterally declared Egyptian independence in 1922, they rejected any legal formula to express Egypt's governing structure. And when Egypt received a constitution, British actions served to undermine its viability. In Iraq and Jordan, the British took a far more direct role in authoring constitutions, but they did so partly to insist that their positions not be challenged by the political structures being established. Monarchical constitutions borrowed European language and structure either directly or indirectly (through the Ottoman constitution). But European powers themselves generally inhibited any movement toward constitutionalism in the Arab world. This inhibition had lasting effect, because it helped establish executive authorities that quickly learned how to evade constitutional mechanisms, often by resorting to the language of the constitution itself. Imperialism was not the sole or even primary cause of the spread of nonconstitutional constitutions in the Arab world. Often, however, it was conscious imperial policy to evade or undermine constitutionalist practices from the beginning.

Second, it was observed in the first chapter that constitutions might serve as ideological proclamations, either in the sense of publicly proclaiming the basis of legitimacy or more narrowly in terms of signaling fundamental policy orientations to the political elite and bureaucracy. Monarchical constitutions in the Arab world have not been highly ideological documents, however. They have often paid obeisance to the idea of popular sovereignty even if they generally avoided (or, more often, encouraged the undermining of) mechanisms to render such a doctrine practicable. More notable than what monarchical constitutions do say is what they do not. Most have failed to go beyond a basic description of the nature of political society. The Kuwaiti constitution of 1962 was written to include lengthier sections on the fundamental duties of the state as well as basic ideological principles that were generally—though quite mildly—socialist in nature. The other documents produced in the Arabian peninsula generally stand at the other extreme, too ideologically timid even to proclaim themselves constitutions. Described more modestly as "basic laws," these documents often appear designed to avoid challenging the more fundamental legal order established by the Islamic *shari'a*. The authors and promulgators appear often to wish to present these constitutions as only technical descriptions of government operations. These extremes aside, Arab monarchical constitutions have generally avoided the ideological loquaciousness of many modern documents. They have often been products of specific ideological environments but rarely appear designed to buttress them.

Finally, the introduction considered that constitutions might serve the purpose of organizing state authority without limiting it. By creating or defining authoritative structures, legal frameworks, and chains of command, a constitution might render a complex state structure accountable to rulers without making rulers accountable to any fundamental law or popular body. Such constitutions should have some telltale features: the absence of real checks on executive authority, poorly developed rights provisions, succession mechanisms that avoid any real accountability, and escape hatches that allow any remaining limitations to be avoided. Arab monarchical constitutions tend to share all these features, though not to an unlimited degree.

First, Arab monarchical constitutions tend to offer loose constraints on executive authority. In general, monarchs have been allowed to retain substantial prerogatives. In some cases, especially those of the Gulf (with the exception of Kuwait), the constitution provides virtually no institutionalized limitation on a monarch's power and ministers have been clearly responsible to him alone. This is not to claim that Gulf monarchs are unfettered, because they are not. But the most effective limits on their authority take operate informally through accountability to the ruling family rather than formally through the constitution (with the limited exception of Kuwait).

In other cases (such as Morocco, Kuwait, and perhaps Jordan), a degree ministerial responsibility to an elected parliament was theoretically established but difficult to exercise (and, in all three cases, parliament was disbanded when it began to consider exercising its weak authority). In Egypt and Iraq, ministerial responsibility to an elected parliament seemed to be more firmly established, as was the principle that the king must rule through his ministers. In both cases, however, it proved difficult to translate these constitutional provisions into real accountability. The reasons for the weakness in Arab parliaments is considered more fully in chapter 4. For present purposes, it is sufficient to note that Arab monarchical constitutions vary in the extent to which checks on executive authority exist in the text, and that even where the principle seemed established it has proved difficult to exercise in practice.

Second, rights provisions exhibit a similar range, but in all constitutions significant loopholes remain. In the constitutions of the Gulf (again with the partial exception of Kuwait), rights provisions tend to be limited and clearly subject to subsequent legislative action. Absolute rights and more extensive catalogues of freedoms turn up in other monarchical constitutions. Such pledges should not necessarily be taken lightly. The internal deliberations of the drafters of two documents (the 1923 Egyptian and the 1962 Kuwaiti constitutions) indicate that constitutional drafters thought carefully about which rights to protect and how. And growing official deference to human-rights concerns in Morocco began with a constitutional provision recognizing international standards. But even in such instances, the majority of enumerated rights are left to legislation to define. The impact of such provisions on enforcement is considered more fully in chapter 5.

Third, regularizing succession is a concern of some monarchical constitutions, especially those of the Arabian peninsula (this time including Kuwait). The purpose of such provisions is clearly to establish monarchical stability rather than accountability. Only in Kuwait does the parliament have a defined role in ratifying a successor; in other states the matter lies wholly within the ruling family. Not coincidentally, Kuwait has had the fewest signs of contested successions. The states with weakest constitutional mechanisms (such as Qatar or Saudi Arabia before the issuance of the Basic Law) have suffered protracted struggles and royal depositions. It has been argued convincingly elsewhere that the surprising staying power of Gulf monarchies is partly due to their ability to craft dynastic monarchies (centered around ruling families rather around a single ruler).[51] Constitutions have sometimes been used to help clarify potentially divisive succession issues and better define relations between the ruler and his family. The current amir of Qatar, who came to the throne by over-throwing his own father (who had himself seized the throne from his own cousin). Mindful of this family history, the new amir showed greater interest in constitutional issues than any of his predecessors. He appointed a committee to draft a permanent constitution for a country that had operated for three decades with a provisional document, and he appointed a formal council for the ruling family to operate alongside older, less formal family mechanisms.

Finally, almost all monarchical constitutions contain provisions for emer-gency rule and rule by decree. Emergency provisions have bedeviled constitu-tionalists throughout the world; it is very difficult to devise ways to allow state authority to suspend some constitutional safeguards in emergencies while still protecting constitutionalist values.[52] Those Arab monarchical constitutions that did contain extensive rights provisions and allowed elected parliaments generally also borrowed emergency provisions from European constitutional documents. Such provisions can vitiate constitutional rule but they should not be regarded too cynically, because they can have the effect of placing real limits on emer-gency action. Typically legislation issued by decree must be submitted to an elected parliament as soon as possible. The problem for would-be constitu-tionalists has not been the emergency provisions themselves. Instead it has been the tendency of some regimes to use them too freely and to ignore constitu-tional limitations on emergency powers. They have sometimes (though not always) been aided by the meekness of many Arab parliaments.

Arab monarchical constitutions therefore might be seen as serving most fully this last objective—defining and organizing without limiting state author-ity. Constitutions offer monarchies some clear lines of authority and smoother succession; and they have many escape hatches for times when their provisions become inconvenient.

Such a conclusion, however, must be qualified with an important obser-vation: many monarchical constitutions still displayed some evidence of con-stitutionalist principles in their drafting and in the structures they established. In some cases, constitutional documents were the subject of extensive public debates and even wide consultation. The 1962 Kuwaiti constitution, the 1952 constitutional amendments in Jordan, and possibly the 1923 constitution in Egypt show such influence. Those who drafted these constitutions showed some interest in constitutionalist principles and generally sought to give such principles as strong an institutional expression as the political situation allowed. Where constitutions were suddenly issued by decree after being drawn up by a narrow group of experts (as in the mandatory constitution in Jordan, most of the basic laws of the Arabian peninsula states, and Morocco until the 1990s), such constitutionalism was generally less in evidence. Only in some of the basic laws of the Arabian peninsula, however, were elected parliaments completely avoided.

The effect was to plant constitutionalist seeds in all but a few Arab monarchies. The primary purpose of the constitution may have been to organize and institutionalize state authority, but in the process other, more liberal and constitutionalist, possibilities were created. In some cases, these possibilities soon loomed large; in Egypt, Jordan, Bahrain, Morocco, and Kuwait, the constitutional mechanisms created led to political crises. Constitutions created to render royal authority more effective also provided some bases to challenge nonconstitutionalist royal practices. In all five of these cases, an attempt was made to resolve the crisis by suspending those parts of the constitution (chiefly those involving parliamentary elections or authority); in all but one of case (Bahrain) this resolution proved temporary.

In sum, monarchical constitutions seem to demonstrate three lessons. First, constitutions were primarily adopted in Arab monarchies for nonconstitutionalist purposes. Second, even constitutions that lack constitutionalist inspiration can encourage constitutionalist movements and contain some constitutionalist practices. Third, most Arab monarchies developed tactics to contain any constitutionalist threat without abrogating the constitutional text, though on several occasions, key parts of monarchical constitutions have been suspended.

In the following chapter, our attention turns to republican constitutions in the Arab world. These constitutions show a similar pattern: they are largely nonconstitutionalist in inspiration but contain some constitutionalist possibilities. Republican regimes quickly learned how to imitate many of the techniques developed by monarchical regimes to contain or suppress such constitutionalist possibilities. In republican and monarchical constitutions, efforts to use constitutions to contain or suppress constitutionalism is highly developed but inherently difficult. In subsequent chapters we turn our attention to the mechanisms of containing constitutionalism as well as their inherent limitations.

THREE

REPUBLICAN CONSTITUTIONS

THE HISTORY OF constitution writing in the Arab world began in the nineteenth century when monarchical regimes agreed to promulgate constitutions primarily in order to regularize state administration and finances. When the results proved less manageable than anticipated (especially when parliaments began to assert and even expand their roles), constitutional experiments were suspended or abandoned. In the twentieth century, many Arab monarchies experimented again, sometimes with similar results: even limited concessions to parliamentarism could prove extremely troublesome.

Arab republics wrote constitutions in a similar context. Indeed, most constitutions were issued by governing systems unwilling to submit to a fully constitutionalist system. In some nascent republics (Syria and Lebanon), the mandatory power allowed a republican constitution (sometimes reluctantly) but worked to ensure that its authority was not subject to constitutional limitations, either procedurally or substantively. In other cases, republics replaced monarchies and grafted republican elements onto monarchical constitutional structures. The effect was to replace one kind of nonconstitutionalist structure with another: presidents supplanted monarchs without any increase in accountability. In fact, presidential systems have often been more inimical to constitutionalism than monarchies. While some constitutionalist openings have emerged in republican systems, they have probably been fewer and less substantial than those that have opened in monarchies. Arab presidents have perfected some tools devised by Arab monarchs for preventing constitutions from becoming instruments of constitutionalism. Why have they still bothered to issue constitutions? This chapter explores the authority-enhancing functions of republican constitutions in the Arab world. It also presents the limited openings they have left for constitutionalism to emerge.

Syria

In the immediate aftermath of the First World War, it was clear that Ottoman suzerainty over most of the Arab world had ended. New political arrangements were sharply contested, however, as Arab political forces contended with Britain and France for control. In Damascus, an Arab government established itself under Faysal, son of the leader of the Arab revolt against Ottoman rule, as king. A group of Arab nationalists (some but not all of Syrian origin) worked to found an independent Arab state. A congress assembled in Damascus and approved in principle a basic law of the "Syrian Arab Kingdom" based generally on the Ottoman constitution.[1] Before the constitution could be put into practice, however, French troops defeated the embryonic state and imposed their rule on Syria. In 1922, the League of Nations formalized French control under the new mandate system, obliging France to allow for a measure of self-government. After a rebellion against French rule failed, local notables finally secured French agreement to elections for a constituent assembly in 1928.[2]

The assembly produced a draft quite similar to past Arab constitutional texts, particularly the Ottoman constitution and the abortive Syrian constitution of 1920. The most striking change had to do with executive authority: while the question of introducing a monarchy to Syria was not yet closed, the drafters of the Syrian constitution wrote a republican constitution. By granting the parliament the authority to elect the president, the authors of the Syrian constitution seemed motivated to ensure that the parliament would not have to struggle as hard as its nineteenth-century Arab predecessors to assert its constitutional prerogatives. Indeed, the prospects for a genuine parliamentary system seemed quite real.

Yet it was not the provisions for republican government that drew most attention. The Syrian Constituent Assembly had written a document that expressed nationalist demands and made no concessions to the French mandate for the country. It defined the territory of the country ambitiously, not only including areas of the Syrian mandate that the French had allowed some autonomy but also extending to Lebanon, Transjordan, and Palestine. It treated the country as fully sovereign over external affairs and not merely internally autonomous. The French refused to approve the draft and dissolved the Assembly. After protracted negotiations, the French high commissioner finally issued a constitution on his own authority in 1930. It was identical to the draft issued by the Constituent Assembly, except for two changes. First, the boundaries were designated to reflect the territorial definition of Syria held by the French. Organic laws were also issued for autonomous regions within the

Syrian mandate, underscoring the point that the French rejected the attempt to establish a unitary state. Second, the draft included an additional article—Article 116—that essentially barred application of any provision incompatible with the French mandate.

This constitution was put into effect in 1932, and a Syrian parliament was elected. When the parliament balked at adopting a treaty to govern French-Syrian relations, however, the French high commissioner suspended it. A general strike in 1936 (coupled with political instability and a change of government in France) finally led the French to agree to reopen negotiations with the Syrian nationalist leadership; a treaty was negotiated and constitutional and parliamentary life resumed. This time, however, it was the French parliament that balked, demanding concessions in the treaty that the Syrian leadership was unwilling to give. By 1939 negotiations had broken down; in July the French high commissioner once again suspended parliamentary and constitutional life.

The German occupation of France in 1940 left Syria's status even more uncertain. With British assistance, the Free French asserted their control over Syria and Lebanon. The French were compelled to pledge eventual independence, however, as the price of British support and as a way of forestalling nationalist disturbances. Parliamentary and constitutional life were restored in 1943. A newly elected Syrian parliament took advantage of French weakness to denounce Article 116 as invalid, imposed without Syrian consent. This amounted to a declaration of independence and the conversion of the Syrian basic law from a French-promulgated (and twice suspended) document into the constitution of a sovereign state. The French did not accept this measure until after the end of the Second World War.

Thus the constitution drafted by the Syrian Constituent Assembly of 1928 ultimately survived the challenges posed by French imperialism. It did not survive independence without changes, however. In 1949, a military coup overthrew the civilian government and the new president, Husni al-Za'im, drafted a new constitution. He himself was overthrown before it could be promulgated, and a constituent assembly was elected to draft still another constitution for the country. The new body retained the framework and most of the provisions of the 1928 document, but it did add considerable detail as well as a lengthy introduction that referred to general principles. This included reference to ideals of social justice (such as progressive taxation) and Islam. This was thus the first Arab constitutional document to adopt lengthier ideological sections that lacked clear legal meaning.

The constitution of 1950 became effective as the influence of the military in politics was growing; accordingly, its provisions for parliamentary government were undermined immediately. In 1951, the military leader, Adib al-Shishakli, suspended parliament, and in 1953 he presented his own draft constitution that placed Syrian politics firmly on a presidential basis. In 1954, al-Shishakli himself was overthrown by a military rebellion and the constitution of 1950 was briefly restored. In 1958, Syria and Egypt agreed to form the United Arab Republic, and a provisional constitution was swiftly issued. This document reflected Egyptian far more than Syrian origins, and provided for only loosely bounded presidential power. Syria withdrew from the union in 1961, however, before a more permanent constitution could be adopted. Once again, the 1950 constitution governed Syria and the resulting parliament distinguished itself as one of the very few to withdraw confidence from a government, forcing its resignation. Yet the result was not a new civilian government but military intervention, resulting in a suspension of the parliament and a new constitution.[3] For the next decade, constitutional life in Syria directly reflected the fundamental political instability prevailing, as regimes rose and fell, generally having little time to enshrine their new order in a constitutional document.[4]

Finally, in 1973, a "permanent" constitution was issued. That document remains in effect to this day. While it draws on past Syrian efforts, the 1973 constitution actually most closely resembles the Egyptian constitution of 1971. This is not mere coincidence: Syria and Egypt had worked briefly to harmonize constitutional systems in 1971 in order to provide the groundwork for a political union that never took place. More fundamental, however, was that the 1971 Egyptian constitution, as will be seen, is a supremely presidential document. While obeisance is given to parliamentary life, human rights, and an independent judiciary, the Syrian constitution of 1973, like the Egyptian constitution of 1971, provides very weak checks on presidential authority. Thus the document reflects political reality in Syria fairly accurately; for the past quarter-century, Syria has been ruled by a constitution that frankly describes a system that operates in a non-constitutionalist manner.

Lebanon

Lebanon's early constitutional development followed (and actually sometimes preceded) that of Syria fairly closely.[5] As in Syria, a republican constitution was promulgated by the French High Commissioner, though unlike Syria much of the initial drafting was done by the French. The Lebanese leadership worked quickly to wrest control over constitutional developments away from the mandatory power, leading to a series of political crises. In 1924, the French issued a draft constitution and arranged for elections to a newly established Chamber of Deputies the following year. Despite resentment of the failure of the French to consult the Lebanese in the drafting process, the Chamber approved the constitution, which was then promulgated in 1926. As with the French draft of the Syrian constitution, the Lebanese constitution explicitly acknowledged the French mandate. The constitution provided for a two-chamber parliament and a parliamentary system, though one with potentially significant presidential prerogatives. The lower chamber was to be elected and the upper chamber appointed. In 1927 the constitution was amended to strengthen the parliament further: the upper chamber (a traditional device for limiting parliamentary authority in the Middle East) was folded into the lower chamber; and a provision explicitly mentioned collective (and not merely individual) ministerial responsibility to the parliament. Yet the modest gains the parliament made at the expense of the cabinet were offset by the transfer of some authority from the prime minister to the president, who generally remained beyond parliamentary accountability after election.

As in Syria, the French authorities did not hesitate to suspend the constitution they had issued. In 1932, rising tensions between the Lebanese government and the French authorities were aggravated when the parliament seemed poised to elect a president unacceptable to the French high commissioner. The constitution was suspended for two years. Negotiations over a treaty to replace the mandate were carried out in tandem with the French negotiations with Syria. The results were similar: a treaty negotiated in 1936 was submitted to a reluctant French parliament without result. In 1939, the French suspended constitutional life once again. The wartime French acceptance of eventual independence for Syria applied to Lebanon as well, and in 1943 constitutional life was restored. In Lebanon, the restoration was coupled with constitutional reform: the appointed seats in parliament (a vestige of the decision to fold the upper house into the lower house) were replaced by elected seats. The reconvened parliament deleted all references in the constitution to the French mandate. As in Syria it was not until the end of the war that the French reluctantly accepted this step.

After independence, Lebanese constitutional development departed from the Syrian path. The country's constitution remained essentially unchanged between independence and 1990. This was certainly not because of political stability: the country was periodically shaken by fundamental political crises that centered directly on the constitutional order. In 1958, the country verged on civil war over the issue of presidential succession; in 1975, civil war indeed broke out over the sectarian issues unmentioned in (but undergirding) the constitutional system. Attempts to bring about national reconciliation centered on constitutional reform. Demands to end the sectarian system (in which parliamentary seats and important positions were informally but rigidly designated for specific groups) were rejected. Attempts to amend the division of positions (and, more importantly, change the authority granted to various positions) were more successful. A conference in Ta'if, Saudi Arabia, in 1989 resulted in an agreement among leading political forces to amend the constitution. The presidency was to remain a Maronite position but lose some of its authority; the premiership (traditionally Sunni) and the parliament (with its Shi'i speaker) were both to be enhanced. Constitutional reform was to be underwritten by the establishment of a new, independent constitutional council with a clear authority to review the constitutionality of legislation. The changes agreed to at Ta'if were inserted into the Lebanese constitution in 1990.

The Ta'if reforms made possible a reemergence of Lebanese constitutional life. While state institutions began to function again (sometimes even more effectively than before the civil war), the continued Syrian military presence in Lebanon sharply constrained the policy choices of Lebanese authorities. As with the French mandate, Syrian influence was exercised totally outside of the constitutional structure. While the Syrians would not have appreciated the analogy, the primary difference between the Syrian and the French was that presence of the former was not even acknowledged within the constitutional text.

Algeria

In Lebanon and Syria, France was led by the logic of the mandate system to bow to local pressure by allowing for the development of written constitutional texts. French suspicions of such texts prevented their effective operation until independence. In North Africa, France was under no similar external pressure; written constitutions were successfully avoided in Morocco (see chapter 2), Algeria, and Tunisia until independence.

The French position in Algeria in particular militated against tolerating significant indigenous constitutional development because of the territory's supposed inclusion into metropolitan France. After the Second World War, a nationalist movement put forward the demand that the country be allowed to promulgate its own constitution. French refusal to meet nationalist demands led to the formation of the National Liberation Front (FLN) and the beginning of the Algerian revolution in 1954.

While nationalist uprisings against imperialism occurred elsewhere in the Arab world, the Algerian revolution was far more violent, sustained, and protracted than any other movement. This had the effect of diminishing the importance of a constitutional text. The Algerian revolution established the country's independence and the regime's basic ideology far more than did any constitutional text; for over a decade (from 1965 until 1976) the regime felt any constitutional text unnecessary.[6] When the ideological force of Algeria's revolutionary legitimacy began to break down in the 1980s, constitutional politics greatly increased in importance. Two new constitutions—issued in 1989 and 1996—were critical elements in the regime's strategies to permit and constrain political opposition by some constitutionalist tools.

Algeria's experience with constitutions began inauspiciously. The FLN finally realized its goal of Algerian independence in 1962. Its president, Ahmad Ben Bella, headed a divided and fractious coalition that began to break apart as soon as it had triumphed. In 1963, a new constitution was written establishing a strong presidency, a single-party state led by the FLN, and a strong socialist ideology. The constitution was designed to solidify Ben Bella's dominance and the country's move toward socialism. One scholar has noted "Ben Bella had managed to concentrate as much power in his own hands as any constitution can grant."[7] The text was so much associated with Ben Bella that when Houari Boumediene overthrew him in 1965, the constitution was suspended.

For eleven years, Algeria was ruled without a written constitutional document. During this period, Ben Bella's radical socialism gave way to state socialism, the FLN remained Algeria's sole party but lost much of its ideological fervor, and state institutions (particularly the military) gained influence at the expense of the party. Indeed, a predominantly military revolutionary council ruled without even a formal trace of accountability.

In 1975, the regime moved toward establishing a firmer constitutional basis for its position. An ideological national charter was written and approved by popular referendum in 1976. Later that year, a constitution was written and also approved by popular referendum. The new constitution reintroduced an elected assembly but otherwise launched only incremental change from existing structures. The FLN remained the sole political party, though the constitution contained no trace of any effort to subordinate state institutions to the party. The president was given great authority: he was to be elected directly; could double as head of government and head of state if he declined to appoint a prime minister; and retained extensive legislative and symbolic authority.

The constitution did contain extensive rights provisions, but Said Arjomand has observed how these were circumscribed within the text itself. The constitution's "bill of rights is superficially impressive in its length. However, not only are there many ideological qualifications, but its last article (Article 73) nullifies the 'fundamental rights' covered by the previous thirty-three articles when they are used 'to the detriment of the Constitution, the essential interests of the national collectivity, the unity of the people [. . .], and the socialist Revolution.'"[8]

Thus, when Algeria reentered the world of states with written constitutions, it clearly did so only to confirm existing political arrangements with some modifications. State socialism, state authority, and rejection of political pluralism were codified by the document but predated it by at least a decade. The new constitution seemed designed to solidify the regime's orientation and offer some popular legitimacy to a regime that claimed to be ruling the country in the people's interest.

In 1979, Boumediene died, giving the new constitution its first real test. A new president, Chadli Benjedid, was designated through the constitutionally mandated procedures: nominated by the FLN, Benjedid was elected in a nationwide referendum. Despite this success, the new constitution could not mask growing divisions in Algerian political life. Economic difficulties, a rising Islamist movement, and the decay of revolutionary ideology (brought not only by the passing of time but also by deliberately allowing the FLN to atrophy) led the regime to embark on a cautious political liberalization in the late 1980s. Political disturbances in 1988 induced the regime to commit itself further to the path of liberalization; in November 1988 a popular referendum endorsed constitutional reform. A new constitution was prepared and submitted for popular approval in 1989. The new document turned its back on socialism (seemingly paving the way for economic reform and perhaps allowing the regime to jettison some of its increasingly expensive populist commitments). More significantly, the new constitution allowed for a multi-party system by abolishing the monopoly of the FLN. Besides offering limited political liberalization, the new constitution actually furthered presidential authority—party and ideological constraints were removed and even the constitutional role for the military was diminished. Liberalization was designed to augment rather than diminish presidential authority.

Yet the dose of political liberalization was far less carefully calibrated than initially appeared. The constitution brought into being processes that the regime could not control.[9] Demonstrating the commitment to political pluralism, the regime allowed Islamist parties to compete. Electoral rules were carefully designed to coax opposition elements into participation without allowing them to assert control over state institutions. Yet in local elections in 1990, Islamist forces, especially the Islamic Salvation Front (FIS), proved far more powerful than expected. National elections in 1991 also pointed to a powerful FIS victory. A military coup deposed President Benjedid and prevented completion of the electoral process. The 1989 constitution, designed to enhance controlled liberalization, augment presidentialism, and decrease the military's role in politics ended in utter failure. Algeria entered a second constitutional interregnum, this one shorter but far more violent than the first.

Rather than accept a coup aimed solely at depriving them of electoral triumph, Islamist forces worked to overthrow the military government. The Algerian regime, now transformed into a thinly disguised military junta, responded forcefully. Even as civil strife increased in ferocity, the regime sought a formula beyond naked repression for confronting the crisis. In 1996, a new constitution was drafted that seemed to have a similar set of purposes to those of the 1989 constitution. The 1996 constitution would allow some measure of political pluralism, though its authors were careful to provide the grounds for excluding Islamist forces: it banned political parties with a "religious, linguistic, racial, gender, corporatist or regional basis" (Article 42). The constitution was both mildly liberalizing and potentially authoritarian: on the one hand it gave state institutions a firm legal foundation and allowed a military regime to transform itself into a vaguely constitutional one; on the other hand, it strengthened the authority of the president, allowing him some legislative powers and constructing an upper house of parliament with one third of its members appointed by the president. Since the upper house must muster a three-fourths majority in order to pass legislation, presidential appointees, if they vote as a bloc, possess a veto over the actions of the lower house.

Most important, the constitution contained only the weakest of concessions to the Islamist opposition. Article 9 banned "practices that are contrary to Islamic ethics and to the values of the November Revolution." As with previous constitutions, Islam was to be the state religion. The High Islamic Council is given a more extensive constitutional basis. While it lacks the mandate and the independence (with members appointed by the president) to serve as an effective check on the authority of other political bodies, the Council is enjoined to exercise independent reasoning (*ijtihad*), presumably with a modernist bent.

The 1996 constitution was approved in a popular referendum and made possible the termination of Algeria's second constitutional interregnum. Some political parties that had stood aloof during the civil war took the return to constitutional life as an opportunity to renew their participation in party and electoral politics, but most of the Islamist opposition completely rejected the new document.

Tunisia

Tunisia experimented briefly with a limited form of constitutionalism in the nineteenth century. In the first half of the twentieth century, constitutionalism was revived among the nationalist Tunisian opposition to the French protectorate. Thus, constitutionalism and independence became linked; in the years after independence, that link was broken. The link between constitutional text and constitutionalism, never completely forged in Tunisia, also shattered completely in the same period. Unlike the other North African countries that suspended their constitutions shortly after independence, Tunisia moved from an early date to establish an unfettered presidential regime by amending rather than abandoning its constitutional text.

Tunisia, when declared a French protectorate in 1881, was allowed to retain its monarchy. French domination of Tunisian governance engendered nationalist opposition, however, and in the wake of the First World War a Tunisian constitutionalist movement arose. Calling for a constitutional monarchy (and implicitly Tunisian autonomy and even independence), the Liberal Constitutional Party encountered French opposition and, at times, suppression. A younger group within the party split off and formed the Neo-Destour [or Constitution] party in 1934.[10]

French attempts to contain or suppress both movements were often successful in the short term, but by the mid-1950s France was ready to relinquish control of the country. A generation of Tunisian intellectuals received an opportunity to bring their vision of an independent, constitutionalist Tunisia into being. In 1955, the Tunisian ruler (the *bey*) committed himself to basic constitutionalist principles (agreeing, most importantly, to rule through his ministers). A constituent assembly was elected the following year. Shortly afterward, France terminated the protectorate, granting Tunisia independence. The Neo-Destour party, led by Habib Bourguiba, dominated the constituent assembly. Bourguiba also served as prime minister. Initially, the assembly worked within a monarchical framework. Early drafts were designed to insure a strong role for an elected parliament and made clear that the bey was not above the law. Yet when a political struggle between Bourguiba and his opponents resulted in Bourguiba's decisive triumph, the assembly moved to abolish the monarchy entirely.

At this point, the work of the assembly shifted sharply in the direction of presidentialism. Parliamentarism was abandoned: an elected parliament was retained but had limited influence over the executive (ministers were appointed by and responsible to the president); and the executive was granted some legislative authority as well. The president retained the authority to preside over the cabinet; to this day, Tunisia has no prime minister in the traditional sense (the figure referred to as the prime minister bears the title *al-wazir al-awwal* or first minister rather than the more widespread *ra'is al-wuzara'* or chairman of ministers). The only effective limitation on the president's authority was temporal: he was allowed to serve three five-year terms.[11]

The constitution was promulgated in 1959. As the limit on Bourguiba's presidential term approached, he moved to have the constitution amended. Beginning in 1971, a series of constitutional reforms was suggested. Those finally adopted had the effect of removing any temporal limitation in return for an extremely ineffective institutional check. Bourguiba assumed the position of president for life. The parliament was given the authority to censure ministers, forcing their removal, but could do so only if it could muster a two-thirds majority (an extremely unlikely occurrence given the Neo-Destour's domination of the electoral process).

With Bourguiba granted lifetime tenure, attention focused on the mechanism to select his successor. This had been a consistently controversial matter in Tunisian constitutional deliberations between those who saw succession as properly an executive branch matter and those who believed the parliament should play the paramount role.[12] The elected constituent assembly and parliaments had generally favored designating the speaker of the parliament while Tunisian cabinets wished to designate one of their own members. Parliamentary advocates, who had lost so much authority in the process of drafting the constitution, were defeated on this issue as well, on the argument that Tunisia's system was presidential and thus any parliamentary role was an infringement on the executive. The practical implications of this were realized when, in 1987, Zayn al-'Abdin Ben 'Ali, Bourguiba's prime minister, claimed that Bourguiba's senility prevented him from continuing in office. Ben 'Ali adduced a vague constitutional provision mentioning incapacity of the president; that provision made no mention of who was authorized to make such a judgment.[13] Ben 'Ali assumed the presidency and gave vague but definite hints that a measure of political liberalization would ensue.

The liberalization that did take place was limited and eventually reversed, but it did include some modest constitutional changes. The presidency for life was eliminated and the occupant of the position limited to two five-year terms. (Ben 'Ali's previous service was not counted; he was elected to his final term—unless the constitution is amended—in 1999). A constitutional council, established by decree in 1987, was given a constitutional basis. (As is seen in chapter 5, constitutional councils are generally weaker and more political than constitutional courts). The succession mechanism was changed in the parliament's favor: a presidential vacancy is now to be temporarily filled by the speaker of the parliament (who then becomes ineligible to be elected to the office).

In 1996, President Ben 'Ali suggested constitutional change in favor of allowing greater freedom and representation for opposition parties. Eventually, the system for electing the president was slightly modified to allow for multiple candidates, though with heavy restrictions. Eligible candidates included only those who were less than seventy years old and had led an officially recognized political party for at least five years. Several existing party leaders were unable to meet these requirements in 1999.[14] And the authority of the president and the cabinet remains quite extensive. The opposition needs a supermajority of two thirds of the parliament before it could bring down a single minister.

Egypt

In July 1952, a group of army officers overthrew the Egyptian government and deposed the king. A self-proclaimed Revolutionary Command Council (RCC) maintained full authority, especially because parliament was suspended and the former king's heir was a minor. Seeking to establish a firmer long-term constitutional basis for the revolution, the RCC appointed a committee of leading jurists and political figures to draft a new constitution.[15] As they began work, the RCC issued a series of constitutional declarations.[16] The first abolished the 1923 constitution on the ironic grounds that it had failed to bring about an executive authority responsible to parliament, leaving loopholes allowing the monarch to dominate the political system. Further proclamations abolished political parties and assigned virtually all authority to the RCC and the cabinet (which was to be headed by the leader of the RCC). At the same time, popular sovereignty was proclaimed as a principle and constitutional democracy promised after a transitional period. In June 1953 the monarchy was abolished altogether.

The committee drafting the constitution nearly completed its work and was on the verge of proposing a fairly liberal draft for republican government. Yet the RCC—itself badly split between advocates and opponents of an early return to constitutional and parliamentary life—procrastinated. Only after considerable delay during which significant changes were introduced did the RCC allow the constitution to be submitted to a popular plebiscite. In 1956, Egypt finally had a fully functioning constitution.[17] The new document was based on the 1923 constitution but introduced many significant changes. Most important was the replacement of the king by a president. The new presidency was not a mere substitution, however, because the constitution ensured that the cabinet would clearly be responsible to the president. The 1923 constitution had built in a rivalry between the monarch and the popularly elected parliament; the new constitution—combined with the introduction of a one-party system—abolished that rivalry. The parliament even found its dominance of the legislative process weakened with the president's ability to issue decrees with the force of law enhanced in comparison to his royal predecessor. With the entire constitutional system under presidential domination, constitutional guarantees and freedoms (most of which were to be defined or regulated by law) lost whatever limited force they had previously held. Egypt had perfected the art of writing anticonstitutionalist constitutions. The document also gave the first hints of the regime's socialist inclinations.

The 1956 constitution was short-lived but its spirit was maintained for at least fifteen years. In 1958, the union between Syria and Egypt produced a hastily issued constitution that resembled the 1956 constitution in structure and content. Its rights provisions were abbreviated and it eschewed any effort at establishing a federal government, opting instead for a unified state with its capital in Cairo. Syria withdrew from the United Arab Republic in 1961; the following year Egypt abandoned the 1958 constitution. A provisional constitutional proclamation gave all authority to the president, a presidential council, and an executive council; accountability in this system was strictly circular. This proclamation, however, was designed to operate only while the regime used the opportunity of the collapse of the union with Syria to reexamine the fundamental political directions of the country.[18] In 1962, a national congress was elected to confirm a new document, the National Charter, which President Gamal 'Abd al-Nasir presented to the delegates in draft form. The National Charter proclaimed the country's basic policy directions and the components of its political system: Egypt was clearly going to remain a presidential republic and a one-party state; the major change introduced by the National Charter was to elevate Arab socialism into the official ideology. The Charter was not designed to serve as a basic law, however. Egypt's new constitution was to be drawn up by a popularly elected assembly. This body was elected in 1964 and swiftly approved a provisional constitution that functioned as Egypt's governing document for the next seven years. This constitution was designed to implement the principles of the National Charter:

> The 1964 Constitution reinforced both the official commitment to Arab socialism and the executive powers of the President. Although his legislative powers were limited to periods of the National

Assembly's adjournment or national emergency the President still retained the power to appoint and dismiss government ministers and to lay down the general policy of the state in all fields and supervise its implementation. Moreover, in practice the President would exercise far more powers than the Assembly and civil rights were not always adequately protected.[19]

The Assembly did retain the power to remove confidence from ministers (or the government). Yet whatever limitations on executive authority the constitution implied were easily circumvented by a nearly continuous state of emergency.

While formally labeled a "provisional" constitution, the 1964 constitution survived until the death of 'Abd al-Nasir in 1970. His successor, Anwar al-Sadat, sanctioned the effort to write a permanent replacement. In May 1971, al-Sadat faced down some rivals with power bases in the security services and the single political party, the Arab Socialist Union. Immediately following al-Sadat's triumph, a preparatory committee began to work on drafting a permanent constitution. Unlike the 1964 constitution, the 1971 constitution was drafted in a fairly fluid political atmosphere. Arab socialism remained dominant but past policy directions could now be questioned; the Arab Socialist Union had fallen out of the president's favor though he seemed unwilling to abandon it; and al-Sadat's rhetorical stress on the rule of law and the necessity to build a state of institutions and rein in the security services, though vague, seemed favorable to constitutionalist values.

The minutes of the 1971 drafting committee survive, providing detailed evidence of the concerns, purposes, and ideological orientations of the drafters of Egypt's longest-serving constitution.[20] The members of the committee engaged in running debates on the relationship between socialism and democracy, the role of Islam, women's rights, the emergency authority of the president, the role and structure of the judiciary, the role for the Arab Socialist Union, and the structure of local and central government. In so doing, they looked to a variety of models: previous Egyptian constitutions obviously served as their starting point, but frequent references were also made to the French constitutional tradition and to constitutional documents of Eastern Europe (generally Yugoslavia, Czechoslovakia, and the German Democratic Republic). Most of these references were positive, though on one occasion a member cited the Soviet constitution as an example of a document that provided no real check on state authority. While authors of other Arab constitutions generally turned to Egypt as well as Europe, the Egyptian drafters displayed very little interest in other Arab experiences. While wishing to give the document both Egyptian and Islamic coloration, the drafters of Egypt's permanent constitution saw themselves operating very much within a European (and also a socialist) constitutional tradition.

Perhaps the central ideological issue confronting (and often dividing) the drafters was the precise nature of Egypt's socialism and its relationship to democratic forms of government. (A second critical ideological issue—the role of Islam and the Islamic *shari'a*—is discussed in Chapter 6.) Critics noted that the term "Arab socialism" was vague and had little meaning; it could also be used to undermine the constitution's guarantees. In a debate concerning the Socialist Public Prosecutor, Tharwat Badawi, a prominent legal scholar, argued:

> The word socialism is always used to eliminate the idea of law. We know what constitutional law scholars did in the Marxist countries. There is no authority, there is no limit on the authority of the Council of the Supreme Soviet, as in the Soviet Union. The Council of the Supreme Soviet does not submit to any law. There are no limits on its powers. It is able to do anything. In the name of socialism the Soviet Union says what it wants and transgresses any law.[21]

Despite Badawi's outburst, the drafters produced a constitution that strongly reflected a socialist orientation, especially in its beginning. The constitution guaranteed work, health services, education, and social insurance; it also required planning, state support for cooperatives, profit sharing with workers, and popular control of the means of production. While some of these provisions remained vague indications of ideology rather than clear limitations on policy, some clauses made more specific promises: education, for instance, was not simply to be available but also free at all levels. On balance, however, the 1971 constitution represented a retreat from Arab socialism even as it codified it. Not only was private ownership protected, but sequestration, nationalization, and confiscation could take place only by law and through the judicial process. The widespread confiscations and redistribution of property that had occurred since the mid-1950s had supported Arab socialism and targeted political opponents; many such actions had been taken by administrative measures. The 1971 constitution did not bar such sequestration but did guarantee due process.

The overall result of the constitutional drafting process was a strange document that gave with one hand and took away with the other. The 1971 constitution was a product of a regime uncertain in its commitment to socialism, wishing to rein in but unwilling to abandon the Arab Socialist Union, and committed to curbing the legal and administrative excesses of 'Abd al-Nasir's regime without seriously restricting presidential power. Thus the document affected Egyptian politics only at the margins but contained strong latent constitutionalist possibilities. The dual nature of the constitution—affirming authoritarianism and presidentialism while hinting at constitutionalism and the rule of law—can be seen in three areas: basic freedoms; judicial organization; and the role of the Arab Socialist Union (ASU).

First, with regard to basic freedoms, the minutes of the drafting committee make clear that its members were very much aware of the gaps and silences which had left rights provisions weak or meaningless in all of Egypt's republican constitutions. Members discussed some rights in general terms, most often viewing them as essential to the sort of society that they wished to see develop. (On occasion, some members would go farther than claiming that rights are socially useful, portraying them as inhering in the individual by nature.) Most fundamental freedoms were still to be defined by law (though a few became absolute), but members explicitly addressed the shortcomings of this approach. The resulting catalogue of freedoms was more extensive than that listed even in the 1923 constitution. The overall effect was not to provide absolute defenses of basic rights but to ensure that legal and judicial processes would be faithfully followed in most cases in which rights were at issue. To be sure, the regime still maintained an impressive number of emergency measures to move outside of these formal legal and judicial channels when absolutely necessary, but most citizens now would be able to take advantage of some legal protections and judicial remedies. Article 68 prohibited any legal provision removing an administrative act or decision from judicial review. Thus, Egypt's 1971 constitution was a very tentative step toward a more liberal order but a much more confident step toward a state of law and institutions.

Second, the ambiguous nature of the liberalism of the constitution, and the much less ambiguous commitment to developing state institutions, is even clearer in the document's provisions for Egypt's judicial institutions. The drafting of the 1971 constitution came at a critical time in Egypt's judicial history. Two years earlier the regime had launched a systematic assault on the autonomy of the judiciary, dismissing many sitting judges and establishing new judicial structures that operated under thinly disguised executive domination.[22] These steps had been taken by administrative actions and presidential decree-laws. The task for the constitution's drafters was to decide which of these changes—and which further changes—to enshrine in Egypt's basic law. Attention focused on several structures. First, public prosecution came under scrutiny. The investigation and prosecution of crimes had been left to the *niyaba*, a body composed of judicial personnel, since the founding of the modern Egyptian legal system in the late nineteenth century. At the time of the drafting of the constitution, consideration was given to establishing a public prosecution system, which would likely have transformed prosecution from a judicial to an executive branch function. Much attention focused on a new office: the Socialist Public Prosecutor. Those protective of the few remaining liberal elements in the Egyptian legal order were very suspicious of such a body, seeking to undermine it or maintain it as a judicial body. They won a partial victory: while the Socialist Public Prosecutor was to be given a constitutional basis and be supervised by the People's Assembly rather than the judiciary, it was to stand alongside rather than replace the judicial *niyaba*. Drafters also were forced to consider the newly established Supreme Council of Judicial Organizations. This body, headed by the president, had replaced the exclusively judicial Supreme Judicial Council, and oversaw hiring, assignment, and promotion of judges. Liberals lost a battle when the Supreme Council of Judicial Organizations was given a constitutional basis. They did defeat efforts to include more than token mention of popular participation in the judicial process, an anathema to Egypt's professional judges. Liberals also successfully argued against the abolition of Egypt's administrative courts; the establishment of this system in the 1940s was regarded as strengthening the ability of Egyptian citizens to contest adverse administrative actions. Finally, the drafters of the Egyptian constitution confronted the newly created Supreme Court, a presidential-dominated body that seemed to guarantee executive oversight of the entire judicial system. The 1971 constitution transformed this new structure into the Supreme Constitutional Court but left all weighty matters concerning appointment and jurisdiction to legislation. As is seen in chapter five, the Supreme Constitutional Court, when finally created in 1979, quickly emerged not as an instrument of executive domination but one of the strongest institutional advocates for constitutionalist values in Arab history.

Finally, the drafters of the 1971 constitution were forced to confront the Arab Socialist Union. While President al-Sadat had not repudiated the organization, the ASU had served as a power base for his opponents. The ASU was not disestablished as the sole political party in the document, but the drafters did take steps to disentangle it from state institutions. Indeed, local government proved a major focus of their discussions: the intent was clearly to diminish the role for the ASU not through the liberalizing measure of allowing party pluralism but by building strong local government (with popular participation) to replace some of the local functions of the ASU.[23]

In the end, the 1971 constitution provided a stronger basis for some of Egypt's state institutions, increased the legalistic orientation of the political system, provided some alternative structures to the ASU, and opened some possibilities for liberalizing political reform without pursuing them. The presidency, which had become the dominant institution in Egyptian political life, was left largely untouched in the scope of its authority.[24]

In 1980, a series of constitutional amendments offered limited enhancement of the latent constitutionalism in the document while simultaneously augmenting the position of the president. Three major changes were introduced related to ideology, political institutions, and the presidency. On an ideological level, the 1980 amendments downgraded without removing some of the socialist language and increased the commitment to Islamic law. Socialism was downgraded by describing Egypt as a "socialist, democratic" state rather than a "democrat socialist state" (Article 1) and by substituting a commitment to "narrow the gap between incomes" while "protecting legitimate earnings" rather than "removing class distinctions" (Article 4). The constitution still retained a strong socialist flavor—the "vanguard" role of the public sector (Article 30), for instance, was left untouched. The commitment to Islamic law was enhanced by a single word: the principles of the Islamic *shari'a* were now to be "the" rather than "a" primary source of law (Article 2).

On a concrete institutional level, the amendments of 1980 abolished the already moribund Arab Socialist Union. During the 1970s, President al-Sadat had allowed ideological "platforms" to form within the ASU; these platforms developed into political parties. The single-party system that had operated since the 1950s was replaced by a system in which a dominant governing party (eventually the National Democratic Party) was joined by a number of small but legal opposition parties. The 1980 amendments recognized the new system by removing any reference to the ASU and stipulating a multiparty system. This step led to further changes: the ASU's official role had extended into a number of fields, including policy guidance and press ownership. Six new articles on the press were added that guaranteed press freedom but made clear that the press had a national duty; a Supreme Press Council was established to assist the press "to uphold the basic foundations of the society and to guarantee the soundness of national unity and social peace as stipulated in the Constitution and defined by law" (Article 211). Many of the functions of the ASU were assigned to a newly-created upper house of parliament, the Consultative Assembly. Upper houses have often been used in the Arab world to balance against lower houses enjoying greater independence; Egypt was to be no different.

Finally, the 1980 amendments enhanced the authority of the president in two ways. First, it removed the two-term limit on the president, allowing him to serve indefinitely (al-Sadat was assassinated before being able to take advantage of this change, but his successor, Husni Mubarak, has been elected to four terms). Second, one third of the Consultative Assembly was to be filled by presidential appointments, allowing the president to dominate the new body.

During the 1980s and 1990s some of the latent constitutionalist possibilities of the 1971 constitution have been realized. The central position of the presidency has remained unchanged, and mechanisms to hold the president accountable have worked only at the margins. But the Supreme Constitutional Court and the willingness of the president to allow some other constitutional mechanisms to work has helped some constitutionalist features to emerge, as will be seen in chapter 5.

Other Former Monarchies

Three Arab monarchies, Libya, Iraq, and Yemen, fell victim to the turbulence that marked regional politics in the 1950s and 1960s. In two of the three cases, the republican successors showed little interest in constitutional texts. When Libya and Iraq did issue constitutions, they were remarkably devoid of any semblance of constitutional government. There was far greater attention given to constitutional development in Yemen, and the country's 1991 constitution provides a fairly strong basis for constitutional government.

In Libya, a constitution was drawn up in 1951, shortly before independence. It established a federal system within a monarchical framework. While the constitution was composed under the watchful eyes of the United Nations (responsible for preparing Libya for independence), Arab neighbors, outside powers, and domestic rivalries (chiefly the country's regions) were the principal determinant of the document's contents. The constitutional architects were often caught between pressures for democratic and parliamentary mechanisms on the one hand and the demands of lesser-populated regions not to be eclipsed on the other. The result was a truly federal system that has few parallels in Arab constitutional history (only the United Arab Emirates made more concessions to regional autonomy).[25] Yet the growing centrality of the monarchy began to undermine Libyan federalism, and the constitution was amended in 1963 to strengthen the central government. In 1969, the monarchy was overthrown. Rather than revive Libyan federalism, however, the new regime concentrated authority in a narrow group of officers. A brief, 37-article constitutional declaration was quickly issued to govern the country until a full constitution was written. This document abolished the old constitution and assigned all previously royal and parliamentary authority to the Revolutionary Command Council (RCC). The self-constituted RCC was indeed authorized to exercise all forms of Libyan sovereignty. The declaration did contain ideological statements supporting Arab nationalism and socialism, but it contained little in the way of concrete provisions. Its few references to any rights and freedoms were often circumscribed—freedom of expression, for instance, was bound by public interest and the principles of the revolution.

The constitution promised in 1969 has not been written. However, in 1977 an even briefer constitutional declaration was issued. The 1977 declaration proclaimed in its second article that the Qur'an was the country's constitution, though since Libya's leader emphatically rejected much Islamic jurisprudence and the body of *hadith* upon which much Islamic law is based, that proclamation carried little meaning. The bulk of the 1977 declaration concerned a network of popular committees and congresses that were to govern the country through direct democracy. While the declaration did describe these committees it devoted little or no attention to their operation or authority nor did it describe any boundaries, limitations, or rights.

In Iraq, constitutional documents written since the overthrow of the monarchy in 1958 have contained no effective means of accountability. Indeed, republican Iraq has been remarkable for its hostility to anything beyond the bare forms of constitutionalism. The leaders of the 1958 revolution established a body, the Revolutionary Command Council, that, like most similarly named bodies in the Arab world, exercised absolute authority. While the composition of the RCC has changed through both violent and peaceful means over the past four decades, Iraq's fundamental constitutional structure remains the same: authority is concentrated in the hands of an unaccountable committee. From 1958 into the 1970s, Iraqi politics was sufficiently turbulent that its various regimes generally had little opportunity to go beyond brief, interim constitutions. For instance, one of the more elaborate efforts, a constitutional document issued in 1964, quickly ran afoul of internal instability that barred its effective operation. While reference was made on several occasions to an elected parliament, the RCC and its president monopolized virtually all state functions either directly or through appointment.

This situation was formalized in the 1970 interim constitution—a document that has been subjected to minor amendments but still governs Iraq. The document contains some ideological provisions too vague to guide governance.

Among the vague clauses was one recognizing the existence of a separate Kurdish national identity in Iraq. This explicit nod toward binationalism, while extremely rare in the Arab world, gave no guidance on implementation and has obviously failed in convincing the Kurdish leadership or population of the regime's intentions. More specific language on rights is restrictive even by the standards of Arab constitutional documents. Freedom of expression, for instance, is regulated by both law and official ideology. Article 26 "guarantees freedom of opinion, publication, meeting, demonstrations and formation of political parties, syndicates, and societies in accordance with the objectives of the Constitution and within the limits of the law. The State ensures the considerations necessary to exercise these liberties, which comply with the revolutionary, national, and progressive trend." In effect, the constitution bans many varieties of political activities rather than protecting them.

The Iraqi constitution clearly presents itself as an authoritarian document. The RCC still monopolizes almost all authority and answers only to itself. This supreme body even names its own members (from the members of the Ba'th party), making it an entirely self-perpetuating body. The president of the RCC doubles as president of the republic; cabinet ministers are responsible to the RCC; and the RCC and president possess extensive legislative authority only partially shared with an elected parliament. In short, the 1970 Iraqi constitution is unabashedly authoritarian, lacking in accountability, and extremely weak on democratic process and liberal rights.

The document was amended in some minor ways in the early 1970s and reaffirmed as Iraq's constitution in 1990. In 1995, an extremely modest step was taken to diminish the monopolization of authority by the self-perpetuating RCC. The RCC amended the constitution to allow its president to be presented to the assembly and then the entire population for ratification. While the amendment may have been a vague nod in the direction of popular accountability, it also augmented the position of the president, even in a strictly legal sense: by confirming the selection of the president by popular election, the amendment removed the authority of the RCC to dismiss the president. Further constitutional change was often hinted by Iraq's leaders, especially in the wake of the 2000 parliamentary elections. While the prospect for some extremely restricted liberalization (on the freedom to form political parties, for example) seemed real, the concentration of authority in the RCC and the presidency was not open for negotiation.

Yemen made a late and inauspicious entry into the group of Arab states with written constitutions, but its efforts have been increasingly serious. In 1962, the imamate ruling Yemen was overthrown by a group of republican officers. The royalists rallied, embroiling the country in civil war for the rest of the decade. The army-dominated republican regime issued a constitution that closely followed the model of post-1952 Egyptian documents in both structure and language.[26] The reliance on Egypt was not restricted to the constitutional field: Egyptian troops entered the civil war on the republican side. Their withdrawal after the 1967 Arab-Israeli war led to a lessening of Egyptian influence as well as a prolonged stalemate in the civil war. The military republicans were overthrown by a group of civilian republicans; this group eventually reached an accommodation with the royalists. A new constitution was issued that became effective in 1971.[27] The circumstances surrounding this constitution made it unusual in Arab history: rather than being issued by a regime in power to define or organize itself, the Yemeni constitution seemed designed to foster national reconciliation among hostile parties. The royalist opposition gave up any attempt to restore the imamate; in that sense, republican government became accepted. But the constitution brought in a heavy dose of Islamization both in the structures it established and in its language. The Islamic *shari'a* was given a definite role in the legal system, for instance: judges were to swear an oath to God (but not the republic or the constitution) and were required to have a *shari'a*-based training; they were to use the principles of the Islamic *shari'a* in commercial matters and when no clear legislative text existed (Articles 146–153). A presidential council was appointed (in which a royalist was given a seat) and a consultative assembly constructed with a mixture of election and appointment.

The constitutional experiment lasted only a few years. In 1974, a military coup brought about a new regime headed by a Revolutionary Command Council. While the military-based RCC continued to dominate the country, civilian participation in cabinets continued (and some efforts were made to keep the Assembly viable). Yemeni politics during the remainder of the 1970s and 1980s was marked by instability and occasionally violent struggle. Yet by the end of the 1980s the Yemeni regime had moved to negotiate union with its southern neighbor, the People's Democratic Republic of Yemen.

As with the national reconciliation that ended the civil war, the Yemeni union was to be expressed in the form of a new constitution in 1991. The document—which survived a brief civil war in 1994—was designed to provide the institutional basis for a true union; its ideological provisions had elements to appeal to the radical politics of the south as well as the more Islamist inclinations of the north. The constitution established an elected national assembly and a five-member presidential council. The assembly is potentially powerful by Arab standards: it elects the members of the presidential council and retains significant authority over states of emergency. Ministers are unambiguously responsible to the assembly, and the assembly's domination of the legislative process is extremely strong (for instance, if the presidential council objects to a law passed by the assembly, the assembly may still pass the law by mustering a simple majority in a second vote). The catalogue of freedoms is not unusually extensive by Arab standards nor is it without some usual escape hatches (in which the law regulates freedoms). However, the provisions for arrest and detention are more complete, and freedom of association is to be limited only by the provisions of the constitution.

Conclusion

Arab republican constitutions have rarely been written to institutionalize constitutionalist values. Constitutionalists have emerged in some countries, such as Egypt, Tunisia, and Yemen, but their accomplishments, while not inconsequential, have been scattered. Because constitutionalism has been a weak and uneven force, if we wish to understand the motivations for writing republican constitutions, we have to look to the other possibilities discussed in the introduction.

Most Arab republics issued constitutions when they became independent or when they overthrew a preexisting monarchy. Constitutions clearly served the purpose of establishing sovereignty or a new political system. But experiments with, and interest in, constitutions have not ended there; other motivations have also been at work.

Arab republics have been especially mindful of the ideological and programmatic functions constitutions can serve. Prefatory sections, enumerating general principles, have grown increasingly lengthy, and major changes in policy directions (such as the introduction or abandonment of socialism) have often been proclaimed through constitutional amendment.

Most notably, Arab republics (with the exceptions of Iraq in the 1960s and Algeria into the 1970s) have carefully avoided extended rule without a clear constitutional basis. Constitutional techniques to limit presidentialism have been avoided; techniques to limit freedoms, democracy, and pluralism (without publicly repudiating them) have been used extensively. Republicans quickly learned the lessons that monarchs had learned with greater difficulty, especially in methods of keeping parliaments weak. In short, constitutions have enabled republican regimes but rarely restricted them.

CONCLUSION TO PART ONE

The Purposes of Arab Constitutions

ARAB CONSTITUTIONS have never been routinely violated facades or mere pieces of paper unconnected with political reality. Neither have they been effective bases for constitutionalist practice. Instead they have served a variety of other purposes less familiar to constitutional scholars but quite important to Arab rulers.

A first possibility suggested in this work is that constitutions might serve as expressions of national sovereignty. If this is an intended goal of a constitution, we should expect this to be reflected in its timing and content. With regard to timing, constitutions with such a goal are issued upon independence (and after revolutionary—or purported revolutionary—change). And with regard to content, such constitutions—whatever the reality of their authorship—present themselves as expressions of the national will.

The ubiquity of constitutions in all regions of the world might lead us to expect that states routinely issue constitutions primarily to underscore their sovereignty in the international arena. Yet while this motivation has been significant in the Arab world, it has played a smaller role than might be expected. Earlier constitutions (and a few current ones) generally presented themselves as royal edicts rather than national expressions. More recently, it is true that most Arab constitutions are purported emanations of the national will. But it is less the language of the constitutions than the circumstances surrounding them that show that establishing sovereignty in an international sense has usually been secondary to domestic goals. Earlier constitutional texts were designed not so much to communicate the idea of sovereignty to an international audience as they were intended to bring about political reforms necessary to maintain independence. The authors of constitutional documents in the Arab world have usually been focused on an internal audience over an external one. Indeed, new constitutions have been issued when the international context did not suggest it. To be sure, most Arab states issued constitutions upon independence, and the Arab states that never experienced direct foreign control (Saudi Arabia and Yemen) were latecomers to the world of states with formal constitutions. Yet by now, even the procrastinating states have constitutions, and many states have had several. Arab republics have often used constitutions to proclaim a revolutionary break with past political forms, and on occasion Arab monarchies have done the same.

In sum, constitutions have served the purpose of underscoring sovereignty, but that does not explain all constitutions or all their content. What then of the second purpose suggested in this work for issuing constitutional texts—that of signaling basic ideological or policy tenets? Constitutions issued with this end in mind might contain lengthy and elaborate preambles or ideological statements and poorly developed provisions for the definition and operation of political authority.

This explanation has much initial appeal. The language of some Arab constitutions ranges from the aspirational to the bombastic. Arab constitutions proclaim the importance of the family with a frequency and vagueness that might even make an American politician blush. Again, however, Arab constitutions are uneven in their ideological content. Early constitutions sought to disguise themselves as reconfirming existing practices and ideas. Monarchical constitutions have generally been fairly timid about holding forth on the basic values of the society. It is typically republican constitutions, especially those that have been issued in the past four decades, that offer garrulous expositions and unenforceable catalogues of ideas, often mixing socialist, liberal, nationalistic, and Islamic elements together in a confusing blend.

The final motivation adduced for issuing constitutional texts in the absence of constitutionalist intentions was the desire to organize or augment state authority. Unchecked executive authority, poorly developed rights provisions, succession mechanisms that fail to make the leadership in any sense accountable, and escape hatches to allow rulers to violate their own rules should be the hallmark of a constitution meant to organize power without limiting it.

Almost all Arab constitutions fit this description. Some are particularly notable for their absence of real restrictions on executive authority. The Iraqi constitution and the Saudi basic law, for example, fail to offer even much of a pretense of accountability, merely describing some basic organs of the state.

Most Arab constitutions are less blatant and offer both restrictions and ways around them. Parliaments are constructed but can be circumvented in the event they balk at legislation; judges are declared independent but deprived of any of the necessary structural guarantees; the rule of law is proclaimed but emergency courts and measures are tolerated when it proves inconvenient. Succession has often been a concern, especially in monarchies. Much of the appeal of constitutions in the Arabian peninsula can be explained in terms of Montesquieu's observation (quoted in the introduction) that even monarchs need to use laws to regulate succession.

In order to organize power and render it more efficient, and secondarily to establish sovereignty and a clear sense of ideological direction, all Arab states have experimented with constitutional texts. All (with the partial exceptions of Libya and Bahrain) currently have some form of constitution in force. And one Arab entity hoping to achieve unambiguous statehood—Palestine—has begun the process of writing a constitution, not once but four times.

Yet while few Arab states feel they can dispense with constitutions, reliance on a constitutional text does present some pitfalls. Even a carefully written text can have unintended consequences. This was apparent in the nineteenth century in the Middle East, when constitutions intended to introduce political reform often resulted in parliaments that were far more assertive than anticipated. In the twentieth century, constitution writers have learned some lessons in how to avoid such developments, but several Arab regimes (in Morocco, Algeria, Egypt, Jordan, Bahrain, Kuwait) have felt compelled to suspend constitutions they had written to their liking when some of their provisions took on unexpected life.

Constitutionalism may have been a weak force in Arab politics to date, but it has not been absent altogether. What is the likelihood that it may emerge, more forcefully, even if not by design? Part Two considers the prospects for constitutionalism in the Arab world, focusing on three possibilities: that popular assemblies will be able to emerge as real structures of accountability; that constitutional courts will rob regimes of their monopoly of constitutional interpretation through judicial review and prevent constitutional meaning from being bent to executive desires; and that the obeisance almost all Arab constitutions pay to Islam will bring into being an alternative form of Islamic constitutionalism. Constitutionalist possibilities are real in the Arab world, but in discovering them we will need to make some corrections in standard constitutional analysis. We must shift from an emphasizing the composition of the document (as this book, like most constitutional analysis, has done up to this point). Our attention must turn to the subsequent evolution and historical development of constitutional practices and institutions. Further, we must disentangle constitutionalism from democracy, and we must even be alert to the possibility of nonliberal constitutionalism, especially in Islamic form.

PART TWO

CONSTITUTIONAL POSSIBILITIES IN THE ARAB WORLD

INTRODUCTION

Constitutions and Constitutionalism

CONSTITUTIONS CAN SERVE constitutionalist principles even when they are not primarily designed to do so. Part One of this book presented several instances in which Arab constitutional documents provided for constitutionalist openings undesired by rulers. Part Two explores how constitutionalism might emerge in the future in the Arab world from existing constitutional structures and approaches. Real, albeit limited, constitutionalist offerings do present themselves. Oddly, they are often strongest when disconnected from a broader movement toward more democratic practice. Proper understanding of these possibilities demands that we recast our image of constitutionalism, stressing bargaining, accident, and evolution more than reason and design. The alternative image of constitutionalism offered here is not generally illiberal, though it is different from prevailing liberal views. The remainder of this introduction presents the nature of this image and its strong empirical basis.

Constitutionalism by Accident

Whereas Part One followed most recent liberal scholarship on constitutionalism, focusing on the composition and content of the text itself, Part Two shifts focus to the evolution of constitutional practice. The distinction is important. The traditional emphasis on constitutional composition effectively stresses intention, design, and rationality more than accident, evolution, and historical development. The traditional, rationalist image of constitutionalism and constitution writing, though abstract, is based on specific historical

97

experiences (the first triumphs of Western constitutionalism in the eighteenth century and the first attempt to write constitutions for sovereign entities at the end of that century). Yet the rationalist image bases itself on an idealized understanding of these historical experiences.

A less celebratory examination of these early Western efforts is therefore quite instructive for our inquiry, because it justifies the shift in our focus away from reason and design and toward accident and evolution. Indeed, a brief excursion into this Western history reveals that constitutionalists have always worked to enhance authority even as they have worked to restrict it. And constitutionalism has always rested far more on accident and evolution than the traditional focus on constitution writing and composition assumes.

In particular, there is one common historical feature of the first attempts at constitution writing that should give many liberal constitutionalists pause: the world's first three written constitutions issued by sovereign political entities—the American, the French, and the Polish—were specifically designed to create more powerful central governments. The authors of the American constitution sought to strengthen the central government and insulate it from direct popular pressures. This political background is widely acknowledged, but the extent to which eighteenth-century Americans understood constitutions not simply as protecting natural rights but as limiting them is less frequently mentioned. In fact, ceding natural rights was critical to the American constitutional experiment from the beginning. Philip Hamburger writes, "Americans usually assumed that the people sacrificed some of their natural rights—that is, some of their natural freedom—in order to preserve the remainder, and these Americans understood written constitutions to be documents in which the extent of the sacrifice was recorded."[1]

Similarly, the French constitution of 1791 empowered the central government. To be sure, the document incorporated the Declaration of the Rights of Man and Citizen. But the constitution not only forbade state authorities from infringing on some spheres, it also required them to act in others. The state was instructed to provide for public relief and education, establish national fetes, and provide a code of civil laws. The authors of the document were concerned not simply with limiting state authority but also with strengthening and removing obstacles in its path.

The Polish constitution similarly sought to diminish aristocratic privilege and strengthen central authority in the face of foreign and domestic impediments. It spoke not only of liberty and equality, but also of order and the preservation of the state: "All power in civil society should be derived from the will of the people, its end and object being the preservation and integrity of the state, the civil liberty, and the good order of society, on an equal scale, and on a lasting foundation."[2]

Constitution writing in the late eighteenth century was not simply about limiting government but about empowering it amidst dire crisis. Such a correction to a historically idealized image of constitution writing should lead us to recast our understanding of constitutionalism, but it should by no means lead us to abandon any interest in the idea. Indeed, some liberal constitutionalists have always recognized that constitutions are concerned not simply with limiting governing power but also about organizing and strengthening it. Montesquieu himself presented despotism, understood roughly as government without law and limits, as destructive of the ruler's own interests: "As people who live under a good government, are happier than those who without rule or leaders wander about the forests; so monarchs who live under the fundamental laws of their country, are happier than despotic princes, who have nothing to regulate either their own or their subjects' hearts."[3]

Stephen Holmes elaborates the power-enhancing features of constitutions even further while retaining his faith in liberal constitutionalism. It is not simply that constitutions and laws make a society more prosperous and governable; they also help government operate effectively. The more sophisticated liberal constitutionalists have never been blind to this aspect of constitutions. Holmes writes:

> The metaphors of checking, blocking, limiting and restraining all suggest that constitutions are principally negative devices used to prevent the abuse of power. But rules are also creative. They organize new practices and generate new possibilities which would not otherwise exist.
>
> Constitutions may be usefully compared to the rules of a game or even to the rules of grammar. While *regulative* rules (e.g., "no smoking") govern preexistent activities, *constitutive* rules (e.g., "bishops move diagonally") make a practice possible for the first time. Rules of the latter sort cannot be conceived simply as hindrances or chains. Grammatical principles, for example, do not merely restrain a speaker, repressing his unruly impulses while permitting orderly ones to filter through. Far from simply handcuffing people, linguistic rules allow them to do many things they would not otherwise have been able to do or even have thought of doing. In other words, flexibility should not be contrasted with rigidity in the conventional manner for the simple reason that rigidities can create

flexibilities. As I have been arguing, a democratic constitution does not merely hobble majorities and officials. It also assigns powers (gives structure to the government, guarantees popular participation and so forth), and regulates the way in which these powers are employed (in accord, for example, with principles such as due process and equal treatment). In general, constitutional rules are enabling, not disabling; and it is therefore unsatisfactory to identify constitutionalism exclusively with limitations on power. . . .

One of the main pillars of constitutionalism, the separation of powers, is routinely described in purely negative terms, as a machine for preventing encroachments. Authority is divided to avoid excessive concentrations of power. One branch of government can "check" another, inhibiting despotism and disclosing corruption. But here, too, the negative connotations of constitutional binding obscure the positive purposes of institutional design.

As a corrective to the conventional view, it is useful to conceive the separation of powers as a form of the division of labor, permitting more efficient distribution and organization of governmental functions. Specializations improves everyone's performance. . . .

Like other constitutional provisions, the separation of powers remains government-enabling: it disentangles overlapping jurisdictions, sorts out unclear chains of command and helps overcome a paralyzing confusion of functions.[4]

While this sort of liberal view of constitution writing is more nuanced and based on a sounder reading of history, does it undermine the constitutionalist vision of limited government? If constitutions are written to organize power, what remains of liberal constitutionalism?

Much remains. First, as constitutionalists since Montesquieu have observed, observing basic laws and limitations on authority does not necessarily diminish that authority. Second, and more subtly, the liberal constitutionalist vision rests fundamentally on a belief in a human ability to regulate power through law and reason. If constitutional law and political power can be likened to grammatical rules and language, then it must be recognized that the language in question is no ordinary one. For the liberals, constitutional language is Esperanto. Writing a constitution, in this view, consists of consciously and carefully creating rules; it is based upon a faith in the ability of human reason to structure society in purposeful and peaceful ways. Constitutions, if they resemble grammar, form the basis of an artificial and highly rationalized language. A recent work on constitutional emergencies goes so far as to argue that the articulation of reasons for exercises of political authority distinguishes constitutional from nonconstitutional government.[5] Holmes's recognition of the power-enhancing capabilities of constitution is not cynical; it rests on a rationalist and idealistic basis.

This more subtle liberal view is based on a better reading of history (though it still leaves much to be desired, as will be seen shortly). The image has begun to gain many sophisticated adherents. Bruce Ackerman describes constitution writing as properly belonging to a higher level of politics. More civic-minded and less self-interested, constitutional politics should be concerned with defining the nature of the political community and the rules that should govern normal politics.[6] Such constitutional politics rests on a broader liberal vision of the proper nature of politics, one grounded in what John Rawls has described as public reason in which citizens deliberate in a framework "that expresses political values that others, as free and equal citizens might also reasonably be expected reasonably to endorse."[7]

Yet such an image of constitution writing, while better grounded than a simple stress on limited government, still rests on an idealized reading of history. Such reasoning has played less of a role than hard bargaining, and much constitutional reasoning that has occurred has been remarkably bad and shortsighted. The French and Polish constitutions were all but stillborn. The inadequacy of the stress on abstract reason can even be seen in the case of the United States Constitution, the only one of the three late eighteenth-century documents to outlive all of its authors. Much more than far-sighted or merely public reason went into the composition of the document.

The United States Constitution presents itself two ways: as the emanation of the sovereign popular will (in its opening) and as the outcome of hard, self-interested bargaining (in many of its detailed clauses). While "we, the people" are the author of the text, there is little way to understand the provision that counts slaves as precisely three fifths of a free person for purposes of apportionment except as an example of the kind of egoistic logrolling and horse-trading that constitution writing—in the idealized version—is supposed to stand above. The authors of the American Constitution were not simply devising rules for the ages; they were striking political bargains and were concerned very much about the short-term impact on the material self-interest of powerful groups. One example of this is Article V, which allows amendments in any area but specifies restrictions in two: constitutional protections on the slave trade cannot be removed before 1808, and "no state, without its consent, shall be deprived of its equal suffrage in the Senate."

To be sure, there is no necessary contradiction between bargaining and reason, but the two are distinct even when combined. In the American case, reason was harnessed to self-interested bargaining; the only two areas deemed of such critical importance that they were placed above the rest of the constitution and outside the normal amendment process related to the underlying bargains between slave and free states and between small and large states. And one of those bargains—regarding the slave trade—was not only explicitly short-term but also based on lack of foresight: conflict between slave and free states took place on the issue of territorial expansion, not on the slave trade.

This actual record of constitution writing should be troubling for liberals but it need not be fatal. Just as liberal constitutionalism can countenance the power-enhancing functions of constitution writing, so can it survive politics based on self-interest and short-term calculation. Constitutions, in such a view, would resemble an unruly language like English, with its multiple origins, inconsistent and almost inexpressible rules, idiosyncratic spelling, and rich vocabulary, rather than Esperanto.[8] Indeed, whatever the case in the eighteenth century, since that time constitutions have been clearly based far more on the human capacity to bargain and adjust than the ability to reason. And when they fail, it is often because the bargains undergirding them have been repudiated or are insufficient. Such is certainly true of two of the most spectacularly violent constitutional failures: the American (as mentioned above) and the German (with the triumph of anticonstitutional parties under Weimar).[9] Ackerman's view of constitutional politics as properly existing on a higher plane may be normatively appealing, but it is empirically misleading.[10] Other theorists (such as Elster or Przeworski) recognize the hard bargaining that constitution writing entails and have fewer expectations that it occur on a higher plane of political life. But even these theorists overstate the importance of constitution writing as an act of conscious political definition.

One metaphor that has recurred in such writing has been that of Odysseus binding himself so that he may hear the sirens' song; constitution writing becomes an exercise in far-sighted self-discipline. Recently another group of scholars has introduced a more helpful nautical metaphor: institutional design is similar to "rebuilding the ship at sea."[11] By this they mean that those who rebuild institutions must do so by using whatever existing institutions are at hand. In this sense, institutional change becomes a matter not only of conscious design but also of evolution, reform, improvisation, and accretion. The metaphor is even more fortunate than its authors realize—not only must constitutional architects use whatever institutional tools exist, but they must also operate under very difficult circumstances that make it virtually impossible to overlook short-term considerations—ignoring the immediate effects of one's actions and concentrating only on ultimate design could easily lead to sinking or scuttling the ship. And our focus must therefore encompass not only the designs of the architects but the effects (often unintended) of their decisions.

Constitutions have often served liberal constitutionalist ends less because their architects were far-sighted than because they lost control of events. Constitutional texts can survive the immediate circumstances of their creation and take on a life of their own, operating in unintended ways. Constitutions often serve constitutionalism best when they escape from, rather than reflect, their authors' wills.

If we widen our historical repertoire beyond an idealized understanding of the American founding and the French Revolution, we will encounter experiences with constitution writing that provide a far sounder basis for understanding the prospects for constitutionalism in the Arab world. There have been numerous constitutions written that ultimately served constitutionalist principles without stemming from a transcendent moment of a people's self-definition. Most immediately, the European experience with written constitutions in the nineteenth century was quite indicative of subsequent global developments in constitution writing. That experience shows how constitutions can be written to express short-term bargains and still serve constitutionalist ends.

Nineteenth-century European constitutions were not abstract attempts to construct government based on reason; they were attempts to arrive at bargains among monarchists, aristocrats, liberals, and democrats. The documents are full of compromises and where no compromises could be reached, constitutions often fell silent—even in crucial places. The Belgian Constitution of 1831—perhaps the most emulated constitution in the history of the world—makes only the weakest of provisions for one of the central constitutional questions of nineteenth-century Europe: whether ministers were responsible to parliament or to the monarch.[12] At the end of the century, Gaetano Mosca noted that despite the spread of parliamentarism, almost all European constitutions and charters still lacked provisions for ministerial responsibility to parliament.[13]

Such constitutions were not promises made by the people to themselves. Instead they were either pacts made among antagonistic political forces or promises made by monarchs desperate to forestall revolution by agreeing to a measure of popular participation. They bear a stronger relationship to the pacts that allowed South American and southern European military regimes to extricate themselves from power in the 1970s and 1980s than to abstract, rationalistic attempts to found political communities.

Indeed, there is an empirical problem in viewing constitutions as constituting documents. While the practice of convening constituent assemblies, purporting to represent the general will of the nation in devising a document for the ages, has spread around the world, constitutions are generally better understood not as constituting new regimes but as being constituted by existing ones. This is especially true in the Arab world, where the motives for promulgating constitutions discussed in the previous section focus on serving existing regimes even more than defining them.

This is not to say that constitutions cannot serve constitutionalist ends, only that they do not always do so as most constitutionalists would have it. More often, perhaps, they limit and define authority by operating in ways their architects never intended. An example of how quickly this can happen is Israel's recent experiment with direct popular election of the prime minister. This constitutional change was promoted by a combination of politicians eager to curb the influence of small parties and activists in the Labor party convinced that their likely candidate (Yitzhak Rabin) was more popular than their party. Yet the change worked to secure the two most fragmented parliaments (in 1996 and 1999) in the nation's history, with a precipitous decline in the share of seats won by major parties, and the triumph of Rabin's opponent (partly because Rabin's assassination prevented him from winning in a system designed for him). Another example of unintended effects is the constitution of the France's Third Republic. That document governed France longer than any other constitution, yet it was consciously designed only to be a provisional document to govern a society too bitterly divided to reach any consensus about governing principles.

Perhaps the most ironic example of unintended consequences is that of parliamentary power. The American constitutional system, based on the fear that "the tendency of republican governments is to an aggrandizement of the legislative at the expense of other departments," was designed to rein in the power of the legislature.[14] European parliamentary systems gave far greater authority to the legislature, including the power to remove senior leaders of the executive for political, and not merely criminal, reasons. European parliaments wrested this authority slowly and, as mentioned above, it was not until the twentieth century that many states attempted to inscribe ministerial responsibility to parliament in constitutional texts. Yet today the American Congress plays a far stronger role in administration (and even in legislation) than European parliamentary bodies.

Institutional and Ideological Bases for Arab Constitutionalism

The emergence of constitutionalist practices rests more firmly on accident and evolution than on foresight; it is the outcome of intense political struggles rather than abstract reason. Is there any prospect that constitutionalism can emerge out of Arab politics in this manner? Does the cultural or intellectual groundwork exist for constitutionalist practices? Do Arab constitutional orders lay the institutional framework that would allow for the gradual and even unintended development of constitutionalism, as occurred in nineteenth-century Europe? Our attempt to understand prospects for Arab constitutionalism focuses attention on the actual workings of constitutional texts and the possibilities that rules will gradually begin to govern and not merely serve their authors (or, more likely, their authors' successors).

The focus here is on the evolution of constitutionalist practices in the Arab world, not their presence or absence in absolute terms. That is, the question is whether existing institutions and texts can move in a constitutionalist direction. If our concern were to explain why constitutionalism is generally weak in the Arab world, we might be inclined to compare Arab political orders with those of other regions; if we were to follow currently dominant trends in political science scholarship, the tendency would be to search for social and economic preconditions for constitutionalism rather than examine political institutions themselves. But chapters 4 and 5 are not concerned with the general weakness of constitutionalism but the possibility of incremental and evolutionary change. We thus turn to existing texts and institutions; in the process, we will find genuine though still conditional possibilities.

Even in Europe and the Americas, constitutional texts often predated constitutionalist practices. Texts took on a life of their own only when the balance of political forces allowed older provisions to operate in newer ways. In many countries, for instance, ministerial responsibility to parliament evolved slowly (and often without amendment of the constitutional text), allowing the constitution to take on new meaning and become an established set of rules for governing rather than a momentary bargain struck by an embattled monarch. Even more radical transformations have taken place through the use of existing constitutional mechanisms.[15]

Are such developments—even at a much more evolutionary pace—possible in the Arab world? Have constitutional structures been created that can take on the task of bringing Arab constitutionalism to life? Part Two focuses first on two such possibilities. The first is that executive-legislative relations will evolve in a way that allows for real balance. Just as ministerial responsibility became the linchpin of the effort to establish constitutionalism in Europe, can the legislature's ability to demand the accountability of the executive emerge out of Arab constitutional practice? Chapter 4 considers this question and uncovers the surprising finding that those Arab parliaments with the least institutionalized links to the broader society seem to offer the best possibilities for the development of constitutionalism.

A second, and surprising, path for the emergence of constitutionalism in the Arab world is through judicial review. Part One showed that Arab regimes generally operate within plausible interpretations of constitutional texts. Since such texts are often vague, however, the ability of regimes to pursue their own interpretations allows them to rob constitutional provisions of any limiting power. The question for much of the world is not whether the constitution will be enforced but whose interpretation of it will be authoritative. It is therefore noteworthy that over the past several decades, judicial review of the constitutionality of legislation and administrative acts has become fairly widespread in the Arab world. Chapter 5 examines whether judicial review can emerge as a promising basis for constitutionalism. Unexpected pockets of constitutionalist practice are presented; their existence is shown to depend partly on institutional autonomy rather than links to the broader society. For both legislatures and judiciaries, democracy and constitutionalism pull in different directions. Full liberal constitutionalism is unlikely to emerge from current Arab parliaments or judiciaries, but there is more potential to move in constitutionalist directions than might initially seem to be the case.

Chapter 6 shifts the focus away from searching for constitutionalist possibilities by institutional analysis (at least in part) and moves instead toward ideological analysis: do Arab and Islamic societies provide suitable ideological ground for constitutionalism to develop? The emphasis on bargaining and evolution makes sense only if such a basis exists. Yet in most writings on constitutions in the developing world, an evolutionary process is implicitly viewed as extremely unlikely. Texts based on mechanical borrowing of European constitutions are almost always held to be unpromising beginnings for non-European societies. Most of the political scientists who focused on constitutional structures a generation ago were themselves far more pessimistic about the emergence of constitutionalism outside of the West then they are remembered as being.[16] In general, constitutionalism was tied either to the historical experience of European feudalism or the Christian tradition of natural law. A recent study of constitutionalism and political culture makes a similar argument in less ethnocentric terms: constitutionalism is unlikely to emerge where the cultural environment is not favorable.[17]

Such pessimism has such intuitive appeal that a brief exposition of the plausibility of an Islamic constitutionalism is required. Elsewhere I have questioned the idea that current legal systems in the Arab world are alien and artificial impositions without indigenous roots.[18] Here I wish to extend the inquiry to cover constitutional documents as well. The arguments generally adduced to show that Islamic political values were particularly inimical to constitutionalism invite special attention because they are often contradictory. A brief examination here of those arguments shows that Islamic constitutionalism is far more plausible than Western constitutionalists have ever been willing to acknowledge.

From the beginnings of Western constitutionalist thought, the political systems of the Islamic world generally (and often the Ottoman Empire and Persia specifically) have been viewed as the antithesis of constitutional government. Western images of these governments served as a useful foil for writers such as Montesquieu:

> Miserable indeed would be the case, were the same man, or the same body whether of the nobles or of the people, to exercise those three powers, that of enacting laws, that of executing the public resolutions, and that of judging the crimes or differences of individuals.
>
> Most kingdoms of Europe enjoy a moderate government, because the prince who is invested with the two first powers, leaves the third to his subjects. In Turkey, where these three powers are united in the Sultan's person, the subjects groan under the weight of tyranny and oppression.[19]

The problem in the eyes of Western constitutionalists has been that Islamic thought and practice—as understood by these Western scholars, often speciously—did not acknowledge the possibility of law governing the ruler. Even when Western writers discovered the importance of Islamic law, Islamic thought was still held to be anticonstitutional by nature: by not recognizing a distinction between religious and secular law, it granted religious sanctification to worldly rulers who then could not be challenged by their subjects.[20]

What makes these claims so odd is that Western constitutionalism was traced by many of these same writers to natural law doctrines and sometimes to Christianity itself. The idea that law can be derived from divine sources, outside the authority of rulers to control, would seem to lend itself fairly easily to constitutionalist interpretations. Yet many writing in this vein have inexplicably restricted their view to Christianity and Judaism. In other words, constitutionalism was held to have roots in religion only so long as that religion was

Christianity or Judaism; Islam, despite its strong legal orientation, provoked no interest among such scholars. Friedrich, for instance, points not only to the tradition of natural law but also to the Jewish roots of Christianity:

> Ancient Judaism in fact played a decisive role in shaping the origins of Western concepts of law. For the One God reveals himself very differently from the gods of peoples surrounding ancient Israel by his preoccupation with the law. The Old Testament is full of acts of legislation, of stories about God's struggle to secure their observation and enforcement, of rewards and punishments.[21]

For similar reasons, Loewenstein claimed "The first of the nations practicing constitutionalism were the Hebrews."[22] Yet if natural law and Jewish law can serve as antecedents of constitutionalism, it certainly seems plausible that Islamic law could do the same. Indeed, many Islamic scholars have drawn an explicit analogy between the Islamic *shari'a* and either constitutional law or natural law.[23]

Two immediate objections might be raised. First, Islamic law might be derived and enforced in ways that limit and regularize the authority of the state, but many of its features are sharply incompatible with contemporary understandings of liberalism. The most oft-cited example in this regard is the requirement that apostates be executed. To be sure, there are ways that this requirement is interpreted and practiced that greatly lessen the starkness of the violation of liberal principles (execution for apostasy has, in fact, been extremely rare). More to the point, however, we should be quite open to the possibility that any Islamic constitutionalism would sometimes be far from liberal in conception and practice—and still be constitutionalist. Those studying Eastern Europe have evinced an interest in the possible amalgamation of liberal constitutionalism with nationalist and ethnic political values. The possibility of an Islamic constitutionalism should similarly pique our interest; it might be more indicative of directions constitutionalism can take in parts of the world where liberal values are far from hegemonic.[24] In fact, outside of the United States, issues of identity have generally been posited outside of a liberal framework, forcing liberal constitutionalism to make significant adjustments.[25]

A second objection to the theoretical possibility of an Islamic constitutionalism is that however much Western constitutionalism might have descended from religious conceptions of law, Western constitutions are wholly manmade. Attempting to construct a new kind of constitutionalism based on divine rather than human sources would be an entirely different enterprise. There is some merit in this objection, since, as much as Western constitutionalism may derive from a natural-law heritage, it did not fully emerge until natural-law doctrines began to decline. Constitutionalism is, in some ways, a response to the demise of natural law. It was when the state emerged as the uncontested source of law that constitutionalism became necessary.[26] So long as other sources of law were viable, whether custom, church, or manor, state authority was contained by law. Constitutionalism became attractive only when the authority to legislate was monopolized by the state.

While there is some historic appeal to this dissociation between natural law and constitutionalism, it probably does not capture how constitutionalism is understood today, especially outside of narrow jurisprudential circles. In other words, the death of natural law may be more apparent than real. In some ways, natural law undertones have grown stronger in constitutionalist thinking, especially with regard to rights and the sources for rights. Prevailing vocabulary concerning rights has subtly shifted in recent years, anchoring them in a vague but real natural law conception: rights are increasingly seen as inherent in nature rather than granted to serve social purposes.

The implicit return of natural law represents a shift in thinking, especially outside the United States. The idea that some rights are natural and thus merely recognized, not granted, by constitutional documents is firmly rooted in the American constitutional tradition. Philip Hamburger has argued, however, that even eighteenth-century Americans accepted limitations on natural rights and distinguished between natural rights and acquired rights.[27] In the past, European constitutionalism has been more willing to countenance the concept that only a positive act of legislation can render a right politically meaningful.[28] This acceptance stemmed partly from a view that rights are grounded in social life and thus, in some sense, bestowed not by nature but by the community.

In the past few decades, however, debates about the sources of rights have been forgotten. The spread of the term "human rights" has carried with it the implication that rights are grounded in transcendent human values and do not differ according to culture, religion, or value system. Once a right is identified as belonging to humans it is far more difficult to argue that it is bestowed (and can be limited) by the community.

Constitutions may therefore be written by human beings but constitutionalism has never been able to shed its natural-law origins. If this is the case, it surely makes sense to explore the possibilities of using other legal traditions as a basis for constitutionalism. Both the Islamic law and natural-law traditions are based on a conception of law that escapes state domination: at least in theory, it is necessary to understand the political order as a product of— and not merely a promulgator of—general legal principles.

Can Islamic law serve as the basis of an alternative, even nonliberal, constitutionalism? Can it provide the basis for concrete constitutional practice? And can Arab constitutional provisions—mostly based on European models—serve as the foundation for an Islamic variant of constitutionalism? In chapter 6, I focus on the Islamic political heritage in the Arab world and assess the degree to which constitutionalism generally, and European constitutional texts specifically, operate on hostile territory in the region. The theoretical basis for Islamic constitutionalism will be revealed quite strong, but its institutional imperfections remain—at least for the present—equally striking. Islamic political thought does offer significant constitutionalist possibilities, but often only to the degree that it embraces Western constitutionalism. As in chapters 4 and 5, chapter 6 demonstrates a basis for the development of constitutionalism that is quite divorced from democratization.

FOUR

PARLIAMENTARISM AND CONSTITUTIONAL POSSIBILITIES IN THE ARAB WORLD

IN 1920, the first Arab parliament of the twentieth century sat briefly in Damascus. Suspicious that the government was not effective in obtaining favorable terms and recognition for the nascent Arab state, the body summoned the prime minister and began formal proceedings to withdraw confidence from him. Faysal (who briefly reigned and later became king of neighboring Iraq) dismissed the cabinet and appointed a new prime minister. This move toward parliamentarism was disrupted by the French conquest of the area and the assertion of mandatory control over the territory.[1] Seventy-eight years later, the Kuwaiti parliament took steps toward removing confidence from the minister of information, a member of the ruling Al Sabah family. Unwilling to countenance parliamentary action against a member of the royal family, the prime minister (who also served as crown prince) submitted his resignation and was forced to form a new cabinet. When parliamentarians continued attacks on leading ministers from the royal family, the amir felt forced to call for new elections.

On August 9, 1998, Jordanian and Palestinian legislatures showed the more pliant side of Arab parliamentary life. The Jordanian parliament reluctantly passed a much-criticized press law introduced by the government after the country's High Court had struck down the government's attempt to mandate the law by decree. On the same day, the Palestinian Legislative Council beat a similarly embarrassing and hasty retreat. Nearly a year earlier, an official accounting of public funds led to charges of waste and corruption against some senior ministers in the Palestinian Authority. Council members were dissuaded from withdrawing confidence in the cabinet only when all ministers were asked to submit their resignation to allow Yasir 'Arafat to form a new government. Yet the promised reshuffle dropped the names of some ministers who had died but none of those accused of corruption; the major change was the addition of a large number of new portfolios, assigned to nearly a dozen new ministers (many from the Legislative Council). After a bitter and sarcastic debate, the Council approved the new cabinet.

Thus the action of the Syrian parliament in 1920 and the Kuwait parliament in 1998–99 stand out in Arab history. In the time between these two actions, Arab parliaments grew much more numerous but very few were even in a position to consider bringing down a government. Indeed, while the Jordanian and Palestinian bodies proved to be more blustery than assertive, even their actions were exceptional. Few Arab parliaments retreat because few have advanced to a position where they might even consider confronting governments.

This chapter has two purposes: explaining Arab parliamentary weakness; and examining the possibilities for Arab parliaments to develop into bases for constitutionalist practice. These possibilities are both real and limited and they depend paradoxically on parliamentary autonomy that is—at least at a formal level—undemocratic in spirit.

Popular assemblies are very common but notoriously weak in the Arab world. All current Arab states have had assemblies, though the states of the Arabian Peninsula have often avoided electing them and assigning them legislative powers. In most of the rest of the Arab world, parliaments are both elected and assigned potentially extensive authority. Yet their prerogatives are rarely used: governments rule as they wish, unimpeded by parliamentary oversight.

There have been some exceptions: Jordan's parliament deposed a king, Kuwait's parliament has brought down ministers, and the Palestinian parliament in the making has already engaged in sharp confrontations with the government over corruption and other issues, even if it has retreated at the last minute. Some Arab parliaments have been so bothersome to the political authorities that they have been suspended: in Egypt, Jordan, Algeria, Kuwait, Morocco, and Bahrain independent governments have shut down obstreperous parliaments for extended (and unconstitutional) periods.

Prospects for constitutionalism in Arab politics are closely tied to the future of Arab parliaments for several reasons. First, parliaments offer one of the few possible instruments to ensure official accountability to established law and procedure (another instrument, the judiciary, is considered in the following chapter). Second, most conceptions of constitutionalism current in the Arab world (and the globe as a whole) rest not simply on accountability to a basic law but also to the people. Thus, most efforts to build constitutionalist institutions and practices will probably involve elected legislative bodies. Third, the experience of another region—Western Europe in the nineteenth century—indicates that constitutionalism can emerge from the contest between elected parliaments and executive authorities or monarchs. As was discussed in the introduction, constitutionalism tended to emerge from bargains in such struggles far more often than it emerged from abstract attempts to define the fundamental principles of the polity.

Thus, parliamentarism forms one of the chief avenues for fostering constitutionalist politics. This makes it critical to understand the reasons for the weakness of Arab parliaments; it makes it equally critical to understand the rare but notable exceptions of powerful parliaments.

Oddly, the past generation of specialists in the comparative politics of the developing world would probably direct us to look outside of parliamentary and constitutional structures in an effort to understand why parliaments rarely limit power.[2] Most specialists in comparative politics have avoided the study of constitutional structures since the 1960s. Especially in the developing world, scholarly attention turned toward the broader society in an attempt to explain politics. Parliaments, like constitutions, were seen as formal structures to mask the more profound social roots of political life. Parliaments in particular came to be seen as disconnected from the society. As pale reflections of the will of authoritarian regimes, parliaments unconnected from a strong social base came to be seen as irrelevant.

Even when interest in formal structures revived during the 1980s, written constitutions and parliaments received little attention. Only when authoritarian regimes collapsed in Latin America and the former Soviet bloc did scholars follow political activists in evincing an interest in constitutional structures and the relations among the various branches of government. Since the Arab world has yet to join the supposed global waves of democratization, Arab parliamentary bodies have continued to languish in scholarly obscurity. There is a cogent basis for this scholarly disinterest: Arab parliaments generally have weak connections to the broader society. Political parties, one of the main instruments for ensuring a connection between social groups and the parliament, are strong in the Arab world only when they serve as a creature of the existing regime. Following the dominant approach, we might expect that viable Arab parliamentarism depends on the ability of a parliament to give organized expression to social demands, perhaps through the system of political parties. Comparative politics scholarship would thus lead us away from examining formal authority and legal texts and toward an understanding of how parliaments might develop structured linkages with the broader society.

In fact, this reasoning, though appealing, remains incomplete for the Arab world. The formal structure of parliaments and the legal basis for their authority can be shown to be a major stumbling block to their effective operation. Constitutional text and established practice do much to undermine parliamentarism in the Arab world. It is true that the weaknesses of Arab parliaments cannot be explained solely in constitutional and institutional terms. The broader social context must be considered. But here we find a surprising result. Those exceptional parliaments that have established their independence from the executive have almost never done so through a strong political party system. Indeed, it is precisely where parties and associational life is weak that parliaments are often difficult to control. In the Arab world, parliaments with inchoate social bases can prove surprisingly independent. Strong party systems tend to vitiate parliamentary strength.

Explaining Quiescent Parliaments in the Arab World

Arab parliamentary bodies are often weak because they are denied constitutional and other tools necessary to operate effectively. They are not deprived of these tools by accident. Earlier assemblies (in the Ottoman Empire, Egypt, and Kuwait) proved to be far too difficult than expected for rulers to master. Sometimes bitter struggle gave way not to constitutionalism but to the development of techniques to undermine parliamentary independence. Rulers conquered rather than compromised with parliaments. In Europe, by contrast, constitutionalism often emerged when parliaments proved too difficult to vanquish and rulers felt forced to make concessions to them.

Imperial powers themselves often deliberately planted the seeds of parliamentary subservience when establishing elected bodies. In Iraq, for instance, the British felt more comfortable with a monarch able to override parliament:

> [G]iven the King's power to prorogue and dissolve Parliament, the King and his Ministers could, in the teeth of an unmanageable Chamber, provide for necessary supplies or decree the legislation necessary to implement treaty obligations.
>
> It cannot be doubted that this is a wise provision, however deeply it may offend against the spirit of pure democracy. It was a matter of great satisfaction that the Constituent Assembly accepted

it without demur. The first Parliaments of Iraq must at the best be untrained and inexperienced. It is vital that, in the last resort, the executive Government, with which alone the Allied Power can deal, should have authority to secure by legal means supplies for essential services and the fulfillment of those treaty obligations on which the very existence of the State depends.[3]

The Ottoman, imperialist, and independent Arab governments in the area developed a rich set of tools to allow parliamentary bodies to operate without restricting executive powers. In general, three sets of strategies were devised to allow for executive domination of the parliament: constitutional, legal, and electoral.

The Weak Constitutional Positions of Arab Assemblies

There are two primary arenas in which parliamentary bodies can exercise political authority: legislation and ministerial responsibility. Popular assemblies can vary widely, but those that have authority in neither of these areas are generally no longer referred to as parliaments at all. Some past Arab assemblies (such as that convened in Egypt in 1866) and some current ones (such as the Saudi Arabian and Qatari) fall in this category. (Arabic terminology tends to be more generous than English here; the term *majlis*, or council, is used for all popular assemblies, even those that are appointed rather than elected.) Yet such assemblies are exceptional in the Arab world: most possess a potentially strong role in the legislative process and few constitutions outside the Gulf allow ministers to serve who have lost the confidence of the assembly. Yet parliamentary authority is still circumscribed in both these areas.

In no Arab state does the parliament have a monopoly on the legislative process. Governments and heads of state often have the power to delay implementation of a law or force the parliament to reconsider legislation it has already passed. And while parliaments play an undeniable role in the normal legislative process in most Arab states, some vital legislation is not adopted through normal channels. In almost all Arab states, the government or head of state has the authority to issue decrees with the force of law in emergency situations. In most cases, such legislation must be submitted to parliament at its next sitting, but this procedure allows rulers the initiative. Precise procedure varies, but it is often the case that the parliament must explicitly reject such a decree-law for it to lose its effect. In essence, this reverses the normal relationship between parliament and executive: it is the executive that legislates, subject to the veto of the parliament. Arab governments declare emergencies with abandon, and this procedure for adopting legislation has been used to pass controversial laws in such areas as personal status or regulation of the press.

An additional constitutional mechanism to diminish parliamentary influence over legislation is the construction of an upper house. As mentioned in earlier chapters, upper houses are often introduced simultaneously with liberalizing political reforms because they can be an effective check on a more pluralist lower house. Members of upper houses are more likely to be appointed or elected indirectly. Precise procedures vary: in some areas (especially Morocco and Algeria), upper houses have been linked to local government; they have also been linked to formally recognized associations. A presidential or royal power of appointment for some seats is also common. Upper houses have rarely engaged in public confrontations with more popularly based lower houses. Yet they frequently must be consulted on legislation (often specific sorts of laws are mentioned, such as those that are necessary for the implementation of constitutional provisions) and stand as a potential barrier against an excessively independent parliament.

Arab regimes have devised a similar variety of tactics to limit ministerial responsibility to parliaments. These tactics were born of experience: as previous chapters showed, ministerial responsibility to parliaments has sometimes been as contentious in the Arab world as it was in nineteenth-century Europe. Some Arab states have simply refused to allow parliaments any effective control over the government. In most of the Gulf states (with Kuwait the most notable exception), the cabinet is responsible to the ruler and the assembly has no mechanism to withdraw confidence from individual ministers or the cabinet as a whole. In some republics, such as Tunisia and Iraq, ministers are clearly responsible to the president (and in Iraq, the RCC), although the parliament could theoretically move to bring down ministers through difficult or cumbersome procedures (in Tunisia, for instance, a supermajority is required). In much of the Arab world, however, parliamentary influence over the government is diminished through more subtle methods. In some countries (such as Morocco, Tunisia, and Iraq), the head of state chairs cabinet meetings. Since the parliament cannot remove the head of state on political grounds, this can move policy outside of the realm of parliamentary accountability.[4]

Even when the constitution provides for a stronger form of accountability, parliaments find it difficult to exercise any effective role. Almost everywhere in the Arab world, elected members of parliament form only a minority of the cabinet. With prime ministers (generally operating under presidential instruction) looking far outside the parliament for ministerial posts, most parliaments are left only the crude tool of refusing confidence to influence the composition of the government.[5]

Where ministers are responsible to parliament, it is common to have the responsibility operate at both the individual and the collective levels. This actually makes accountability to parliament slightly more viable. In most Arab countries, parliaments have never even debated withdrawing confidence from the entire cabinet. Individual ministers are less portentous but therefore more likely targets; even so, only in a few Arab countries have parliaments even considered moving against a minister. Arab parliamentary practice provides for three kinds of measures for a parliament to hold a minister accountable. The first measure is the parliamentary question; this is often used by individual members of parliament to mention concerns of particular constituencies and occasionally to raise policy issues. The second measure is interpellation [*istijwab*], a more weighty step requiring the support of a significant number of deputies (such as ten). Interpellation requires that the minister present himself in parliament, explaining and defending his action and addressing often hostile or politically charged questions. Since it is a prelude to a vote of no confidence, interpellation is regarded as a confrontational step and rarely used. Finally, the third and most serious measure is a vote of no confidence. Only the exceptional Arab parliament has even held a vote on such a step. Even the possibility of parliamentary debate on such a motion moved leaders to close down parliaments in the Ottoman Empire, Morocco, and Kuwait.

Indeed, the effective concentration of authority in the head of state blurs the line between political opposition and sedition, both in republics and monarchies. Parliamentarians who seek to withdraw confidence from the cabinet, based on constitutional mechanisms for ministerial responsibility, effectively target the head of state (who is not accountable to the parliament) as well. Legally and constitutionally, a parliament would be acting within its prerogatives by withdrawing confidence from a minister or an entire cabinet supported by the head of state, but politically, such a move does not obscure that the head of state and his policies are the real target. This is especially (but not exclusively) the case where the president chairs the cabinet or where the prime minister doubles as crown prince. This feature of Arab constitutional life helps explain the odd combination of truculence and reticence often characterizing parliamentary challenges to the government. When assertive parliaments have moved against governments, they generally do everything to avoid a vote of confidence. In Jordan in 1992 and 2000, a majority of parliamentarians signed a petition to the king asking him to dismiss the government. The same majority could have easily brought the government down directly but elected instead to act as a supplicant to avoid having their action appear as aimed against the king. In 1997, the Palestinian Legislative Council issued a report charging many ministers with corruption and called for their prosecution. Rather than withdraw confidence from them, however, it asked the president to form a new cabinet. In 2000, the Kuwaiti parliament engaged in a heated debate about a decree suspending two of the country's newspapers for publishing a false report. The decree had been drawn up by the cabinet but not issued. One former minister sitting in the parliament described the draft decree as "insane." The prime minister (who also served as crown prince) and the foreign minister (often assumed to be next in line for the throne) absented themselves from the debate in order to avoid embarrassment. The government's defenders criticized attacks on "the symbols of the nation;" that is, members of the ruling family.[6] Yet rather than bring down the government, the parliament toned down its criticism after ministers threatened to resign. Arab parliaments, even when they wish to criticize ministers or even force them out of office, almost always shy away from a formal vote of no confidence.

Still, most parliaments are not completely toothless. While there are ways for executives to avoid parliaments in sensitive legislative matters, most ordinary legislation must move through the parliament. Parliaments have the ability to debate issues in public in societies where open political discussions are often risky. Their ability to hold ministers accountable, even if atrophied, is still often as strong on paper as it is for their European counterparts. A complete explanation of the weakness of Arab parliaments in the face of the executive branch must look beyond the constitutional texts that still generally allow the parliaments some authority. Indeed, in many republics the parliament has a strong role in nominating the president (who is generally elected by popular referendum). Parliaments may be robbed of many tools, but they usually do not use the ones they do have to ensure any true measure of accountability in the political system. Earlier Arab parliaments could often prove more vigorous than later ones that theoretically possessed more extensive authority. To understand why, we have to move to different levels: the legal and institutional environment; and the party and electoral system.

Legal and Institutional Sources of Weakness

Arab parliaments are generally poorly structured to make use of the authority that they do have.[7] In order to originate legislation, for instance, parliamentarians would need to be able to call on a body of technical expertise that is generally beyond their individual means. Drafting a complex piece of legislation requires a combination of legal training and substantive knowledge. Parliamentarians generally work on their own, although some parliaments (such as the Kuwaiti) do allow for small personal staffs. Even the most generous parliaments do not provide sufficient staff for an individual member of parliament to draft a complex law.[8]

Instead of supporting individual parliamentarians, Arab parliaments tend to concentrate their support services at the level of the parliamentary body as a whole, centralizing authority within the parliament. While parliamentary officials insist that support services are made available to all members, it should not be surprising that centralization enhances the position of specific officials—most notably the speaker. Thus the ability of the parliament to serve as an independent body hinges on the inclinations of a few officials. And in systems in which a majority party controls both the speakership and the cabinet, the parliament will have difficulty developing an independent legislative voice.[9]

Indeed, Arab parliamentary traditions grant the speaker a collection of powerful tools to steer the parliament. The speaker controls the agenda, which, while circulated in advance, can be changed when the speaker finds the need arises.[10] Speakers also intervene actively in the course of parliamentary debate, ordering members to keep their comments short, avoid repeating themselves, and stick to the topic. Those who disregard such commands find themselves interrupted and ordered to be silent.[11] Such heavy-handed intervention indicates that it is the speaker, and not the parliamentarians, who dictates the terms of the debate.

Parliamentarians can turn to the broader society for support and expertise, though significant obstacles are placed in their path. First, in countries with strong party systems, such direct contact is often mediated by the party. Unless the cabinet is backed by a viable parliamentary coalition (a rare occurrence in the Arab world), a single major party is likely to hold sway over the parliament and the cabinet. Thus members of parliament from the majority party—which generally has strong links with the upper echelons of the bureaucracy—are unlikely to develop strong independent bases of expertise and support. Second, parliamentary committees, which function in some countries as an institutionalized mechanism for building contacts between the parliament and interest groups, rarely play such a role in the Arab world. Generally, most committee meetings are held *in camera*, making it difficult to call on outside expertise. And Arab parliaments are generally expected to have officials from interested ministries present when discussing legislation. The effect is to have the government far more strongly represented than any outside body or interest group.

Thus it should be no surprise that the vast majority of legislation in the Arab world is prepared in ministries. While this is often the case in parliamentary systems, Arab parliaments are especially weak in their ability to examine or amend significantly legislation submitted to them.[12] Parliaments are often derided in the Arab world as mere rubber stamps; their generally meek role in the legislative process is probably the primary source of this image.

Some Arab parliamentarians have become frustrated in recent years by their inability to build strong external bases of support. In some countries, parliamentarians have held government domination of news media responsible. Such domination is uncontestable, especially in broadcast media, leading some parliaments to attempt to establish their own direct mechanisms for insuring adequate coverage. These efforts have encountered strong opposition from governments. In Kuwait, parliamentarians have pressured the government to broadcast their sessions and sought to establish their own publications. The significance of such steps was not lost on the government. When the parliament passed a law in late 1998 requiring the broadcast of parliamentary sessions, the government threatened to refer the issue to the Constitutional Court on procedural grounds before finally acquiescing. And the Information Ministry long resisted attempts by the parliament to establish its own publications, sarcastically asking if all government offices were to have their own magazines and newspapers. Members of the Palestinian Legislative Council have been particularly vocal in this regard, though they have been only marginally more successful. While Palestinian print media are not official censored by the Palestinian Authority, heavy-handed official actions have made clear that journalists must operate within limits in publishing information that might seem to cast negative light on official actions. This has deadened press coverage of the very lively (and often critical) parliamentary debates. Frustrated, the parliament arranged to have its parliamentary sessions broadcast by a Jerusalem-based television station. With foreign financial support and a broadcast base outside the area controlled by the Palestinian Authority, parliamentarians had seemed to find a public voice—until the broadcaster was summoned to Ramallah (controlled by the Palestinian Authority) and detained until the broadcasts stopped.

Without the resources, organizational capacity, or public standing to establish a firmly independent outlook, most parliamentary bodies fall under bureaucratic domination in the legislative process. This subordinate position is encouraged by—and probably deepens—a deferential attitude toward the head of state. In most Arab countries, public restrictions on speech render the head of state beyond safe criticism. While most kings and presidents allow prime ministers and cabinets to become the day-to-day defenders of government policy, an unambiguous directive from the head of state is difficult to ignore. Thus parliamentary bodies often lose whatever independent spirit they might possess when given a firm push by the king or president.[13]

The deference to the bureaucracy is accentuated by the continental European legal framework adopted by most Arab states. In bureaucracies created on a continental model, the potential scope of administrative regulations and actions is often much wider than in Anglo-American countries. Bureaucratic actors are given far greater latitude in the administration of areas falling within their purview. In general, such systems distinguish among various levels of rules: the constitution, statute, administrative regulations or ordinances, and administrative decisions. Administrative regulations refer to general policies; administrative decisions refer to more specific acts related to individual matters rather than general policies. The scope for administrative regulations and decisions can be very broad. In the United States, bureaucratic actors generally must adduce a specific statutory authority for the regulations they issue. In continental systems, bureaucratic actors generally receive a more general authority (and thus far greater discretion) in issuing administrative regulations and decisions consistent with their constitutional or statutory mandate. Under the 1958 constitution, the French parliament is even restricted to specific areas; rule making outside those areas is left to administrative decisions.[14] Arab constitutions often do not go so far, but the prevailing ethos still allows ministers wide discretion within the loose boundaries set by constitutional and statute law. And prevailing legislative practice is to grant such discretion explicitly over a broad range of cases. Indeed, the Egyptian parliament on one occasion unconstitutionally delegated its authority to set taxation rates. To be sure, the growth of bureaucratic capacity in the United States has been accompanied by a pattern of Congressional delegation of administrative authority, but Arab ministers still are granted far more latitude and areas of competence than their American counterparts. Thus, much rule making over critical areas is traditionally ceded by Arab parliamentary bodies to the ministries.

Electoral Laws and Parliamentary Weakness

Arab parliaments, hamstrung as they are by the constitutional and legal framework, still retain much potential authority on paper. In most (though not all) of the Arab world, the electoral laws prevent them from developing the independence necessary to realize their potential.

The roots of parliamentary ineffectiveness extend to all components of the electoral process. First, party systems are generally severely restricted. Most Arab constitutions provide for freedom of association but only within bounds defined by law. In all Arab countries, political parties operate in a restrictive legal environment. Some countries (such as the Gulf states, including relatively liberal Kuwait) permit no political parties. Some (such as both Egypt and Algeria in the past) formally established one-party states; others (such as Syria, Iraq, and Tunisia) have made it virtually impossible for opposition parties to operate effectively. Some (such as Egypt) have banned political parties based on religious or ethnic lines, effectively forbidding the major dissident political orientations from organizing themselves in party form.

The electoral laws themselves are generally structured to favor governing parties. This is accomplished through numerous mechanisms. First, electoral boundaries and representation can be designed to favor the government. Rural areas—where bureaucracies and notables are often especially effective in mobilizing voters—are often overrepresented in parliaments relative to urban areas where opposition parties are often stronger. In some elected bodies (especially upper houses), representatives are not selected on the basis of geographically determined districts but instead through syndicates, trade unions, or regional councils that are themselves dominated by the government. In Kuwait, the government responded to rising opposition among the urban population by incorporating the outlying bedouin districts into the electorate. Tribal primaries were allowed in order to guarantee that the bedouin population would vote in a unified manner during parliamentary elections. Bedouin deputies thus came to represent tribes (although they were formally elected by geographical district) and their reelection came to depend on their ability to provide services to fellow members of the tribe.

When political parties are allowed to operate, governments generally prefer dividing the country up into geographical constituencies to translate smaller electoral majorities into larger parliamentary majorities. Egypt stood as an exception: in the 1980s, a series of proportional representation schemes were devised that seemed at first to allow for small parties to gain entry to parliament. But the bar for entry was fixed at 8 percent of the national vote. As a result, opposition parties were forced into coalitions. This system was struck down as unconstitutional by the country's Supreme Constitutional Court on the grounds that it forbade independent candidates from running (violating a constitutional right to seek office). A new, completely geographical system was devised to replace it. This undermined discipline in the governing National Democratic Party (NDP): local notables whom the NDP declined to nominate entered the race as independents. An ingenious solution was devised: NDP nominations became a closely guarded secret until the deadline for filing candidacies. The first time this technique was used, would-be candidates waited hopefully to be tapped by the NDP; those passed over had no time to file as independents.

Finally, governments have manipulated elections in far cruder ways. Indeed, in countries in which political liberalization has allowed some space for opposition candidates to operate, the voting process often comes under greater pressure. Egyptian elections display this phenomenon: court decisions legalizing parties and overturning electoral systems have led the government and the NDP to rely on an extraordinary amount of interference with balloting itself.

Egypt's Interior Ministry, hardly a bastion of liberal or democratic practices, oversees the election. And the parliament itself—the product of questionable electoral practices—acts as the arbiter of electoral disputes. The constitution suggests otherwise: Article 88 states that balloting "shall be conducted under the supervision of the members of a judicial organ." Yet members of the judiciary were unable (and many unwilling) to undertake full supervision until very recently. The number of polling places far exceeds the number of judges. Full judicial supervision necessitates polling over several days. Some leading judges were reluctant to insist upon full supervision, mindful of the burden but also unenthusiastic about involving themselves in questionable procedures.

A losing candidate in Egypt can challenge an election result before the judiciary, but this route is eventually blocked by the parliament itself. Article 93 of the Egyptian constitution provides that the parliament shall decide on the validity of membership. It further designates the Court of Cassation (Egypt's highest judicial body for civil, criminal, and personal status cases) as competent to investigate the validity of challenges. The Court refers its findings to the speaker of the parliament, which has sixty days to consider the matter. Membership can then be revoked by a two-thirds majority of parliament. Yet when the Court of Cassation actually refers cases, parliament almost always ignores the results. In most circumstances, the speaker does not even allow the parliament to discuss the Court's findings. Defeated candidates are powerless to force the issue. They may only sue for monetary compensation for their exclusion from parliament (and have actually won on occasion). The gap between judicial investigation and parliamentary inaction reached staggering proportions in 1995 when the Court of Cassation ineffectually recommended invalidation of the election of close to half of the deputies.[15] Attempts to challenge prevailing practices in the courts have brought uneven results. For instance, not until 2000 did the Supreme Constitutional Court find the minimal judicial involvement in overseeing voting unconstitutional. Having lost control of voting in the 2000 elections, Egypt's executive authorities became more heavy-handed during the campaign, arresting opposition activists and would-be monitors.

Oddly, limited political liberalization often increases official reliance on blatant electoral manipulation in the Arab world: with parliamentary elections more open to competition, some governments have felt forced to resort to underhanded methods to maintain their majorities. Electoral fraud has, on occasion, become an essential element of regime survival.

Weak Parties and the Seeds of Arab Parliamentarism

The lengths to which some governments have gone to maintain control over the parliament reveals a surprising feature of Arab parliaments: despite being robbed of many constitutional, institutional, and legal tools to establish their independence, such bodies retain substantial authority. While regimes have numerous methods of preventing parliaments from realizing their potential to assert this authority, ultimately a parliamentary body determined to make full use of its remaining tools could obstruct government action, hold it accountable, and even change its composition and basic policies. Arab executives are very aware that much latent power still lies in the hands of most parliamentary bodies and act decisively at early signs that a parliament will make use of its cumbersome but extant prerogatives. As seen in chapter 1, early constitutional efforts led to crisis whenever parliaments began to take ministerial responsibility seriously. Similar political crises have erupted in the twentieth century leading to suspension of parliamentary bodies in Morocco, Algeria, Jordan, Kuwait, and Bahrain. An assertive parliament (or, in the Algerian case, the probability of one) confronted the regime with the prospect of a greater amount of political accountability than it was prepared for. Fidelity to the constitutional text would have led to a level of parliamentarism that these regimes were not prepared to accept.

Parliaments that attempt to use their limited tools to assert their independence and hold governments accountable are thus rare but not unknown. What explains their emergence? Most such bodies have shared a common feature: a weak or nonexistent party system. Arab parliaments are often disregarded by Arabs and external observers because they seem to have such a shallow base in the society. Ironically, it may be this shallow base—at least on an institutional level—that is the secret of their occasional strength. Regimes that establish (or are established by) dominant parties have little trouble subduing parliament: in Iraq, Syria, Egypt, Algeria, and Tunisia, the regime has been identified with a single party, sometimes for close to two generations. Opposition parties might be tolerated at times, but the regime's ability to assert control over the parliament has been unquestioned because of the existence of a state-sponsored political party able to draw on the full weight of the state's distributive, coercive, and administrative apparatus to guarantee a subservient parliament.

On the other hand, systems in which successful candidates emerge based on family ties, notable status, or constituent service, often produce parliaments that have great difficulty acting cohesively but still assert a great degree of independence. Such a system often seems—even to the participants—old-fashioned and even traditional. Yet the results can be impressive: such bodies have engaged in confrontations with executive authorities and may offer the most realistic route to a fuller parliamentarism in the Arab world. The anomaly that weak parties can allow stronger parliaments to emerge can be illustrated by a consideration of the experience of three Arab parliaments: the Egyptian, the Kuwaiti, and the Palestinian.

The Egyptian People's Assembly

Egypt has the longest parliamentary tradition in the Arab world. The country's first popular assembly was established in 1866 (only a few years after the Tunisian constitution). While originally a consultative body, the assembly had begun to assert its authority over the budget and the cabinet when it was disbanded by the British occupation. The British did permit the establishment of very weak assemblies during the occupation. The 1923 constitution established a firm basis for parliamentary control over the legislative process; it also provided for a modicum of ministerial responsibility to parliament.

Parliamentary elections held under the 1923 constitution did have real effects on Egyptian governance, although the parliament itself, once seated, acted as little more than a public forum and an electoral college for the cabinet. This is not unusual in parliamentary systems, in which the cabinet makes policy and presents legislation to a parliament where it has a secure majority. Thus, the parliament had the potential to exert real influence over Egyptian politics, but primarily by expressing or withdrawing confidence from the government. The mechanisms described earlier in this chapter by which the parliament is removed from much of the legislative process (the drafting of legislation in ministries, the wide scope of administrative law, and the limited capability to draft or examine proposed legislation) operated even under the relatively liberal 1923 constitution.

In this respect, the Egyptian parliament was similar to its European counterparts. Yet even this electoral college role was substantially diminished in several ways. First, the king asserted a stronger role in selecting ministers than was anticipated by the authors of the 1923 constitution; he also did not shy from dismissing parliaments that had inclinations very different from his own. Second, the king, working with some civilian politicians, periodically engaged in electoral manipulation, in order to ensure a pliant parliament. Third, the king suspended the constitution on two occasions in order to prevent a hostile parliament from sitting.

The regime that came to power after the overthrow of the monarchy in 1952 was thus heir to two very well established traditions: lively parliamentary life and avoidance of the consequences of parliamentarism. Many Egyptian liberals hoped that the coup would lead to a full-fledged (and republican) parliamentary government. Some of the frustrated civilian political leaders of the old regime saw the removal of the monarchy as an opening to full parliamentary sovereignty.[16] Their decisive defeat in 1954 laid the groundwork for a period of parliamentary subservience more extended than at any time since the British occupation. The following two decades saw total executive dominance of the parliament through both explicit constitutional mechanisms (such as granting the president extensive emergency and legislative authority) and a host of legal and nonlegal tools that left parliament little option but to ratify decisions and legislative changes developed elsewhere. Underlying this parliamentary subservience was the one-party system eventually mandated by the constitutional text itself. With members of parliament owing their election to their nomination by the party headed by the president, any possibility of parliamentary independence was removed.

Under both Anwar al-Sadat and Husni Mubarak, parliamentary subservience has continued, though it has been reduced by the abandonment of some of the most egregious tools of executive domination. The president retains extensive emergency powers and most of the institutional mechanisms of parliamentary weakness discussed earlier in this chapter have remained unchanged.

The most fundamental shifts have involved the disestablishment of the Arab Socialist Union and the reassertion of judicial power.[17] These developments have left a slight opening for parliamentary assertiveness but their chief effect has been to force the regime to hold parliamentarism in check through increasingly heavy-handed electoral manipulation. The abolition of the one-party system came during the 1970s. It was not replaced with a fully pluralistic order but instead one in which the National Democratic Party (NDP), headed by the president and supported by the full administrative weight of the state, dominates the political order while allowing a limited number of political parties to contest elections. In order to ensure that the new party pluralism would be contained within sharply defined limits, a number of restrictions were placed on political parties. First, a political parties law banned groups that were based on religion or duplicated existing parties; for a period, opposition to the peace treaty with Israel was also placed beyond the bounds of party contestation (that ban was overturned by the country's Supreme Constitutional Court). Second, an electoral system was designed that would guarantee NDP majorities: candidates were to be elected by party list and only those parties receiving 8 percent of the national vote could claim seats in parliament. This barrier was sufficiently formidable that only a revived Wafd Party in alliance with the Muslim Brotherhood (itself unable and perhaps unwilling to register as a party because of its religious platform) was able to obtain a modest share of seats.

While this system seemed well designed to guarantee both an insurmountable NDP majority and a tame and loyal opposition, it was soon undermined by a series of judicial decisions. First, many parties who were refused licenses successfully resorted to the administrative judiciary. Most of the political parties extant in Egypt today were established only after such court decisions. These new parties may have only weakened the parliamentary opposition by making it impossible for any single opposition group to cross the 8 percent threshold were it not for a series of decisions by the Supreme Constitutional Court overturning the voting system. Claiming that the Egyptian constitution guaranteed individuals the right to stand for election, the Court struck down electoral laws, including the list system, that prohibited independents from registering as candidates. The effect was not only to allow smaller parties a more significant chance of entering parliament but also to fragment the NDP: candidates with strong local standing now might run under the NDP banner but owe much less to the party endorsement. Thus, once elected, some deputies operated in a manner that might seem excessively independent by the NDP leadership. In many circumstances, candidates passed over by the NDP (whether because of their excessive independence or for other reasons) could run as independents. And in 2000, the Court ruled that elections carried out under less than full judicial supervision were unconstitutional. The effect of this decision was to force the government to use its heavy-handed techniques before the elections (by suppressing opposition groups) rather than on election day. And the first elections carried out under judicial supervision, in the fall of 2000, led not only to some members of the Muslim Brotherhood obtaining seats, but also to unusual success by those deemed "NDP independents"—candidates who did not run under the NDP banner but joined it hours after their election. NDP independents do support the government but often only after being coaxed, and the behavior of many has deeply embarrassed the government in past parliaments.

To make matters more critical, another series of court decisions began to call into question some of the tools that executives had traditionally used to bypass parliament. In 1985, the Supreme Constitutional Court voided a presidential decree amending the personal status law. The Court did not challenge the clear constitutional basis allowing the president to issue decrees with the force of law during parliamentary recesses but held that such actions only applied to pressing emergencies. The Court effectively asserted the right to judge such emergency situations (whereas it might have asserted that the presidential obligation to submit such decrees to the next session of parliament left the authority to judge emergencies in the hands of the legislature). Several other rulings by the Court undermined the ability of the parliament to skirt its constitutional role. A sales tax law was struck down on the grounds that the parliament had unconstitutionally allowed rates to be set by decree rather than by parliamentary legislation. The Court also held that laws passed by referenda still had to conform to the constitution, robbing the president of a favorite tool of ensuring adoption of constitutionally questionable legislation.

The effect of these rulings should not be exaggerated. In 1998, the Supreme Constitutional Court itself discovered that the president's emergency powers remained strong when the president amended the law governing the retroactivity of its judgments by decree. The decree was issued shortly after the parliament went into recess; the ostensible emergency was that the Court was preparing rulings on some taxation cases in which retroactive invalidation would cause fiscal chaos. The president did consult the General Assembly of the Court (consisting of member judges) as he was legally required to do, but with the presidency of the Court vacant (and members anxious to have Mubarak follow traditional practice by turning to a member of the Court to fill the post) it was not the time for political boldness. The decree-law was dutifully submitted to parliament when it reconvened; the parliament was given the choice of affirming or overturning the measure; its expected affirmation came after little debate.

Thus the judicial rulings did not fundamentally reconstitute Egypt's political system. But they did have the twin effects of making executive control of the parliament both more important and more difficult to obtain. The result has been a series of measures taken to ensure appropriate outcomes not through law but through manipulation (both legal and illegal). As mentioned above, the NDP has sometimes held off announcing its candidates until the very last moment in order to prevent those unsuccessful aspirants for NDP nomination from registering as independents. Candidates associated with undesirable groups (especially Islamists) have found their poll watchers detained or the telephones not working on election day. And crackdowns on opposition before election time have become more common.[18] Such measures were unnecessary during the 1960s when there were no opposition candidates; they were not even needed so extensively during the 1970s and 1980s when the electoral system helped guarantee appropriate outcomes.

Realizing that such methods are critical to the electoral success of the governing party, opposition parties are increasingly unwilling to contest the NDP on these terms. Leading parties have frequently boycotted recent elections because of the electoral rules. Thus, the recent Egyptian experience demonstrates that the electoral and party systems are the critical element in executive domination of the legislature. The judicial decisions mentioned have made such domination depend on increasingly heavy-handed measures but they have not changed the fundamental situation.

The importance of the party and electoral system can be seen by a comparison of the effect of similar judicial decisions in Jordan, where the party system is fragmented and candidates run as individuals or as representatives of loosely defined ideological tendencies. In both Egypt and Jordan, increasingly assertive judiciaries have launched a similar challenge to the breadth of executive prerogatives (the challenge has been far broader and more sustained in Egypt, though not necessarily more successful). In Egypt, the Supreme Constitutional Court's 1985 decision placed limits on the executive's authority to issue decree-laws in the absence of parliament by claiming the authority to review the extent to which such actions were based on true emergencies. The Court's action, overturning a change in the personal status law that had drawn Islamist fire—was extremely inconvenient for a regime whose Islamic credentials were being increasingly questioned. Islamist members of parliament, who had gained seats under the brief electoral alliance between the Muslim Brotherhood and the Wafd, were launching a noisy campaign to apply the Islamic *shari'a*. Yet with its secure parliamentary majority, the government was able to push through an amended law fairly quickly, giving parliamentary approval to most of the changes earlier made by presidential decree.

In January 1998, Jordan's High Court issued a ruling similar to the 1985 decision by the Egyptian court. Earlier, the government had issued an amended press law by decree greatly increasing the financial requirements for the publishers. This had the deliberate effect of forcing some of the more lurid and sensationalist weeklies out of operation. The Jordanian government was resorting to a tool it had used before: limits to liberalization were legislated by the executive when parliament was not in session. A weak and divided parliament was unlikely to overturn the legislation when it returned. In this case, however, the government's actions were disrupted not by the parliament but by the High Court: ruling that the action was not justified by any emergency, the Court struck down the decree-law. The government reacted angrily. The president of the Court was forced into retirement by the justice minister.[19] Initially the government hesitated to accept the ruling and, even after it did so, seemed to be moving to seek a parliamentary majority to support the change. Even while announcing acceptance, the king took the unusual step of issuing a sharp, public denunciation. In an open letter to the prime minister, the king called the verdict a "dangerous precedent which we hope will not happen again."[20] Accepting the ruling forced the government to turn back to the parliament for ratification of the law. Yet the inchoate party structure and institutional weakness of the parliament inhibited any action. Before the court ruling, when an affirmative step would have been necessary to repeal the decree-law, the parliament had been unable to act. But now the High Court had transformed the situation by requiring the parliament to affirmatively act to approve the law before it could be applied. And the government found the parliament a sullen obstacle. The unpopularity of the law and its restrictions on freedom of the press made it difficult to muster a parliamentary majority in favor of any change; only after months of wrangling (and a committee recommendation to loosen many parts of the law), did the parliament finally give the government what it wished.

In Egypt, the stronghold of the NDP on the parliament has enabled the government to produce a parliamentary majority whenever it needs one (in 1995, the Egyptian government managed to obtain parliamentary approval for legislative changes in the country's press law without even allowing parliamentarians sufficient time for anything more than a cursory reading of the draft). In Jordan, the government is forced to operate without the same sort of ability to produce easy majorities. The parliament does not systematically block the government but neither does it automatically support it. The result is that the Jordanian body is less decisive but actually more of a stumbling block to unfettered executive authority than its more established (and theoretically more powerful) Egyptian counterpart. Disorganization and party weakness in Jordan have led to a stronger—or at least more obstinate—parliament.

The Kuwaiti National Assembly

The National Assembly in Kuwait has been one of the most obstreperous assemblies in the Arab world. At no time has it been able to institute a fully parliamentary system, but it has successfully resisted government attempts to render it more pliant and continuously threatened to use some of its constitutional tools to bring about a greater level of accountability. Perhaps more than any such body in the Arab world, the Kuwaiti National Assembly shows how well parliaments can be simultaneously frustrating and frustrated. The Assembly frustrates the executive by blocking, delaying, or criticizing its actions but also leaves its own members feeling powerless to pursue any alternative agenda.

During its first decade, the National Assembly served as forum for a wide variety of ideological tendencies, but it did not launch any challenge to the government (although the first parliament successfully objected to a cabinet including merchants on constitutional grounds, as described in chapter 2). In a tumultuous period in Arab politics, the Assembly actually seemed to help cement a distinctive Kuwaiti national identity.[21] And the government managed to stave off any challenge to its policies and authority by bringing new groups into the electorate. Most notable in this regard was the population of "outer Kuwait," which tended to be more recently settled, less educated and cosmopolitan (and therefore less motivated by Arab nationalism and Nasserism), and more oriented toward tribal loyalties. In order to ensure some measure of representation for this population, parliamentary elections were preceded by the tribal primaries mentioned above in which members of the tribe would select candidates to stand for election. In multimember districts, these tribal primaries greatly assisted the election of tribally based candidates. Many parliamentarians, especially those from "outer Kuwait," became known as "service deputies" because of their positions as mediators between the bureaucracy and the population; they gained reelection through provision of employment and access to their constituents. The Kuwaiti government, awash in oil revenues, found little difficulty gaining the political loyalties of the tribal and service deputies. It also was able to balance various ideological trends against each other: with the parliament containing liberals, Arab nationalists, Islamists, business leaders, and Shiʻi Muslims it became difficult for any single group to lead a challenge to the composition or the policies of the government. In recent years, for instance, the government has been able fairly successfully to guide national debate toward issues that divide liberals and Islamists (such as women's suffrage) and away from those that might unite them (such as corruption).

Even if the Kuwaiti parliament was rarely capable of concerted action, it still was a more difficult body to manage than the Egyptian People's Assembly. While Kuwait's parliament has always contained various ideological tendencies they have never been organized into formal parties; nor has the government made any attempt to form its own party. Without a structure like Egypt's National Democratic Party to call on (indeed, without even the ability to bargain with party leaders possessing clear authority), Kuwait's governments have generally managed to prevent a strong opposition bloc from developing by a mixture of balancing, provision of services, and exploiting divisions. The government has not always been successful: at times, parliamentarians have threatened to form fleeting majorities around specific issues (such as the oil industry or corruption). By the mid-1970s, an increasingly assertive parliament had emerged. On one issue (involving judicial review of the constitutionality of an administrative order), the parliament was poised for the first time to pass legislation over a government veto (which the constitution allows if the proposal obtains a supermajority on a second vote or—if the second vote is held in the following parliamentary session—a simple majority).[22] An Assembly that availed itself of the full range of its constitutional authority was an extremely intimidating prospect for the government, which reacted by dissolving the assembly, suspending parts of the constitution, and ruling by decree.

In 1981, motivated perhaps by the need to generate a broader basis of domestic support, the government restored the constitution and the Assembly (although it made an ineffectual attempt to bring about some modifications).[23] Yet the restored Assembly proved as difficult as its predecessors: by 1985, it had gathered a majority against the minister of justice (a member of the ruling family) who resigned to avoid dismissal. Parliamentarians then began to move against others (including 'Ali al-Khalifa, another member of the ruling family, whose tenure as minister of oil was marked by allegations of enormous corruption).[24] In 1986, the government responded as it had a decade earlier: the Assembly was suspended along with parts of the constitution and the cabinet was given the authority to rule by decree. In 1989, former parliamentarians spearheaded a movement to reinstate the Assembly and the constitution. The government responded with a mixture of repression and compromise and, as described in chapter 2, only agreed to a full restoration during a national congress held in Saudi Arabia during the Iraqi occupation.

When parliament was fully restored in 1992, new elections were held in a very different atmosphere: while formal political parties still did not operate, some former tendencies had coalesced. Liberals and leftist Arab nationalists had been drawn closer together (the Iraqi invasion having rendered any talk of Arab unification not simply unrealistic but extremely unpopular, leaving little distance between liberals and former radicals). Islamist forces were increasingly popular in a traumatized society and made significant inroads both among the college-educated and the districts of "outer Kuwait." The parliament that resulted sparked ambitions of a real constitutional monarchy in Kuwait; some even broached the idea of a prime minister who was not crown prince. Certain members of the royal family were clearly unacceptable to the parliament: leading parliamentarians hung a *persona non grata* (*shakhsiyya ghayr marghuba*) label on 'Ali al-Khalifa (whom the parliament insisted be tried for corruption) and the interior minister blamed for the suppression of the constitutionalist movement in 1989–90. Members of parliament only reluctantly accepted others that it held responsible for Kuwait's lack of preparation for the Iraqi invasion. In return, the prime minister named six members of parliament to cabinet seats, a higher number than had ever served in the past. Among the new ministers were Islamists, radicals (including a former would-be revolutionary, Ahmad al-Rub'i, as minister of education), and leaders of the constitutionalist movement of 1989–90 (including Mishari al-'Anjari in the critical justice ministry).

Yet the newly elected Assembly proved to be no more imposing than its predecessors. Liberals and Islamists soon locked in conflict over a number of issues, and when Islamist deputies narrowly failed in ousting Ahmad al-Rub'i from the cabinet, the conflict between the two camps turned bitter. In Assembly elections in 1996, key liberals (including some who had served as ministers) failed in reelection bids; Ahmad al-Khatib, a former radical who had served in the Founding Assembly and most parliaments, retired. Islamist forces fared far better, but the "service deputies" and tribal representatives seemed to be the biggest victors. The Kuwaiti system seemed as if it had pulled back from the fuller parliamentarism that had threatened to emerge in the wake of the Iraqi invasion. The defeat of the constitutionalists was symbolized by the need of one of their leaders, Ahmad al-Sa'dun, for support from government ministers to secure reelection as speaker.

Yet the newly elected parliament proved to be one of the most troublesome for Kuwait's government. It abolished the tribal primary system, probably ensuring that future parliamentary elections would be more difficult for the government to manage (though illegal primaries were in fact held in 1999). Some liberals moved to launch parliamentary proceedings against the minister of finance, though Islamists refused to support the move. Instead Islamists targeted the minister of information, a member of the royal family. A very prominent personality (and a former ambassador to the United States), the information minister came under criticism when books not normally permitted in Kuwait (as offensive to Islam or public morals) were displayed at a book fair. Comments made by leading Islamists made clear that the book fair itself was less a concern than the belief that the minister had surrounded himself with liberals who were controlling state-run media. In short, a real policy difference had arisen between a parliamentary faction and the government. Vague threats that the parliament would be dissolved did not prevent a parliamentary majority from forming that would likely have removed the minister (partly because the government held back the threat of suspending parliament altogether so that dissolution would only result in new elections). Rather than accept this result, the prime minister submitted his resignation and formed a new cabinet. Having accepted defeat, the government found itself involved in a series of new wrangles: the parliamentary leadership complained that the new cabinet had not properly detailed its program as required by the constitution and an Islamist member moved to interpellate the minister of interior for allowing moral corruption and drug abuse to spread. The prime minister finally approached the amir and declared himself unable to cooperate with the parliament. With a clear and explicit threat to dissolve the parliament (probably, though not certainly, constitutionally; that is, with new elections to follow immediately), parliamentary leaders agreed to a series of steps to lessen the confrontational tone of executive-legislative relations, including moving the discussion of the interpellation of the interior minister into secret session.[25] The compromise was short-lived, and in 1999 the amir finally dissolved the parliament constitutionally. Seeking to show what it could accomplish, the government then issued a series of decree-laws on controversial matters (including granting women the right to vote). All these matters would require the approval of the incoming parliament, however, virtually guaranteeing that the past contests between government and Assembly would be renewed.

The Assembly elected in 1999 marked a triumph for the liberals. Yet the dynamic of government-parliamentary relations changed little. As with the supposedly more pliant Assembly elected in 1996, the body found little difficulty confronting the government but much more difficulty taking concerted positive action. The parliament rejected virtually all the decree-laws issued by the amir after the dissolution of the parliament, as some liberals (who favored many of the measures) voted on procedural grounds that such changes were an abuse of the amir's authority to issue emergency legislation. Some parliamentarians even complained about constitutional issues raised by the ill health of the prime minister—while his position as crown prince had moved him beyond most direct criticism in the past, his prolonged absence from the parliament seemed to undermine any accountability. In January 2001, parliamentary pressure was an apparent factor in the cabinet's decision to resign (although Al Sabah rivalries were probably the primary cause). Yet beyond blocking the government and launching criticisms, the new parliament seemed unable to construct or pursue its own agenda.

Thus the Kuwaiti National Assembly, often regardless of its particular composition, acts sporadically to insist on political accountability. It has been unable to dictate the composition of the cabinet (always dominated by the royal family) though it has sometimes been able to affect some of the portfolios. Too fragmented to articulate its own policies (except on occasional issues), the parliament has sometimes been able to criticize controversial government policies and even bend them. Unable to muster the resources needed for full political and budgetary supervision of the government, the parliament has been able to confront and sometimes embarrass the government on specific issues. By and large, the government has been able to contain parliamentary ambitions, but the process has been extremely frustrating at times. On a few occasions, parliamentary actions went so far as to aggravate conflicts within the ruling family, particularly by moving against Al Sabah ministers. More frequently, however, the parliament has been extremely annoying but not threatening. The current prime minister and crown prince has made clear his continued contempt for the body by absenting himself from most of its meetings (even before his health became a problem) and leaving others to explain and defend official policy. Ministers complain that parliamentarians launch long-winded and ill-informed attacks, pepper them with innumerable petty or tendentious questions, irresponsibly block needed reforms (especially those involving prices and finances), and talk recklessly, without regard for consequences. These complaints are not surprising: the political and electoral systems in Kuwait seem designed to produce precisely this kind of parliament.

What explains the odd combination of episodic boldness with inability to exercise full constitutional powers? Why is the Kuwaiti parliament so bothersome to the government without being able to institute full accountability? The secret lies largely in the party system, or lack of one. Having created an elected parliament but barred political parties from forming, Kuwait ensured that individual deputies would be elected as independents. On rare occasions, the government has intervened heavily in the electoral process to guarantee a pliant parliament. For the most part, however, it has relied on the fragmentation and rivalries within parliaments along with a practice of co-opting some of the members and groupings. This cumbersome process does not always work efficiently. And it rewards precisely the grandstanding (even demagogic) bluster that so frustrates the government. Unwilling to tolerate a body that would exercise its full constitutional responsibility of holding the government accountable, Kuwait's leaders have created a body that they are bound to find irresponsible. Able to affect policies and composition of the government through inflaming public opinion, and able to secure reelection only by strident language or providing services, parliamentarians unsurprisingly engage in behavior that seems egoistic and often uncooperative. While they lasted, tribal primaries did introduce the functional equivalent of government-dominated political parties: by allowing themselves to be co-opted by the provision of government services, tribal leaders muted the stridency of parliamentary debates.

Mindful of these criticisms but supportive of parliamentary democracy, one Kuwaiti constitutional scholar has advocated a stronger party system as a solution.[26] A truly pluralist party system not dominated by the government might have this result, but the suggestion misses the point that the parliament's stronger performance and its limitations have the same cause: by granting the National Assembly strong prerogatives on paper but robbing it of the tools necessary to act as a coherent body, parliament is difficult to dominate even as it cannot bring rulers fully to account.

The Palestinian Legislative Council

The Palestinian Legislative Council is an anomaly in the Arab world.[27] Its legal basis is far weaker than that of any other assembly, but it has already emerged in just a few years of operation as an independent body willing to embarrass and confront the executive. Even though the Council has a strong record by Arab standards, it remains similar to the Kuwaiti National Assembly: willing to pressure the government to change its policies and even its composition, able to launch a few limited legislative initiatives, but ultimately unable to impose its will on an executive authority suspicious and resentful of parliamentary boldness.

The origins of the Council lie in the Oslo Accords. While the initial agreement between Israel and the Palestine Liberation Organization signed in September 1993 anticipated some measure of Palestinian self-government (an autonomous "Palestinian Authority"), a considerable amount of wrangling preceded more complete arrangements. Israel agreed with the PLO on an interim period during which the Palestinian Authority would expand its competencies and geographic scope. During the interim period, a permanent settlement was to be negotiated. Even the interim arrangements were difficult to negotiate, however, because both sides viewed them as prejudicing a final settlement. Virtually every issue became the subject of protracted and complex negotiations.

The authorities granted to the Palestinians obviously attracted great attention, but there was also some coverage of matters of internal governance in the Oslo Accords. The Israelis were anxious to forestall any symbolism of statehood, so terms like parliament, cabinet, and constitution were avoided. The result was the creation of a new body, the Palestinian Council, which could be viewed in many different ways. In its structure, the Council seemed to be halfway in between a parliament and an oversight committee; certainly, no separation of powers is anticipated in the text, which designates the Council as the governing authority and the successor to the Palestinian Authority. However, the Council was granted the authority to make laws (including a basic law for Palestinian governance) that made it resemble a legislative body. And when the elections were held and the members seated, the Council immediately began to act as a provisional parliamentary body.

The Palestinian elections of 1996 brought into being an independent council that still seemed likely to be supportive of the elected president, Yasir 'Arafat. Most political parties opposed to the Oslo Accords boycotted the elections, leaving the field open for members of 'Arafat's party, Fatah, and independents. Even if supportive, however, the new body consisted of individuals who had gained election on their own. Many of the Fatah members were elected despite failure to receive the party's endorsement; they ran anyway, confident of their popularity in their own districts. As a result, the Council members showed little ideological opposition to the president, but neither did they owe their election to him or his party.

The Council set to work immediately, writing some internal regulations (that resembled those of other Arab parliamentary bodies) and electing a speaker, Ahmad Quray'. In both cases they quickly showed their independence by ignoring 'Arafat's wishes (the president disagreed with the oath of office selected by the Council and reportedly favored a different candidate for the speakership). And members began referring to the body as the Palestinian Legislative Council, implying that it was the legislative arm (rather than the successor to) the Palestinian Authority. The president, defined in the Oslo Accords as the head of the Council, operated completely independently of that body as a freestanding executive. And Palestinian ministers were treated as forming a cabinet rather than the Council's executive committee.

The next major law taken up by the Council was a basic law, regarded as an interim constitution for the Palestinians. A considerable amount of preparatory work had already been done on the law and by the time the Council took up the issue, several proposed drafts were being circulated. These drafts had been prepared by legal officials of the PLO and independent legal and academic figures. A committee of experts formed by the Palestinian Ministry of Justice had been due to draw up a draft document for submission to the Council; a prolonged closure of the West Bank and Gaza in 1996 had made it impossible for the committee to meet. Some members therefore took up the task independently.[28]

In the summer of 1996, the Council took up the Basic Law with enthusiasm. Members regarded the matter as critical: up to that point, newly emerging Palestinian institutions based their legal existence only on signed agreements with Israel. Even strong supporters of those agreements wished to root institutions in Palestinian laws rather than agreements with Israel. Many members of the Council regularly gave expression to the desire to establish a Palestinian state with a stronger democratic and constitutional basis than prevailed elsewhere in the Arab world. But this quickly led to a clash with President 'Arafat who claimed—despite the Oslo Accords, which gave the Council the duty of writing a basic law—that it was the Palestinian National Council, representing Palestinians everywhere, that should take the lead. The conflict broke out in a public confrontation between Quray' and 'Arafat in July 1996, leading Quray' to resign in protest over 'Arafat's behavior.[29] Quray' was dissuaded from carrying through on his resignation, and the Council resumed its discussion of the basic law, but 'Arafat did not retreat from his position that the Council was acting prematurely.

The Council debated the basic law and approved its first reading in the fall of 1996. The law was then referred to the relevant ministry and president for comment, following Arab parliamentary practice. Rather than comment and refer the draft back to the Council, however, 'Arafat failed to act. Relations between 'Arafat and the Council became quite strained. In the minds of many Council members, this dispute only accentuated the need for immediate passage of a basic law: in its absence, the precise delineation of authority between the Council and the president remained unclear, leaving the Council unsure of whether or how it could pursue the matter further. In 1997, the Council finally decided to resume discussion of the basic law and passed it on its second and third reading. Once again 'Arafat simply ignored it. By 1999, the PLO's Executive Committee signaled the abandonment of the Council's draft by asking the Arab League to appoint an advisory committee to assist in drafting a constitution for an independent Palestinian state.

Disputes between 'Arafat and the Council began to extend into other fields. The Legislative Council often came under criticism for working too slowly to establish a legal framework for Palestinian self-government, so its members found it particularly irksome that the few laws they were able to pass generally lingered on the president's desk for months before any action was taken. Judgments of courts were sometimes ignored and Palestinian security officials were frequently accused of torture, offending many human-rights–oriented Council members. Officials of the Palestinian government were often accused of corruption, increasing the determination of the Council to play a watchdog role. When a report detailing widespread corruption was issued by an autonomous Palestinian auditing bureau, Council members angrily confronted the government and demanded that 'Arafat dismiss those ministers most guilty of abuses. 'Arafat then met with the Council in a more conciliatory move, announcing that all members of the cabinet had submitted their resignations and that he would form a new cabinet shortly. New promises of cooperation mollified Council members only for a short period. The following spring the cabinet submitted a budget that members of the Council found insufficient and the promised cabinet reshuffle was endlessly delayed. The most prominent member of the Council resigned in protest at 'Arafat's behavior and the ineffectual response. Remaining members of the Council vowed to consider withdrawing confidence from the cabinet. 'Arafat finally presented a new cabinet to the Council in August 1998. Despite the fact that the only significant changes involved the addition of new ministers without the removal of old ones, the Legislative Council (several of whose members gained cabinet positions), approved the new body after a bitter debate.

The Palestinian Legislative Council thus emerged as a body very similar to the Kuwaiti parliament (and to the Ottoman parliament a century ago): its constitutional basis was weaker, but it insisted on its privileges and attempts at times to ensure official accountability. While the Council stood ready to confront individual ministers and sometimes the entire cabinet (and 'Arafat himself), it did not emerge with any significant victory from its confrontations. Typical in this regard was the battle over the 2000 budget: the Council's Budget Committee provided a detailed and scathing report citing financial irregularities, inadequate reporting, and even violations of the law. After a heated debate that put the government very much on the defensive, the Council passed the budget. Similarly, physical altercations between vocal members of the Council and Palestinian security forces prompted thundering rhetoric and embarrassed the Authority internationally, but the Council was unable to bring any official to account after such incidents.

The attitude of the Palestinian executive toward the parliament grew similar to the attitude displayed by the Kuwaiti government: members of the parliament were viewed as amateurish, obsessed with petty privileges, threatening to national unity, and damaging to government efficiency. Ministers were frequently quizzed on minor local matters rather than significant policy issues as Council members struggled to maintain a reputation for protecting the concerns of their constituencies.

After over four years of operation, the Palestinian Legislative Council accumulated a record that might seem impressive: it has written a constitution and passed a series of laws establishing a basic political and legal framework for the country. But even more notable was the Council's swiftness in engaging in a series of public confrontations with cabinet ministers and the president. Since most members of the Council were either independent nationalists or Fatah members, this record might initially seem surprising. But members of the Council were elected as individuals and must cultivate strong individual reputations to maintain their positions. Such a collection of individuals proved difficult to dominate; the Palestinian government succeeded only in fending off the Council rather than subjugating it.

Conclusion

Arab parliaments have generally been denied the tools to become more than the rubber stamps their critics generally view them as. Experience with elected assemblies in the nineteenth and early twentieth centuries led Arab executives to design—sometimes by trial and error—the constitutional, legal, and electoral tools to rob such bodies of the ability to bring about a full parliamentary system. Establishing such a parliamentary system would represent (and probably require) a revolution in Arab politics.

Yet a degree of parliamentary oversight and accountability to an elected assembly can develop even within the constitutional framework existing in most Arab states. In the absence of a clear establishment of parliamentary sovereignty (which in Europe has often transformed parliaments into electoral colleges), Arab parliaments have been successful to the degree they have resembled the American Congress in their focus on local issues, dispersion of power, willingness to influence policy through obstruction, proclivity towards grandstanding and bombast, and search for individual rather than collective influence.

With only limited exceptions, executive authorities have succeeded in robbing constitutional structures of their ability to institute any genuine measure of political accountability. Critical to this success has been their willingness not only to write constitutions to their liking but also to interpret them as they need. In the past few decades, this monopoly on constitutional interpretation has been challenged by the surprising emergence of judicial review. Will Arab judiciaries be more effective than parliaments in holding government accountable—if not to the people than at least to the law?

FIVE

JUDICIAL REVIEW IN ARAB CONSTITUTIONAL SYSTEMS

ARAB CONSTITUTIONAL TEXTS authorize executives more than they limit them. They do so not only by explicit authorization but also by their silences, gaps, and vagueness. Rights are guaranteed but not defined; separation of powers is declared but easily circumvented; and procedures are designed with escape hatches built in for instances in which their implications become politically inconvenient. Arab governments do act unconstitutionally but only rarely; most are able to operate consistently within plausible if illiberal interpretations of the constitutional text.

Arab executives can generally do what they wish precisely because the vagueness of the constitution can be bent to their advantage. This makes constitutional interpretation especially important: if Arab executives were to lose their ability to bend the constitution when they saw fit, a genuine basis for constitutionalism could be built. Independent and authoritative judicial review of the constitutionality of legislation and administrative acts would seem to offer precisely such a basis for constitutionalist politics. Precisely for this reason, Arab regimes might be expected to be very suspicious of ceding the task of constitutional interpretation to independent judiciaries. Yet surprisingly, such judicial review is arising and spreading in the Arab world.

Political scientists have displayed little interest in judicial review in recent decades. At the heart of the disciplinary skepticism toward judicial institutions lies a hoary attitude: how can judicial actors, even if independent and bold in their interpretation of law, enforce their vision without reliance on other actors? Two centuries ago, Alexander Hamilton noted in Federalist number 78:

The Executive not only dispenses the honors, but holds the sword of the community. The legislature not only commands the purse, but prescribes the rules by which the duties and rights of every citizen are to be regulated. The judiciary, on the contrary, has no influence over either the sword or the purse; no direction either of the strength or the wealth of the society; and can take no active resolution whatever. It may truly be said to have neither FORCE nor WILL, but merely judgment; and must ultimately depend upon the aid of the executive arm even for the efficacy of its judgments.[1]

Political scientists who focus on political institutions effectively echo Stalin's question regarding the Pope: how many divisions do the courts have? Without either enforcement power or an obvious social base or constituency, courts seem of marginal interest, especially when critical political questions are to be determined. Thus, even when the "new institutionalism" emerged in the 1980s, banks, bureaucracies, and welfare systems tended to draw attention rather than judicial structures.

Judicial review has become widespread in the Arab world, however. Every Arab state outside of the Arabian peninsula has at some point conceded some form of judicial review. Even within the peninsula only a minority of states has eschewed judicial review altogether. In two ways, the spread of judicial review is not as remarkable as may initially appear. First, there is a strong global trend toward greater acceptance of judicial review; the practice spread earlier in the Arab world than some other regions but is now the rule rather than the exception throughout the world. Second, judicial review has spread without becoming politically important in most of the Arab world. Regimes seem to have given up little in most cases by ceding some authority over constitutional interpretation to judiciaries.

We thus need to define the puzzle concerning judicial review in the Arab world more precisely: first, how has judicial review emerged in most of the Arab world without serving as a basis for constitutionalism? Second, if politically weak judiciaries are the rule, how can we explain the exceptional cases in which judicial review has restricted executive action?

A close study of the Arab experience reveals that the explanation for politically weak judiciaries as well as the politically strong exceptions lies in the oft-submerged tension between judicial review and democracy. Democrats have generally been suspicious of judicial review until fairly recently. Only since the Second World War has judicial review been viewed as essential rather than inimical to democracy. This transformation has been assisted by a set of procedures designed to make judicial review safe for democracies. Adopting similar procedures in the Arab world has made judicial review safe for authoritarianism instead.

The exceptional cases of strong constitutional judiciaries lie in a different sort of tension between judicial review and democracy: strong constitutional judiciaries, like strong parliaments, have emerged when they are able to escape (at least partially) from executive domination. Such an escape has been possible by insulating them from formal democratic structures. In other words, the more judicial structures are isolated from other structures—especially those that are formally democratic—the greater role they can play.

The Emergence of Judicial Review

Judicial review is a remarkably recent innovation in most political systems where it has been adopted or emerged. Prior to the Second World War, a very small and quite disparate group of political systems had unambiguously instituted some form of judicial review. Among the very few were the United States, Austria, and a few Latin American countries. Even in these cases, the authority was rarely exercised. A few other countries (such as Iraq and Norway) had taken the step of entrusting constitutional interpretation to bodies with judicial representation. Judicial review was a peculiarity of a small group of countries that shared no other common features.

Currently, however, judicial review is the norm, rather than the exception, in Europe, North America, South America, and the Middle East. Judicial review is thus no longer a peculiarity—it has been adopted by a large number of polities that still share little else in common. Most states of the former Soviet bloc—even those in which democratic procedures are shaky at best—recently established functioning (and sometimes quite bold) constitutional courts, as has South Africa. In this they follow the path of earlier transition states, most notably Spain, which created its constitutional court in 1978, and Portugal, which brought one into being in 1982.

Prior to the Second World War, judicial review was generally viewed as a limitation on democracy. Granting unelected judges the right to measure the actions of democratically elected legislatures made no sense to many democrats: who better than the people's elected representatives could interpret the will of the sovereign people expressed in the constitution? Similar reasoning was adopted in communist countries.

Indeed, it was precisely because judicial review limited democracy (and its perceived excesses) that it appealed to those seeking to build constitutional limits around democratic structures. It should not be at all surprising that judicial review thus first emerged in the United States, the first country to attempt to contain democratic practices within constitutional limits.[2] In Sweden, a European pioneer in judicial review, the practice was specifically advocated in response to universal male suffrage and parliamentary supremacy in governance.[3] Constitutional interpretation was moved from the parliament to an independent (partially judicial) body in France under the Fifth Republic in order to check the parliament and augment presidentialism.[4]

A less adversarial relationship between democracy and judicial review was pioneered in Austria where a constitutional court was introduced in 1920 as part of a new, democratic constitution. While the Austrian innovation eventually proved quite influential (and remains, directly or indirectly, the model emulated most often in the rest of the world), the construction of the Court was less bold than initially appears. Only a few official actors were allowed to raise cases; thus, rather than limit the authority of state structures, the Court initially served only to mediate relations among them.[5] Further, judges were directly elected by the parliament, significantly lessening the derogation of parliamentary supremacy. Indeed, precisely because the Court could cancel legislation, it was seen as having a mixed legislative-judicial character. It was in this subtle way that the Austrian experiment was most innovative. By placing the Court under the wing of the parliament and deliberately insulating it from the executive, the architects of the Austrian constitution lessened the perceived contradiction between parliamentary sovereignty and judicial review. The experiment barely lasted a decade, however, before the Court was brought under executive control and eventually abandoned under fascist rule.[6] The experience of fascism (and later communism) helped most Europeans forget any tension between constitutionalism and democracy.

Very gradually judicial review emerged (or was consciously instituted) in order to secure rather than restrict democratic gains. In Costa Rica, judicial review emerged in the late nineteenth century and early twentieth century based on constitutional text, judicial assertiveness, and finally statute. The impetus to define judicial review by law came as a result of the confusion over the status of legislation issued under a short-lived constitution written in the aftermath of an authoritarian coup.[7] This possible link between judicial review and democracy was somewhat weakened, however, by the struggle in the United States between Franklin Roosevelt and the Supreme Court; in the birthplace of judicial review it was widely perceived in the first half of the twentieth century as operating to protect privilege and frustrate popular desires.

It should therefore be no surprise that even as judicial review was increasingly asserted or adopted, often in the form of specialized constitutional courts, different political systems experimented with devices to guard the guardians of constitutionalism and induce the constitutional judiciary to be responsive to other actors in the political system. In some countries, the standing to bring a constitutional case was limited to official actors; often objections could only be raised before approved legislation went into effect (prior review). Some courts (such as Cost Rica's) were required to muster a supermajority to declare a law unconstitutional; others could have their judgments overturned by legislative action. In almost all cases, rulings could of course be overturned by amending the constitution itself. The lone (albeit partial) exception has been India, where the Supreme Court has actually declared some constitutional amendments unconstitutional.[8] The use of constitutional amendments to modify or overturn judicial rulings entails some cost (perhaps minor) to constitutionalism, because it often involves enshrining ephemeral policy concerns into a document purported to constitute the polity itself. Courts can also be made responsive to other actors in the political system through the appointment process. A system of presidential or parliamentary appointment (or some combination) is virtually universal among constitutional courts; in some instances (especially when tenure is shorter or appointments are made on a partisan basis), the result is an overtly political court.

These new methods of rendering judicial review more accountable to democratic forces and procedures have made it possible for democracies to regard the practice more benignly. Accordingly, the half century since the Second World War has seen a tremendous expansion in judicial review. The defeated Axis powers (Germany, Italy, and Japan) all adopted some form of judicial review; the architects of their constitutional orders regarded the practice as an obstacle to untrammeled executive authority. The tension between democracy and constitutionalism began to fade from public (though not always scholarly) view about this time. Judicial review was seen less as a method of limiting democratic excesses and more a technique to institute and protect democratic practices. Concern shifted from the tyranny of the majority to the tyranny of dictators.[9] The new view transformed judicial review from an isolated institutional peculiarity to a perceived condition for the rule of law. In subsequent years, judicial review spread to many (eventually most) of the newly independent states. After 1989, most former Soviet bloc states rushed to adopt judicial review, often before they wrote new constitutions. In 1994, the president of the Romanian constitutional court proclaimed "After the

Second World War, and especially in the past four or five years, it has become increasingly obvious that there is a need to establish specialized institutions to analyze and decide on compliance of laws with the Constitution. This is an indispensable requirement for the consolidation of a constitutional democracy."[10]

Judicial Review in the Arab World

Judicial review emerged almost imperceptibly in the Arab world. The 1920 Syrian constitution created a supreme court to hear important cases but it was not explicitly accorded the right of reviewing the constitutionality of executive or legislated action.[11] Neither was it allowed to assert such a claim on its own because the imposition of the French mandate prevented the constitution from becoming effective. (Three decades later, however, the Syrian Supreme Court was explicitly given such constitutional authority and judicial review of some kind has operated in all subsequent Syrian constitutions.) In 1925 Iraq's first constitution included the earliest explicit mention of judicial review.[12] In Egypt, a lower court asserted the principle of judicial review in 1941 only to have its reasoning rejected by an appeals court.[13] In 1948 the Supreme Administrative Court in the country issued a decisive ruling affirming the right of judicial review.[14] This action made Egypt one of a small group of countries where the principle was introduced solely by judicial action rather than explicit constitutional text or statute (other such countries include the United States and Israel).[15] A committee charged with drafting a new constitution after the 1952 overthrow of the monarchy proposed a specialized constitutional court, but the new regime balked at the idea. The 1952 Jordanian constitution allowed the High Court to be consulted by parliament and the cabinet when constitutional interpretation was needed, and its rulings were binding.

In Kuwait, the 1962 constitution (largely drafted by a leading member of the earlier Egyptian committee that had first suggested a constitutional court) mandated the designation of a specialized judicial body for constitutional disputes but left details to implementing legislation. It took eleven years for the court to be established.[16] In the interim, Kuwaiti courts made no claim of any right of judicial review.[17] Thus, while the Kuwaiti constitution was the first in the Arab world to require a constitutional court, by the time that the requirement was met several countries had already established their own courts. Morocco's 1962 constitution created a special and largely judicial constitutional chamber.[18] Egypt's Supreme Court, established by presidential decree-law in 1969, was given jurisdiction over constitutional cases; it was renamed the Supreme Constitutional Court in the 1971 constitution. The United Arab Emirates established a Supreme Court for the Union upon its formation in 1971; while the Court's jurisdiction was not limited to constitutional matters, the country's federal structure was seen to necessitate a designated body for constitutional disputes.[19] Egyptian influence was probably behind the creation of specialized constitutional courts in Yemen in 1970 and Sudan in 1973 (though in 1992 Yemen moved to give jurisdiction in constitutional cases to a nonspecialized supreme court).[20] In 1973 Syria adopted a specialized constitutional court structured very similar to its Egyptian counterpart.[21]

None of these bodies was initially viewed as a defender of constitutionalism. Beginning in the late 1970s, however, limited political liberalization in parts of the Arab world brought possibilities for bolder uses of judicial review and stronger structures capable of exercising it. In 1979 Egypt adopted legislation to implement the 1971 constitutional reform, and the Egyptian Supreme Court was reconstituted as a far more independent body, the Supreme Constitutional Court. In 1987 a lower-level Tunisian court asserted the ordinary judiciary's right to review the constitutionality of legislation. The same year the president created an advisory constitutional council.[22] Algeria and Lebanon followed with constitutional councils modeled partly on the French example.[23] In 1991 Jordan proclaimed a (still unfulfilled) desire to create an independent constitutional court with potentially greater independence than its counterparts in several other Arab countries. In 1998 the Jordanian High Court asserted a right to review the constitutionality of legislation in the course of normal litigation and not merely when asked by the government to do so. The substance of the ruling was as startling as the assertion of the right to review legislation in normal litigation; it rejected a restrictive press law issued by the government during a parliamentary recess on the grounds the constitution only authorized such actions in emergency situations. The court took it upon itself to define such emergencies.

The latest bout of experimentation with judicial review has begun to have significant effects, most notably in Egypt. Egypt's Supreme Constitutional Court has thrice struck down electoral laws and necessitated new parliamentary elections; it has invalidated some restrictions on political parties and nongovernmental organizations; and it has even enforced restrictions on the president's authority to issue emergency decrees with the force of law. Outside of Egypt, the docile Kuwaiti Constitutional Court has found itself confronted with sensitive issues such as women's right to vote and even the issue of constitutionalism itself—on two occasions the country's amir suspended several clauses of the 1962 constitution (including the clause specifically preventing him from suspending any clauses of the constitution), disbanded parliament, and assigned to the cabinet the right to issue decrees with the force of law. On both occasions the constitution was eventually restored, leading to a complex struggle between the parliament and the cabinet over the status of legislation passed during the constitutional interregnum. While the Court has managed to escape any ruling on the essence of the dispute, its ability to continue avoiding the matter has been severely threatened.[24]

The decisions of the Egyptian Supreme Constitutional Court, coupled with the seemingly growing potential for bold decisions elsewhere, has led some to see constitutional judiciaries as a potentially strong actor in the struggle to establish constitutionalism and democracy.[25] Yet the obstacles to using constitutional courts and judicial review to achieve such goals are formidable. This is especially the case with the appointment of judges and the standing necessary to bring a case.

Appointment

Appointment to constitutional judicial and quasi-judicial bodies has generally occurred in ways that seriously limit their independence. In Europe, attempts to make judicial review compatible with democracy often focused on allowing some parliamentary oversight in the process. Heads of state, themselves often elected (directly or indirectly) are also often accorded a role. Borrowing these procedures in the Arab world (and allowing judges only limited tenure in office) has seriously undermined their independence. The Syrian Supreme Constitutional Court created under the 1973 constitution is composed entirely of members appointed by presidential decree. The Syrian constitution is also the most unabashed in the use of short tenure: members serve for renewable four-year terms. Such judges are hardly likely to develop a strongly independent record and could easily be shunted aside if they do.

Yet even with lifetime appointments, the appointing authority naturally influences the composition of the court and affects its political direction. In many political systems this is not seen as undesirable: it helps ensure that the constitutional court is generally in accord with other political forces in the country. Thus, staggered appointments, parliamentary supermajorities, and diversity in appointing authorities (sometimes, for instance, bar associations are allowed to make nominations) are used to ensure that various political trends will have a role in determining the composition of a court without any of them exclusively controlling appointment. Yet these methods are unlikely to have the same effect in nonpluralist political environments, such as those that prevail in the Arab world. With little change in the holder of executive authority, legislatures under executive domination, and heavy restrictions on independent political organizations, it becomes very easy to mask executive domination of the judiciary without diminishing it. Algeria's constitutional council constructed in 1989 had members appointed by all three branches of government—the president, the parliament, and the judiciary. All the initial appointments, however, were members of the governing party.[26]

Egypt has the one constitutional court in the Arab world that can claim to have avoided direct or indirect executive domination over appointment. The method used would be unattractive to many democrats because it limits the accountability of the Court to elected officials. Vacancies in the Egyptian Supreme Constitutional Court are filled by the current judges of the Court (who forward their choice to the president who retains the legal power of appointment), making the Court self-perpetuating, unlike any supreme or constitutional court in the world.

The importance of the appointment process can be illustrated by comparing the record of the Egyptian Supreme Constitutional Court to the Kuwaiti Constitutional Court. The former received its independence in 1979; during the prior decade, appointment had been very similar to the Syrian procedure, bringing the Court under executive domination. After 1979 (especially after the mid-1980s when the new appointment procedure had begun to seriously affect the composition of the Court), the Court rapidly distinguished itself as the boldest and most independent judicial actor in Arab history, leading some political leaders to complain about the emergence of a "government of judges."[27] Kuwait's Constitutional Court, by contrast, shows more signs of executive domination. Appointment to the Kuwaiti Court is hardly the Arab world's most egregious example of executive domination: members are selected by a judicial council. That council, however, is dominated by senior judges and other officials who owe their positions to ministerial appointments. The resulting Constitutional Court has consisted of senior judges with a record of political timidity: at various times they have been faced with challenges to executive actions involving almost every controversial constitutional issue in the country: press censorship, citizenship, women's right to vote, suspension of parliament, and even the structure and procedures of the Court itself. It has either turned back these challenges or dismissed them on procedural grounds. Critics of the Court generally point in private to the method of appointment to explain its pusillanimous record.[28]

Further evidence of the importance of appointment came at the end of the 1990s in Egypt. The presidency of the Supreme Constitutional Court fell vacant with the retirement of the activist 'Awad al-Morr. The vacancy was used to pressure the Court into accepting a diminution in its authority to issue retroactive judgments (see chapter 4).

Standing

The second critical issue for the political importance of judicial review and constitutional courts involves the procedure and standing for bringing a case. In cases in which judicial review is decentralized (and potentially within the jurisdiction of any court), any individual involved in a case at any level can raise a constitutional issue. Concentrating review in a single court requires determination of who may bring a case to that court and how. Typically, standing is limited to the president, the cabinet (or specified ministers), or a group of parliamentarians. Such actors are generally permitted to pose abstract questions regarding the constitutionality of laws; they need not wait until a concrete legal dispute arises. Often trial courts are allowed to refer constitutional aspects of concrete cases to a specialized court. The origins of centralized review with limited access lie partly in the fear held by European democrats: decentralized review would render the parliament subordinate to the entire judiciary; centralized and restricted review would let a small number of judges, themselves often selected by the parliament, rule only on questions that the parliament (or ministers serving with the confidence of parliament) chose to submit.

Arab systems have chosen to follow the path of centralized judicial review, either in the form of specialized constitutional courts (on the Austrian model) or constitutional council (on the French model). In cases in which courts asserted a right to decentralized review (Egypt, Tunisia, and Jordan), the executive has generally discouraged such a trend. Central bodies for judicial review will have difficulty asserting themselves in the Arab political context. With legislatures weak, it is unlikely that they would pass a law that executive authorities wished to challenge on constitutional grounds. It is also unlikely that the parliaments in the Arab world will show the political independence necessary to bring an executive action to a constitutional court. (The sole exceptions thus far have been the Kuwaiti and Lebanese parliaments. Both bodies have some independence from the executive for reasons explored in the previous chapter. Even the Kuwaiti parliament, however, has been too fearful of the Constitutional Court to initiate action.) It is therefore not surprising that the Arab courts or councils that act on constitutional issues only when called upon by designated officials have gone almost unnoticed in their own countries. The Algerian and Tunisian Constitutional Councils have not been very active (though the Algerian Council has been more active, even if it has not challenged the government like its Egyptian counterpart). In Jordan, pending the creation of a true constitutional court, constitutional questions are to be raised before the country's High Court by government or parliamentary initiative; the political role for judicial review resulting from this constitutional mechanism has been negligible.[29]

With official actors generally unwilling to bring cases to a constitutional court, only those bodies allowed to rule in concrete legal disputes will likely play a significant role. Unsurprisingly, such judicial action has been restricted. In no case in the Arab world can an individual or private actor, even one involved in a concrete dispute, bring a case directly to the constitutional court. Constitutional courts exist to determine the law, not to try a case, and one can gain access to them only through the court with original jurisdiction. Referral is not automatic. Generally the trial court assesses the seriousness of the constitutional argument and then makes a decision on referring it. The result is not simply to keep frivolous constitutional claims out of court; in all countries where such screening operates, some critical constitutional issues have simply never reached the court supposedly erected to adjudicate them.

In Egypt, for instance, the law grants the president the authority to transfer crimes involving civilians to military courts. Some constitutional authorities claim that this is a violation of the constitutional right of citizens to their "natural judge."[30] The records of the drafting committee for the 1971 constitution give little clue as to the meaning of the phrase "natural judge," but it would seem to indicate that court cases should be referred to an appropriate court based on clear legal principles rather than the desires of officials. Despite the constitutional ambiguities, no military court referred the issue to the Supreme Constitutional Court, even after President Mubarak began to exercise his authority in 1992 in an attempt to suppress Islamist violence. Only after three years did lawyers for some of those tried managed to convince an administrative court to refer the issue.[31] In Kuwait, access to the Constitutional Court is the most liberal in the Arab world. If the court with jurisdiction declines to refer a constitutional question, a private party can appeal to a body called the "Committee to Examine Challenges" [lajnat fahs al-tu'un], consisting of a panel of judges from the Constitutional Court. Yet the Committee has never referred a case to the entire Constitutional Court.[32] And even when the trial court refers the case, the Constitutional Court has often sought to dodge a decision (as it did in 2000 and 2001 in the face of a fairly cogent constitutional challenge to the bar to women's suffrage—the Court dismissed the cases on procedural grounds). Thus access to constitutional courts has often been obstructed in the Arab world—and often the judiciary has participated in such obstruction.[33]

Possibilities for Judicial Review in the Arab World

The structures and procedures invented in Europe to make judicial review more democratic have operated in the Arab world in order to undermine the viability of judicial review—and thus generally allowed Arab executives to interpret ambiguous constitutional texts to their advantage. Arab judges will only become more genuine instruments of constitutionalism if they are insulated from presidents and parliaments in both appointment and jurisdiction. Thus the key to judicial efforts to support Arab constitutionalism rests not on anchoring the judiciary in other social and political forces; those forces are already dominated by the regimes. Instead, political and social isolation is required. Such isolation has arisen in a few cases: the Egyptian court is most notable in using its institutional autonomy to embark on a constitutionalist project.

Should other courts join the Egyptian (and the Jordanian, Lebanese, and Kuwaiti courts are probably the most promising candidates in this regard) in establishing their distance from other structures, what basis would they have for supporting constitutionalism? In general, two factors seem most important: the constitutional text itself, and the judiciary's ability to develop a constitutionalist interpretation of ambiguous elements of the text.

Constitutional Text

Some Arab constitutions simply give very little basis for any constitutional challenge. For instance, Qatar's "Temporary Amended Basic Law" has so few procedural and substantive restrictions on the amir and the government that it would be very difficult for an individual to challenge an official action on constitutional grounds. Even if a challenge were made and supported by a court, the constitution can be amended by decree.[34]

The weakness of constitutional texts in most Arab countries is more subtly expressed than in Qatar. Most do provide for substantial rights and freedoms; democratic procedures are also spelled out. However, no Arab constitution can really be said to have constituted the political system; in almost all cases the constitution is the product of a specific regime and very much reflects its desires and concerns. The text of constitutions in most countries in the Arab world therefore generally include many authoritarian measures (such as bringing judicial appointments under executive control) or make such measures easily available to executive authorities (such as the power to rule by decree in loosely restricted emergency situations). Equally notable is that important elements of Arab constitutions are not self-executing but need implementing legislation to be effective or completed. Articles on the judiciary often simply call for independence to be guaranteed by law. This gives wide latitude to the legislature, which generally operates under executive domination. If the legislature fails to act there is often no effective remedy (the article in the Kuwaiti constitution regarding a judicial body for constitutional disputes was ignored for close to a decade).

Moreover, the limits implementing legislation must observe are often quite vague. For instance, while the first amendment of the American constitution forbids Congress from abridging freedom of the press, the Kuwaiti constitution requires the parliament to guarantee (and in a sense define) freedom of the press by legislation: "Freedom of the press, printing and publishing shall be guaranteed in accordance with the conditions and manner specified by law." The American text bars legislative action; the Kuwaiti text demands it and appears to leave the parliament considerable discretion in the matter. By insisting that the right be guaranteed "in accordance with the conditions and manner specified by law" important qualifications can be introduced. The Constitutional Court is thus given fewer weapons if it is inclined to strike down legislation restricting freedom of the press. In extreme situations the need for implementing legislation comes close to reversing the relationship between constitutional and statute law. Rather than have the constitution limit and define the scope for statutes, it can be statutes that define the limits of the constitutional text.

Existing constitutional provisions were not written by accident; they were often designed to make guarantees and limitations vague and ineffective. In many instances, such language was developed by trial-and-error. Earlier chapters explored the reasons for this in more detail; for now it is enough to note that from the beginning of constitution writing, textual silences and vagueness were designed to undercut constitutionalism. Many of these techniques were already developed before the imperial era, but British and French practice in Egypt, Iraq, Syria, and Lebanon developed them still further. As Elizabeth Thompson writes of the imperial-era constitutions in Syria and Lebanon: "While assigning sovereignty to the people, they also granted supreme power to a nonelected official who stood above the law, the French high commissioner, who could decree laws, dismiss parliaments, and even suspend the constitution itself."[35]

Constitutional evolution has often accentuated the vagueness and contradictions of the text. In the era since independence, most Arab constitutions have moved beyond defining rights, obligations, and procedures to proclaiming general programmatic statements and goals. When new constitutions are issued, they are often based on older ones; they both modify older language and add new clauses reflecting prevailing political realities or ideologies. Thus they often have liberal, nationalist, monarchical, parliamentary, presidential, socialist, and authoritarian layers. They also contain tremendous tensions—between private property and socialist goals; between individual freedoms and presidential or royal prerogatives. Tensions in the text greatly increase the number of plausible interpretations. Judges seeking to use such a document to guarantee a constitutional or a democratic order may be able to find what they wish, but so may judges seeking to undermine or (more likely) avoid such a reading. Executive and legislative authorities will similarly be able to adduce a constitutional basis for actions inimical to constitutionalism and democracy. In order to act as a restraint in such circumstances, a constitutional judiciary must see its task as going beyond ruling on the plausibility of constitutional arguments submitted to it, because authoritarian interpretations may often be quite plausible. Instead the court must be sufficiently bold to erect its own constitutional jurisprudence. Such a sense of mission might develop, but it requires political audacity of a kind that judicial independence may allow but can hardly guarantee.

Constitutional Jurisprudence

This leads to the final obstacle that inhibits judicial review from supporting constitutionalism and democracy: the jurisprudence and culture of the judiciary. Judicial decision making always involves some interpretation, however minimal, in the application of law. With constitutions written in general language and Arab constitutions especially indeterminate, constitutional judiciaries in the Arab world have many possibilities open to them. And since it is not uncommon to go outside of the constitutional text itself in order to explicate the text, the field for interpretation is particularly wide. Constitutional judiciaries may not be able to claim that the constitution says whatever they want it to, but they can certainly have it say many different (and quite contradictory) things. Judiciaries characterized by weak political will and deference to the executive might undermine constitutionalism. Yet other courts in the Arab world have begun to develop innovative and assertive constitutional visions.

An example of weakness is the widespread Arab constitutional doctrine that "acts of sovereignty" fall outside the jurisdiction of the courts. An act of sovereignty is something that states do by virtue of their nature as sovereign actors; the idea is so vague that it has been used to justify virtually any measure that can be presented as having a connection with foreign policy or internal security. To be sure, many Arab judiciaries are prevented by law from examining acts of sovereignty, but such legal provisions could be interpreted narrowly or even deemed unconstitutional with some plausibility. They are based on the rarely articulated belief that the executive is sovereign and that the holder of executive authority can take whatever action is necessary—according to the most extreme versions, without any accountability or restrictions.[36] It is difficult to think of a view of executive authority more at odds with constitutionalism.[37] Arab courts do regularly resort to the doctrine of "acts of sovereignty" to avoid ruling on an executive action in nonconstitutional cases. The Kuwaiti Constitutional Court has been faced with cases in which the doctrine has been cited in its most extreme forms to justify actions that were incontrovertibly unconstitutional. The Court has not endorsed the argument that the executive's violation of the constitution is an act of sovereignty, but it has not repudiated it either.

By contrast, other courts in the Arab world have taken efforts to place restrictions on acts of sovereignty.[38] Syrian courts have taken the position that a declaration of a state of emergency is an act of sovereignty that cannot be reviewed by the judiciary. They still claim the right to review actions taken under the state of emergency and overturn them if they bear no relation to the emergency at hand.[39] The Egyptian Supreme Constitutional Court has been bolder. It has begun to abandon the term "acts of sovereignty" in favor of the American term "political questions." The difference is subtle but it has the effect of locating the determination of jurisdiction firmly in the hands of the judiciary. The newer term implies that there are certain issues that are inappropriate for the judiciary either because the court lacks the proper tools or because they necessitate executive or legislative discretion. These issues, however, are excluded from the purview of the judiciary not by executive right but because of judicial self-restraint. Designation of an issue as a "political question" is a court decision. And one judge on the Court admits that "neither in its earlier or in its recent decisions has the court given precise criteria for both acts of sovereignty and/or political questions, preferring to give itself, case-by-case, the power to determine whether or not the challenged law is considered an act of sovereignty or a political question."[40]

The determination of the Egyptian Supreme Constitutional Court to recast the doctrine of "acts of sovereignty" is characteristic of a broader boldness in judicial interpretation. It is instructive that the Court's judges do not look to the intent of the authors of the country's constitution; since the 1971 constitution was the product of an authoritarian regime undertaking only the most tentative steps toward liberalization, a jurisprudence based on original intent could easily lead to illiberal results.[41] While judges of the Court certainly do not feel that they can exceed the bounds of the text, they do not hesitate to look outside of the text of the constitution to elucidate constitutional principles. Thus, in trying to sort out the 1971 constitution's various clauses on socialism and private ownership, the Supreme Constitutional Court has generally favored private property by insisting that only those restrictions specifically authorized by the constitution are allowable. The chief justice cites in support of this view not the text of the constitution itself—which contains contradictory orientations—but the Egyptian constitutional tradition.[42] Potentially more ambitiously, the Egyptian Supreme Constitutional Court has begun to use international human-rights instruments to interpret provisions of the Egyptian constitution. The Supreme Court, the predecessor to the Supreme Constitutional Court, ruled in 1975 that the United Nations Declaration of Human Rights is not a treaty (but merely a nonbinding recommendation) and, even if it were, treaties have the force only of legislative texts and can therefore be limited by subsequent or more specific legislation. The Supreme Constitutional Court has not challenged this argument directly, but it has insinuated the text of international human rights documents into Egyptian constitutional law by using them as aids in interpreting vague constitutional guarantees. In striking down an article in the Customs Law that punished as smugglers those who simply could not produce appropriate documentation that duties were paid, the Court ruled that this violated the presumption of innocence, guaranteed in the constitution, as explicated in international documents.[43]

Conclusion

Judicial review is now well established in much of the Arab world but it has not emerged as a significant constitutionalist force except in some isolated cases. The problem is not that judicial rulings are ignored; even inconvenient rulings are generally implemented. Instead, the power of judicial review is undermined by the inability of courts to free themselves from political domination. Independence of courts, like independence of parliaments, is best established in the Arab context by isolating them from the nonpluralist order prevailing in the polity. Arab courts need to become less democratic (in the sense of distancing themselves from formally democratic executives and legislatures) not more so if judicial review is to become a constitutionalist force in Arab politics.

SIX

ISLAMIC CONSTITUTIONALISM

Aʀᴀʙ ᴄᴏɴsᴛɪᴛᴜᴛɪᴏɴᴀʟ ᴛᴇxᴛs have been written primarily to enable, organize, and justify political authority. They have provided at best a fragmentary basis for a constitutionalist order in which such authority is also regulated and contained within consciously established and articulated limits.

Perhaps the Arab world is simply infertile ground for constitutionalism. Constitutional scholars have often stressed that written constitutions are hardly a sufficient (or even necessary) condition for the emergence of constitutionalism. Those who wrote of "paper," "facade," and "semantic" constitutions had in mind constitutional documents that did not result in constitutionalist practices. According to such views, constitutions cannot be viable documents in the absence of the political, ideological, and cultural prerequisites for constitutional life.

The argument presented thus far stands at odds with this traditional view. First, Arab constitutions have been shown to be viable documents even when they do not serve constitutionalist ends. Second, the obstacles to constitutionalism in the Arab world lie partly in the constitutional texts and structures themselves rather than the broader society. Structures that elsewhere work to hold executive authority accountable (courts and parliaments) have failed to do so in the Arab world because they have been consciously and deliberately deprived of the tools that would allow them to play such a role. Third, prospects for constitutionalism have sometimes been enhanced by insulating judicial and parliamentary structures from society. Rather than requiring a firmer social foundation, structures of accountability need greater autonomy in the Arab world in order to function effectively. Finally, Western constitutionalism has been presented in this work as growing out of intractable political struggles as much as out of Enlightenment rationalism. Its institutional mechanisms might be more easily detached from the supposed philosophical basis than is generally believed.

Yet we have yet to confront the core of the cynicism concerning constitutionalism in non-Western societies: how can constitutionalism emerge in societies in which liberalism is so far from hegemonic? There is a rich tradition of Islamic political thought and practice; must this tradition be swept aside in order to provide the basis for constitutionalism in the Arab world? Or can Islamic principles—enshrined in most Arab constitutions according to a variety of formulas—be employed to build a different kind of constitutionalism? At first glance, it would seem to be easy to make a constitutionalist argument in Islamic terms, especially given the tremendous interest by Islamic scholars in developing law. The idea that the supreme source of law lies in religious texts would seem to encourage the view that earthly political authorities can be held to standards far higher than the ones they might set for themselves.

In this chapter, we consider how Islamic political thought does indeed provide such a basis for constitutionalism, and how an Islamic constitutionalism might differ from more familiar liberal forms of constitutionalism. Then we return to the practical and institutional focus that has informed much of this study thus far: what have been the actual results of attempts to create an Islamic constitutional order? The evidence presented here supports the idea that Islamic political thought is increasingly inclined toward constitutionalist ideas. Attempts to put these ideas into practice have not been successful, however—not because of any inherent flaw in the concept of Islamic constitutionalism but because of an insufficient attention to structures of political accountability. Islamic constitutionalism is theoretically possible but has yet to be instituted in practice.

The Emerging Islamist Constitutionalist Consensus

Modern Islamic political thought presents an array of doctrines, approaches, ideologies, and strategies. Arguments among various orientations have frequently left the realm of theoretical debate and entered the arena of political action and even violent struggle. The stridency and cacophony that occasionally occur should not deafen us to a surprising consensus that has steadily emerged over the past century among a wide array of approaches; that emerging consensus insists on the fundamentally constitutionalist nature of Islamic politics. Indeed, the analogy between government in accordance with Islamic law and constitutional government has emerged as a staple in modern political writings by Muslims.

Yet while the possibilities for Islamic constitutionalism might seem obvious to many in recent years, they tended to remain submerged for centuries. Islamic political writers have always insisted on the theoretical supremacy of the Islamic *shari'a* while often accommodating themselves to almost any political system that did not involve its blatant repudiation.[1] Even sympathetic writers have felt compelled to admit that the latent constitutionalism rarely found historical expression:

> Historical precedents are even less helpful because again, except for the period of the Prophetic mission and of the Rightly-Guided Caliphs, they indeed give more weight to the cynics' taunting that, for the better part of their history, Muslims have known no political system other than the most arbitrary. As regards the *Shari'ah*, it was never implemented as an integral system, and the bulk of its provisions remained as legal fictions.[2]

This judgment, though sound, is probably excessively harsh. First, the experience of prophetic government and the early caliphs, as it is understood by Muslims, does at least constitute a political ideal that would-be constitutionalists are able to cite. Indeed, as will become clear, modern Islamists generally devote far more attention to this early period than any subsequent historical experience. Second, there were writers who explored formulas that would have lent themselves more to constitutionalist practices.[3]

The latent constitutionalism failed to develop not so much because the Islamic *shari'a* was ignored but because it was pursued as a set of institutions and practices partly autonomous from the process of governing. In other words, the *shari'a* did not form the basis of the political order but was allowed to function in its own realm of legal scholarship, education, and courts. Rulers and the institutions embodying the *shari'a* encroached on each others' affairs only on rare occasions. This arrangement did entail practical limitations on the rulers' authority but not in any constitutionalist guise: it was based not on explicit and well-articulated fundamental principles but on unspoken mutual deference between governments and *shari'a*-based institutions.

That deference showed some signs of decay in the nineteenth century when various states in the Middle East began to infringe on institutions of Islamic learning, legal scholarship, and courts. Because of the sensitivity of the relationship, most states initially left the institutions and practices related to the *shari'a* autonomous but built new schools, courts, and law codes by their sides. In the twentieth century, however, governments in the Middle East have generally forgotten past deference completely and either abolished or (more often) moved to control formerly autonomous *shari'a* courts and institutions of Muslim learning.[4] And the increasing reach of the state in all spheres of life has left many residents of the area frustrated with the lack of political accountability characteristic of Middle Eastern governance.

It is no coincidence that as older relationships broke down, new attempts arose to recast the role of the Islamic *shari'a* in political life. These attempts have taken on an increasingly constitutionalist flavor. Already in the nineteenth century, Khayr al-Din al-Tunisi's writings were designed to spark the political involvement of the *'ulama*. Khayr al-Din sought to construct political systems based on accountability and the rule of law (see chapter 1). In the twentieth century, however, most of the initial attempts to recast Muslim politics came from outside of the traditional sites of Muslim learning. Until recently, the *'ulama* were engaged in a losing battle to retain their autonomy rather than construct new political systems. Yet in the late twentieth century, even many leading members of the *'ulama* joined the debate over the proper political order.

The debate, while contentious, has led to the development of a surprising consensus supporting an Islamic constitutionalism. To be sure, there are real differences among various thinkers and leaders. Yet those differences should not obscure some underlying similarities. Rashid Ghannushi was arrested and exiled by a secularist Tunisian regime; his ideas bear strong similarities to those of Kamal Abu al-Majd who has served a similar Egyptian regime as a minister. 'Abd al-Qadir 'Awda was executed in Egypt in 1954; a generation later, his views are quoted favorably by intellectuals like Muhammad al-'Awwa who securely propounds his ideas as a university professor in Egypt and Saudi Arabia. Muslim thinkers have differed on their diagnosis of the nature and severity of the political crisis in the Muslim world, and they are badly divided on tactical issues—that is, how to best bring about the Islamicization of law and society. They thus pursue strikingly different means. But a brief exposition of the views of some leading writers can serve as the basis to show the emerging consensus among Islamist intellectuals (and even among many of their opponents) on the ultimate end of constitutional government.[5]

In the middle of the twentieth century, intellectuals outside of the traditional centers of Islamic legal scholarship began to criticize the sharp turn away from Islamic law in the Muslim world. These same intellectuals often criticized traditional Islamic legal scholarship as excessively rigid and closed to new interpretations. In doing so, they were accepting views developed by Western scholars that have since come under severe attack but were increasingly accepted even among Muslim intellectuals at the time.[6] These intellectuals sought to build a legal and political order that was more authentic in two senses. First, it would be based not simply on Western models, but also on the region's Islamic heritage. Second, it would strip away the perceived accretions and stultifying rigidities of centuries of overly abstract legal scholarship and seek out the broad range of legal thought long buried by obscurantist *'ulama*. Rashid Rida and 'Abd al-Razzaq al-Sanhuri moved in this direction from two different starting points. Rida began with a firmer basis in traditional Muslim scholarship; al-Sanhuri was a jurist trained in France. These different starting points led to different emphases. Rida sought an Islamic state governed by the *shari'a* (supplemented by positive law within its boundaries), involving consultation as well as an active role by an invigorated *'ulama*.[7] Al-Sanhuri saw the *shari'a* not as the basic framework of government but as a rich legal source that needed only to be modified to be applied to modern circumstances. Turning away from the *shari'a* would be turning away from Egypt's Islamic, Eastern, and Arab heritage. Al-Sanhuri sought to draw on Islamic law as he modified legal codes not only for Egypt but also for other Arab countries.[8] Indeed, al-Sanhuri not only accepted the analogy between the Islamic *shari'a* and constitutional law, he also saw legal reform as a functional successor to the caliphate: the Islamic world could be unified by a common legal framework informed by the Islamic *shari'a* but borrowing also from other legal systems.

The arguments advanced by al-Sanhuri and especially by Rida had potentially radical implications. If Muslim societies were to be governed by the Islamic *shari'a* to a much greater extent, how could the existing political and legal orders—which were quickly minimizing the role of the *shari'a*—be seen as appropriate or legitimate? Al-Sanhuri was too comfortable in the world of French jurisprudence to explore this question any further. But for Rida, in particular, the implication was clear that the *shari'a* posits clear constitutional limits: those practices and legal innovations inconsistent with its provisions are illegitimate and must be removed.

These potentially radical arguments were advanced by Abu al-A'la Mawdudi, a Pakistani intellectual, and 'Abd al-Qadir 'Awda, an Egyptian judge and chief ideologue of the Muslim Brotherhood. Both Mawdudi and 'Awda considered Islamic law not simply central to an Islamic political order but the defining difference between Islamic and non-Islamic politics. For Mawdudi, God is sovereign in any truly Islamic political order, and therefore all official actions must be consistent with His Law. The effect is to render Islamic law as a kind of constitution—one Mawdudi found superior to Western constitutions.

'Awda similarly accepted the idea that the *shari'a* was the defining feature of Islamic politics. He wrote: "The basic constitution for the Muslim is the Islamic *shari'a*" and "Islam forbids each Muslim from obeying a law or command that violates the *shari'a* of Islam and exceeds limits established by God and his prophet."9 Positive legislation thus has a sharply limited role. Not only must it be contained within the bounds of the *shari'a*, it is only legitimate for one of two purposes:

> The first: implementing legislation that aims at guaranteeing the implementation of the texts of the *shari'a* of Islam. The second: organizing legislation, to organize the group, defend it, and meet its needs on the basis of the principles of the Islamic *shari'a*. This legislation can only exist where the *shari'a* is silent and there are no particular texts. Such legislation must agree with the general principles of the *shari'a* and its legislative spirit.10

'Awda did not shy away from a militant implication of this viewpoint: it was the duty of Muslims to resist laws violating the *shari'a* and the governments that were behind them. Indeed, he hinted that those responsible for promulgating laws in violation of the *shari'a* were apostates.11 Taqi al-Din al-Nabahani, a Palestinian judge similarly troubled by the disjuncture between the law in force and the *shari'a*, developed similar arguments at about the same time.12 Such writings have succeeded in elevating the importance of the *shari'a* in Muslim politics so much that Muhammad al-Ghazzali, an Egyptian religious scholar, testified that even those who merely advocated laws violating the *shari'a* lay outside of the Muslim community and therefore deserved punishment.13

The centrality of the *shari'a* has come to dominate contemporary political debates. This has expressed itself in several ways, not all of which have received equal attention. The most prominent expression of the new *shari'a* politics follows directly on the heels of the writings of Mawdudi and 'Awda: a revolutionary call to overthrow political systems that do not base themselves fundamentally on the *shari'a*. Perhaps the most influential statement of this perspective has been Sayyid Qutb's *Milestones*, in which he argued that the abandonment of the *shari'a* and of divine sovereignty has thrown humanity back into a form of pre-Islamic ignorance (*jahiliyya*):

> If we look at the sources and foundations of modern ways of living, it becomes clear that the whole world is steeped in Jahiliyyah, and all the marvelous material comforts and high-level inventions do not diminish this ignorance. This Jahiliyyah is based on rebellion against God's sovereignty on earth. It transfers to man one of the

greatest attributes of God, namely sovereignty, and makes some men
lords over others. It is now not in that simple and primitive form of
the ancient Jahiliyyah, but takes the forms of claiming that the
right to create values, to legislate rules of collective behavior, and to
choose any way of life rests with men, without regard to what God
has prescribed. The result of this rebellion against the authority of
God is the oppression of His creatures.[14]

Positing existing governments as rebelling against God carries revolutionary
implications that have attracted great attention—and not simply from scholars.[15]
Activists made some of these implications explicit in the form of sometimes
violent oppositional movements that rejected the existing political order. Governments were hardly blind to the revolutionary implications: both 'Awda and
Qutb were executed.

Yet the centrality of the *shari'a* has expressed itself in other ways as well.
Qutb's own writings urge not simply revolutionary political change but an
inward-looking personal change as well; indeed, the personal change seems to
be a prerequisite for the later political change.[16]

It is therefore necessary—in the way of the Islamic movement—that
in the early stages of our training and education we should remove
ourselves from all the influences of the Jahiliyyah in which we live
and from which we derive benefits. We must return to that pure
source from which those people derived their guidance, the source
which is free from any mixing or pollution. We must return to it to
derive from it our concepts of the nature of the universe, the nature
of human existence, and the relationship of these two with the
Perfect, the Real Being, God Most High. From it we must also
derive our concepts of life, our principles of government, politics,
economics and all other aspects of life.[17]

Such an introspective approach might be followed to at least a temporarily
apolitical attitude while individual Muslims and groups rediscover their faith.

Yet alongside the revolutionary and the introspective expressions of the
new *shari'a*-mindedness, a third trend has emerged here that can only be
termed constitutionalist. Many Islamist intellectuals have tried to discover in
Islamic sources the duties, limits, and procedures of governance. These writings have received much less attention in the scholarly literature, yet they are
widely read and debated in the Muslim world. While the Islamic constitu-

tionalists have severe critics, they have succeeded in establishing the framework for discussions of Muslim politics.

In order to explore this emerging constitutionalist consensus, four leading figures will receive particular attention: Kamal Abu al-Majd, Rashid Ghannushi, Muhammad al-'Awwa, and Tawfiq Shawi.[18] These four writers have been selected because their writings have attracted attention outside their country of origin (all but Ghannushi are Egyptian) and because they represent the breadth of the constitutionalist perspective. Abu al-Majd is a former minister and equally at home in Western constitutional law and in Islamic jurisprudence; he is generally regarded as very much an establishment figure. Ghannushi lives in exile, vilified by the Tunisian regime as a would-be revolutionary. Al-'Awwa and Shawi fall between these two poles; both are associated with the Muslim Brotherhood but also have reputations as independent thinkers.

One of these figures might serve a regime, one might seek to overthrow a similar regime, and two might fall between these poles, but such differences do not obscure a fundamentally similar understanding of the role of the Islamic *shari'a* in a modern political order. The sole purpose behind selecting them here is to show the contours of the emerging constitutionalist consensus. All four are thoughtful, articulate, and even original, but they are selected here because they do not stand out, except as they express this constitutionalism in slightly different ways. Rather than give a broader account of modern Islamic political thought, the purpose here remains much more modest: to show how diversity within the family of Islamic political approaches should not obscure a convergence of understanding regarding the proper role for the Islamic *shari'a*.

While the political orientations of these and similar writers may vary greatly, they all are fundamentalist in a technical sense: a strong common element is the desire to discover what is fundamental to a proper Muslim political order by delving back to the foundation of the first Muslim society in Medina. Indeed, the tremendous emphasis on the Medinan polity has become a staple of Islamist political writings. While there were individual Muslims before they fled to Medina in 622, such writers hold there was no society governed according to Islamic principles. In the years after the flight, the prophet was able to establish a political order based on the moral teachings of Islam. Muhammad al-'Awwa goes so far as to call the Medinan polity the world's first state:

> The Islamic state in Madinah was the oldest example of a political society organized in the form of 'state.' This claim rests on the fact that it was an organized society based on 'rule of law.' The supremacy

of 'rule of law' is a distinguishing factor between a 'state' and other forms of organized political societies. It presupposes that all organs and agencies of the government are subject to and will abide by the rules of the same legal system which govern the individual citizen.[19]

Other constitutionalist writers frequently observe that those Qur'anic verses that deal with social organization and human relations are generally among those designated as revealed in Medina; it was only after the creation of an Islamic polity that the full legal and political teachings of the religion became the subject of divine revelation. Those who wish to discover the nature of Islamic politics should direct their attention to Medina; those who wish to doubt any political role for Islam are refuted by the definitive counter-example of Medina.

From this starting point, Islamic constitutionalist writers follow Mawdudi and Qutb in affirming the idea that Islam requires the sovereignty of God.[20] They distinguish between ideologies that locate ultimate political authority in human beings (either individuals or the people as a whole) and Islam in which such authority lies only with God. Absolute monarchy and untrammeled democracy are both deemed to place some human beings in control of the lives of others without benefit of divine guidance.

If sovereignty lies with God, so does legislative authority, leading Islamic constitutionalists to affirm the absolutely binding nature of the *shari'a*. Any action by any human government has to be measured against the requirements of the *shari'a*, and any man-made rule, policy, or regulation that contradicts any provision of the *shari'a* is invalid. Ghannushi writes that "Islam makes the binding nature of legal provisions a basis for legitimacy of the state and makes the ruler bounded—in the decisions he takes, the procedures, and the commands he issues—by the provisions of the Islamic *shari'a*."[21] Tawfiq Shawi makes the constitutional argument even more explicit:

> When our peoples demand application of the Islamic *shari'a*, some might think that the goal of that is to apply the Islamic *fiqh* to relations among individuals in the society, whether in civil, commercial, criminal or other aspects. But this is insufficient, because the first goal is that the state itself be bound by compliance with the sovereignty of the *shari'a*. All the organizations, institutions, and individuals who represent [the state] must be bound to comply with its principles and rules and apply them on themselves and on their own exercise of authority before they apply them on the general population and the individuals within society.[22]

The *shari'a* can thus be portrayed as the basis of an Islamic constitutional order, a metaphor frequently invoked. Indeed, many writers explicitly accept the term "constitution" while insisting that the basis of the order lies in law ordained by God rather than a constituent assembly. For many, the *shari'a* is thus more constitutionalist than any man-made constitutional order. Tawfiq Shawi observed that interpretation of the constitution is often left to the very authorities that the constitution is supposed to limit (or those appointed by them), whereas a true *shari'a*-based system would involve specialists in Islamic law and the population as a whole in interpreting the law.[23]

Yet establishing the *shari'a* as the basis of a constitutional order raises some difficulties. It is only fairly recently that the *shari'a* has come to be identified as a specific body of legal rules (rather than a set of institutions and methods) so that it does not translate easily into a specific constitutional order.[24] The *shari'a* does not lend itself automatically to constitutional law. There is, of course, over a millennium of *fiqh* [Islamic jurisprudence] on which to draw. Yet few *fuqaha'* [specialists in *fiqh*] devoted systematic attention to questions of political structure. And the turn away from Islamic legal sources toward codes of Western origin—begun over a century ago—discouraged the extension of *fiqh* into new areas in many Muslim societies. Islamic constitutionalists have therefore developed an ambivalent attitude towards the existing body of *fiqh*. While it cannot provide them all the legal and institutional guidance they feel is needed, to abandon *fiqh* while proclaiming fealty to the Islamic *shari'a* could lead to an Islamic ideology devoid of content.

Accordingly, Islamic constitutionalists are not only best viewed as fundamentalists but also as modernists: they explicitly call for a reinterpretation of classical positions in terms of modern needs. Ghannushi has stated:

> We should distinguish between *Shari'a* and *fiqh*. *Fiqh* is the word for jurisprudence. Islam can be understood to be a synonym of the word *Shari'a*. However *fiqh* or jurisprudence is the understanding of the people in society, and this may develop and change from time to time. It may also vary with the level of education and civilization. In one historical period a jurist like Al-Shafe'i moved from one geographical location to another, changed many of his ideas or his opinions and only left 15 questions the way they were. So what would happen if Al-Shafe'i came to this world today? What would happen to his ideas?[25]

A sharp distinction is often made between the Qur'an and the *sunna* on the one hand and other sources of *shari'a*-based law on the other. The Qur'an is the unalterable word of God; the *sunna* is similarly unalterable because it represents the statements and actions of the prophet. Other sources of law, however, are of human origin and inevitably bound by the particular time and place in which they arose. A rule based on a clear Qur'anic text or an unambiguous statement of the prophet cannot be changed by later interpretation; all else is the subject of legitimate scholarship and debate. Such efforts must be based on an acceptance of the principles of Islam rather than by a desire to make Islam conform to an alien ideology or system, but Islamic constitutionalists can be fairly wide-ranging in their acceptance of new interpretations of law. Shawi insists that an effort to render the *shari'a* in codified form, for instance, does not close the door to *ijtihad* or new interpretations developed by those trained in Islamic jurisprudence.[26] Al-'Awwa even goes farther: he is no more willing than others to abrogate any clear rules in the Qur'an or the *sunna*, but he notes that even the sunna contains rules not intended to be permanent but instead designed for the society of the time.[27]

Islamic constitutionalists make use of this injunction to develop Islamic law by engaging in their own efforts to design a proper Islamic state. There is an irony in these efforts, in that 'Ali 'Abd al-Raziq, who argued that Islam required no specific political order, is a major foil for most of the Islamic constitutionalists, yet some stop just short of his position. There is such a thing as a proper Islamic political order, the constitutionalists claim, but the *shari'a* provides only general guidance on the subject. It is up to each age to apply these general principles in the form most appropriate. Al-'Awwa writes:

> For if we assume that the Prophet had established some specific system of government, or had designated a person as the *Khalifa* (Caliph or head of state) to succeed him or determined one single way of choosing him then that course of action would undoubtedly have suited the Islamic *Ummah* after his death and would, most probably, have remained so for many generations after him. But it is doubtful whether one system could continue to be applied to generations of Muslims in different countries where Islam had spread and where their diverse social, economic and other circumstances would have effected changes in the political system.
>
> For this reason, the Prophet left the matter of choosing the ruler and the determination of the system of government (also left without specifying details) to Muslims to decide according to their interests and the requirements of time, place and changing circumstances; and nothing decreed was binding on them except the general rules of

Islamic law in regard to consultation, justice and equality, and the ordinances and moral values which the Prophet had promulgated during the Madinan period, that is, from the inception of the first Islamic state until he passed away.[28]

These general principles cited by al-'Awwa—consultation, justice, and equality—recur in the writings of Islamic constitutionalists. The final principle, equality, refers to the insistence on the equal status of all who submit to God's will; that is, all Muslims. The status of non-Muslims receives great attention from these writers (especially Ghannushi) and remains a topic of controversy and discussion.[29] Justice is a traditional and unsurprising concern.

Yet the emphasis on consultation (*shura*) is more problematic. To be sure, there are a few mentions of consultation in the Qur'an and the *sunna*, but most Muslim thinkers have been uninterested in transforming this into a full constitutional theory. Instead, the more common view in the past has been to view consultation as limited (to *ahl al-hall wa-l-'aqd*, literally, the people or loosen and bind, or leading figures often equated in recent years with the *'ulama*), desirable (but not obligatory), and advisory (but not binding). Khayr al-Din al-Tunisi began to try to transform the concept of consultation in a constitutionalist direction over a century ago; the more contemporary writes cited here have picked up the task with enthusiasm.

Central to the newly emerging Islamic constitutionalism is the idea that consultation is obligatory on the ruler and binding. Different sorts of questions should be submitted to different groups: questions of Islamic law should go to those qualified to interpret (the *'ulama* or the *mujtahidin*, those who engage in *ijtihad*); technical questions should go to those with the necessary expertise, and general questions that are left open by the *shari'a* should be submitted to the community as a whole. This raises some further difficult questions—regarding, for instance, the participation of non-Muslims and women—but barring any explicit text, the Islamic constitutionalists presented here tend to address these questions in a fairly liberal fashion. A strong measure of popular participation is not deemed to diminish from God's sovereignty so long as the letter and spirit of the *shari'a* are observed. Kamal Abu al-Majd has even gone so far as to speak of "dual sovereignty": absolute sovereignty belongs to God, and limited sovereignty within the boundaries established by the *shari'a* lies with the mass of Muslims.[30]

These writers therefore build on the radical ground laid by previous thinkers but move the center of the debate to issues of government structures and accountability. It is not difficult to understand the attraction of such ideas in the Arab world, where political alienation is coupled with resentment of corruption and feelings that holders of political authority seek only their own benefit. In arguing for an authentically Islamic political order, the Islamic constitutionalists have laid the basis to graft some of the structures of Western constitutional orders—elected presidents and parliaments, guarantees of rights, and written and codified limitations on governmental authority—on Islamic roots. There are sharp limitations and subtle changes in this grafting process. A pluralist party system, for instance, poses real problems for writers in any Islamic political tradition because of the strong traditional suspicion of partisanship or any organized division of the community (a suspicion at odds only with more recent liberalism; it has strong echoes in earlier generations of Western liberal thought). Despite such tensions and transformations, the goal of the Islamic constitutionalists is clearly to render political authority accountable, primarily to religiously sanctioned standards, but also to the people.

These writings have attracted a great deal of attention among Muslims concerned with politics. Some have been quite critical; others are simply suspicious. These responses come from two sources: a leftist critique that sees the attempt to bring about a *shari'a*-based system as anachronistic and illiberal; and a traditionalist critique that finds constitutionalists insufficiently faithful to Islamic traditions. Even as debate has turned bitter, the intellectual distance among the various positions has actually decreased, as an examination of each critique in turn will show.

At the core of the leftist suspicion of the Islamic constitutionalists is a strong skepticism concerning its claims. Many liberals, leftists, former leftists, human-rights activists, and secularists feel that the constitutionalism of the Islamist writers is a ruse. By coating their calls for an Islamic state with the more palatable material of consultation, accountability, and rights, Islamists seek only to assuage their opponents while seizing political power. Even if the sincerity of the constitutionalists is not questioned, the idea of the sovereignty of God is held as impracticable. Who, after all, is to determine God's will but human beings? Allowing such fallible figures to act in the name of God might only worsen problems of accountability. The past and present of the Islamic world seem to bear out these suspicions: Islamic history has known few governments that can be truly deemed constitutional, and when Islamic symbols are used by contemporary rulers they generally serve only to mask or justify harshly authoritarian regimes (Saddam Hussein and Ja'far Numayri are frequently cited as particularly cynical rulers in this regard).[31]

In many ways, these suspicions are but manifestations of a more profound intellectual debate on the nature of Islamic *fiqh*. The critique of the

Islamic constitutionalists from the left presents a far more negative evaluation of the modern applicability of Islamic jurisprudence. Many stop little short of calling for a wholesale repudiation of the entire body of *fiqh*; most see the existing body of *fiqh* as a product of the circumstances prevailing in the societies where it was developed. Calling for the application of *shari'a* is therefore tantamount to advocating an anachronistic legal system based on frozen and outdated interpretations of religiously-sanctioned sources. Some have even claimed that the *shari'a* itself is best understood not as a body of law but only a set of moral teachings.[32]

Yet when many critics develop their positions more fully, they seem to differ from the Islamic constitutionalists only by degree. Both camps accept that clear texts from the Qur'an and the *sunna* are binding, that other law is based on fallible and time-bound human insight, and that Islamic law must be developed in ways to make it appropriate for the modern age. The constitutionalists must take such a position because their emphasis on consultation and other themes involves precisely such a reinterpretation of texts in ways unanticipated by older legal scholarship. The critics on the left push the inappropriateness of the body of traditional legal scholarship much farther. Yet the following statement by Abdallah An-Na'im, a Sudanese human rights activist and law professor, differs from the writings of Rashid Ghannushi only in tone:

> It is my conviction, on the one hand, that Islam itself is capable of sustaining a modern constitutional state where all citizens enjoy equal rights, without discrimination on grounds of race, color, sex, language, religion, or politics. I am equally convinced, on the other hand, that the prevailing view of Islamic Shari'a law, as developed by early Muslim jurists, is fundamentally inconsistent with modern notions of constitutionalism and the rule of law. The following criticism of Shari'a should therefore be seen as part of a plea for Islamic law reform in the best interests of Islam itself as well as the interest of my own country, the Sudan.
>
> I maintain a distinction between Shari'a and the sources of that law, mainly the Qur'an, believed by all Muslims to be the literal and final word of God, and Sunna, or traditions of the Prophet. It would be heretical for a Muslim, and completely unacceptable to all the Muslims he or she may hope to influence, to attribute inadequacy or deficiency to the sources of Islam itself. It is not heretical, and should therefore be acceptable to all Muslims, that Shari'a in the sense of the law developed by Muslim jurists through their

own interpretation of Qur'an and Sunna, is open to debate and criticism. Shari'a is not identical with the sources of Islam as such, but rather the way those sources were historically interpreted and applied.[33]

Thus many critics of the Islamic constitutionalists have in fact affirmed their basic argument: an Islamic political order must be based on the *shari'a*; but the *shari'a* must be reinterpreted (and distanced—to some extent—from existing *fiqh*). This agreement is real but masks some further divisions. How much of existing *fiqh* is appropriate? Who is authorized to develop new interpretations? What methods are most appropriate? All but the avowed secularists profess obeisance to the binding nature of the *shari'a*, but for many this simply means that any legislation not explicitly contravening the Qur'an or the *sunna* is permissible. As will be seen, this has emerged as a very influential view in Egypt. It is a position Islamic constitutionalists would find very difficult to accept: it would empty both their emphasis on the *shari'a* and their constitutionalism of content. Yet in insisting on a more demanding orientation, the Islamic constitutionalists encounter some real difficulties. To appreciate these fully, it is necessary to consider the critique of Islamic constitutionalism from the right.

Despite the arguments of the Islamic constitutionalists dating back to Khayr al-Din al-Tunisi, some Muslims have been suspicious of the enterprise of developing an Islamic constitutional law. Such suspicions were probably dominant among many of the *'ulama* until quite recently. While accepting (and insisting on) the view that the *shari'a* must be enforced, more traditionally minded *'ulama* have developed few remedies for any violations.[34] This weakness of remedies is evident even among members of the *'ulama* sympathetic to some of the radical arguments.[35] Further, traditional legal scholarship, to the extent it focuses on constitutional questions at all, covers only the rights and obligations of rulers rather than any procedural questions. Thus many of the recent constitutionalist writings have an unfamiliar (and, in the minds of some, insupportable) tone: the desirability of rulers engaging in consultation is taken for granted and rests on a firm Qur'anic foundation, but the arguments that advice must be sought, that it is binding, and that the community as a whole must be consulted on some matters are departures from understandings prevailing in the past. When constitutionalists move beyond reinterpreting such political matters to call for a reinterpretation of all of Islamic *fiqh*, they enter what many traditionalists consider very dangerous territory indeed.

The disinterest of many of the *ulama* in constitutional matters is deepened by a suspicion of positive legislation. While nobody would contest that rulers must issue orders and regulations as part of the governing process, elevating those orders and regulations to the status of law risks obscuring the proper role of the *shari'a*. Writing a constitution that is designed to be consistent with Islamic law misses the point: only the *shari'a* itself can have such fundamental status. Thus, traditionally minded *ulama* have actually been far more reluctant than many Islamists to engage in the process of constitution writing. Hasan al-Banna, founder of the Muslim Brotherhood in Egypt but not a member of the *ulama*, made clear that he accepted the Egyptian constitution of 1923 and criticized it only for the matters it had omitted (and thus, by implication, permitted, such behavior as consumption of alcohol and illicit sexual relations).[36] Yet as late as 1962, the highest religious official in Morocco denounced the country's draft constitution because it granted the government an un-Islamic right of legislation.[37] Feeling similar pressures, several states of the Arabian peninsula have issued "basic laws" but avoided the term "constitution."

Such traditionalist suspicions of Islamic constitutionalism have diminished in recent decades, and many members of the *ulama* have come closer to adopting some of the constitutionalist arguments. Yusuf al-Qardawi, an Egyptian religious scholar influential throughout the Arab world, exemplifies this trend. While he stands uncompromising in his demand for implementation of *shari'a* law, he shows little interest in general constitutional questions. Nevertheless, he has affirmed that Islamic teachings denounce unlimited rulers, endorsed democracy that operates within the bounds of Islamic law, and argued that Muslim rulers must not only consult but accept the advice that follows from consultation.[38]

Some Islamic writers identified with those labeled here as "constitutionalist" have been influenced by these traditionalist views even as they have receded among the *ulama* themselves. Most notably, Taqi al-Din al-Nabahani, the Palestinian founder of the Islamist *Hizb al-Tahrir* drafted a constitution for an Islamic state that stated starkly "The president of the state is the state."[39] This supremely anticonstitutionalist declaration was not borrowed from Louis XIV but instead based on the absence of constitutional or procedural checks on the authority of the ruler in Islamic history and legal thought. Yet despite such influence, the vast majority of constitutionalists—even those who view al-Nabahani favorably—denounce this view. (Ghannushi, for instance, respectfully but firmly rejects it.)[40] Thus the Islamic constitutionalist consensus displays an often-unconscious ambivalence: it is based on an affirmation of the relevance of Islamic tradition even as it questions much of it.

This ambivalence should not be surprising because it stems from a difficult conundrum for would-be constitutionalists. To affirm the constitutionalist nature of Islam requires the establishment of firm and definite rules for governing. Those rules cannot easily be identified from traditional Islamic political thought. It is possible—as the constitutionalists have done—to develop such rules, but it requires them to engage in an enterprise not part of traditional Islamic legal thought. For the traditionalist critics from the right, the application of the *shari'a* involves simple adoption of known rules. For the more liberally minded critics from the left, the application of the *shari'a* involves only the acceptance of general principles or incontrovertible statements. The Islamic constitutionalists are caught in the middle. Their call for unyielding application of the *shari'a* is accompanied by a call for comprehensive rethinking of basic *shari'a* principles; for both traditionalists and liberals, this is taking a leap into the unknown. To laud the *shari'a* for the firm limits it places on rulers seems to be an odd claim from those who simultaneously emphasize its flexibility. Indeed, it leaves the constitutionalists open to charges of insincerity from both sides. Traditionalists can charge that the constitutionalists use Islam but do not understand it; for liberals, the constitutionalists seek to cloak calls for Islamic rule in less threatening guise. The criticism from the right has been tempered in recent years, and constitutionalist ideas are probably increasingly acceptable to members of the *'ulama* alarmed by perceived official secularism. On the other hand, the popular appeal of Islamist movements has probably heightened liberal suspicions that constitutionalism is but the latest guise for theocrats and religious totalitarians.

Islamic constitutionalists vary in how they approach this problem. In a sense, their proposals form a continuum based less on their explicit ideology— which betrays a common conceptual foundation—than on their sensibilities. Key to understanding their approach is their attitude toward positive law: is the *shari'a* a set of general guidelines that can accommodate a wide variety of legislative solutions, or is it a set of fairly strict instructions that can only be supplemented as a last resort?

Some constitutionalists are far more willing to incorporate liberal and democratic mechanisms into their preferred political order and less willing to defer to the *'ulama* and traditional *fiqh*. In short, they come closer to the more liberal critique that seeks to identify the *shari'a* with the most general principles and rules out only those arrangements that stand directly in contravention of the Qur'an and *sunna*.[41] Others seek to preserve much more of traditional *fiqh* and rely more heavily on the *'ulama* or *mujtahidin* in their preferred structures. This group betrays a greater suspicion of procedures, structures, and laws not specifically sanctioned by the *shari'a* but stemming from a foreign orientation.[42]

At its root, this problem points to a key difference between Islamic constitutionalism (or any system based on divine commandments and natural law) and Western constitutionalism. Basing a political system on religion invites a focus on substantive law: what is permitted and what is prohibited by God? Such a system is constitutional because it separates legislative authority from the power to rule. Western constitutionalism, by contrast, has generally focused on procedural rather than substantive law. To be sure, there are limits (most notably in rights provisions) on the substance of state legislative authority. (It might be noted, however, that even such substantive limitations are sometimes justified in procedural terms: free speech is not only presented as an individual right but also a necessity if democratic procedures are to become meaningful). Yet Western constitutionalism, like Western constitutional documents, devotes far greater attention to the workings of government. Political authority is limited in that it must operate in accordance with certain procedures. A leader who exceeds his or her authority in order to pursue good policies violates such constitutionalist principles; it is the means by which authority is achieved and exercised that differentiates constitutional from unconstitutional action.

Adherents of a more procedurally oriented view of constitutionalism would thus find fault with attempts to limit political authority solely through substantive law. If the *shari'a* is to set the boundaries of individual and state action, then who is to interpret the *shari'a* and determine the existence of violations? God may be sovereign, but who holds power-holders accountable in this world? There are pitfalls at both sides of the continuum just described. Those who cast the Islamic *shari'a* as a set of general guidelines, abandoning much of traditional *fiqh*, in effect grant far more authority to those who interpret Islamic law. Whose new interpretations are binding? Does allowing such new interpretations in effect allow rulers to do as they please, confident that some new interpretation of the *shari'a* will allow their action? Such an orientation seems to risk a toothless constitutionalism, one that insists political authority has limits but is ineffectual in determining them.

Those who hew more closely to traditional *fiqh*, on the other hand, risk a different set of problems. Traditional *fiqh* is quite poor in mechanisms of political accountability. And it is difficult to see how the *shari'a* could actually be implemented in this form without transferring political power from the hands of unchecked autocrats to the *'ulama*. Knowledge of the Islamic *shari'a* would become a technical matter, and only those who underwent long and specialized training would be equipped to speak authoritatively on the limitations and obligations of political authority. The *ulama* would not necessarily rule directly, but their political authority would increase greatly without any real mechanism of accountability having been instituted.

Most Sunni constitutionalists adamantly deny that they wish to create a theocracy dominated by the *ulama*. Yet to the extent they make good this denial by seeking to move authority over legal innovation out of the hands of the *ulama*, the more they risk robbing constitutionalism of any meaning. And the more insistent they are on applicability of traditional *fiqh*, the more they either empower rulers (by abandoning mechanisms of accountability) or the *ulama* (by making their interpretations binding) without instituting viable limits on either.

Can Islamic constitutionalism confront such dilemmas and work in practice? Are such attempts to establish a clearly articulated set of purposes and limits for political authority bound to collapse in the face of internal contradictions? In fact there have been attempts to bring about constitutional orders based on the principles of the Islamic constitutionalists. In 1980, Egypt amended the second article of its constitution to proclaim that "the principles of the Islamic *shari'a* are the principal source of legislation," in a sense sanctioning the more liberal version of Islamic constitutionalism. In 1979 revolutionary Iran adopted a constitution based on a far more extensive and ambitious attempt to implement an Islamic republic. Most Islamic constitutionalists would disassociate themselves from both experiments: the Egyptian as insufficient and insincere, the Iranian as based on Shi'i doctrines (or on doctrines alien to both the traditional Sunni and Shi'i Islam). In fact, however, both experiments provide valuable lessons about the viability and pitfalls of pursuing an Islamic constitutionalism.

Before a brief consideration of these two experiments, however, it is necessary to emphasize that the effort will be to understand whether Islamic constitutionalism is practicable, not whether it is liberal. It is a simple matter to show that on key points Islamic constitutionalist doctrines differ from some contemporary liberal and democratic ideals. They are based, as their proponents constantly emphasized, on divine rather than popular sovereignty. And they endorse a view of freedom that seems alien, even Orwellian, to many liberals both inside and outside of the Muslim world: Islam requires total submission to God and His order in order to remove subservience of human beings to each other. To describe acceptance of *shari'a*-based rules as freedom and to be concerned with the rights of the (Muslim) community over those of the individual is very much at odds with most current understandings of liberalism.

That does not make such ideas anticonstitutionalist. Constitutionalism might be based on different sorts of political orientations, including those with a more nationalist or communitarian flavor.[43] Allowing individuals to speak freely only so long as they do not insult or repudiate Islam would violate most contemporary liberal conceptions of religious freedom. Such an approach seems unfamiliar, but it is actually to be found not only among nationalistic and Islamic constitutionalists, but even among earlier generations of liberal Western constitutionalists. Montesquieu, for instance, endorsed a view of liberty that could have easily been advanced by Ghannushi or even Sayyid Qutb:

> political liberty does not consist in an unrestrained freedom. In governments, that is, in societies directed by laws, liberty can consist only in the power of doing what we ought to will, and in not being constrained to do what we ought not to will.
>
> We must have continually present in our minds the difference between independence and liberty. Liberty is a right of doing whatever the laws permit; and if a citizen could do what they forbid, he would no longer be possest of liberty, because all his fellow citizens would have the same power.[44]

If Islamic constitutionalism can be considered liberal at all, it would only be according to older standards than are generally prevalent today. But the question for present purposes is not whether Islamic constitutionalism is liberal but whether it is possible: can attempts to base a political order on the *shari'a* in fact result in a state governed by law? Are Islamic principles able to serve as a clear guide to governing procedures and actions? Two attempts—a limited constitutional revision in Egypt and an ambitious Islamic revolution in Iran— help us understand the practical possibilities for, and pitfalls of, a constitutionalism based on Islamic principles.

Egypt

Egypt has embarked on a modest attempt to ensure that political authority is exercised within the boundaries of the Islamic *shari'a*. The effort is fairly recent, although Islam's dominant status in the country has not been in doubt for over a millennium. The 1923 constitution granted Islam official status without making any mention of the Islamic *shari'a*. This formulation, however weak it appears in retrospect, was in fact proposed by Egypt's former *mufti*, Shaykh Muhammad Bakhit (often identified as a conservative); the failure to cite *shari'a* law was not publicly criticized for decades.[45] As previously mentioned, even Hasan al-Banna described Egypt's constitutional system as close to Islam, criticizing it only for failing to ban some behavior prohibited by the *shari'a*.[46]

Yet by the time of the 1971 constitution, the idea of applying the Islamic *shari'a* had gained sufficient salience that it was a major topic of discussion. Indeed, since the drafting of the 1971 constitution was carried out in a far more open process than all of its predecessors (probably including even the 1923 constitution), the summer of 1971 saw a very lively debate, both in the drafting committee and the press.[47] The issue of the role for the *shari'a* arose in several different ways. For instance, provisions for women's rights provoked a debate between those advocating strong and definitive language and those who were concerned that this would lead to violations of the *shari'a*. The most direct attempt to address the issue came in the discussion of Article 2 of the constitution. The original draft stated: "Islam is the religion of the state; the Islamic *shari'a* is a basic source of law-making [*taqnin*], and Arabic is the official language." This language provoked criticism from two camps. For some this did not go far enough, because it left the role of the *shari'a* ambiguous and vague. An alternative was proposed making the *shari'a* *the* source of law-making. For others, the proposal was not too vague but too definite, opening the door to widespread legal change. The final version retreated only slightly, stating that "the *principles* of the Islamic *shari'a* are a principal source of legislation [*tashri'*]"[48] [emphasis added].

The setback for *shari'a* advocates was only temporary. In 1980 the constitution was amended, inserting a definite article so that "the principles of the Islamic *shari'a* are *the* basic source of legislation" [emphasis added].[49] Yet the meaning of the text remains unclear. What is the difference between the Islamic *shari'a* and its principles? What is the positive content of the *shari'a* and how is it to be defined? What does the absence of any reference to *fiqh* indicate? What does it mean to proclaim the *shari'a* the source of legislation: is it to offer encouragement to the legislature to consult the *shari'a* before drawing up legislation? What is the fate of legislation that is not based on the *shari'a*: is it unconstitutional?

It may have been that the intent of the regime in offering this change was simply to enhance its Islamic credentials. Yet the new constitutional language came shortly after the Supreme Constitutional Court, created by the 1971 constitution, was given real independence (see chapter 5). Those unhappy with legislative provisions of various kinds thus had a new forum to which they could resort in order to enforce their conception of the meaning of the Islamic *shari'a* and the revised second article of the constitution.

In a series of decisions, the Court has pursued a consistent interpretation of the revised article. While not robbing the provision of all of its content, the Court has not used it to enforce real limits on Egyptian legislation and the legal order. In effect, the Islamic *shari'a* has increased in symbolic importance, but political authorities have found few obstacles placed in their path. Indeed, the Court has actually authorized the executive and the parliament to develop binding interpretations of Islamic law. Granting such authority makes it very unlikely that Article 2 can serve as the basis for an Islamic constitutionalism in Egypt.

The Court began to hear challenges to existing legislation based on its supposed incompatibility with the Islamic *shari'a* beginning in the 1980s. In the past few years, such challenges have become nearly continuous. The Court has staked out a clear position on the meaning of Article 2, reaffirming it with striking consistency.[50] While the amended text is open to numerous interpretations, the decisions of the Court endorse the argument that it prohibits any legislation that explicitly contravenes the Islamic *shari'a*. This reading of the revised text is hardly inevitable, and it seems to hand the advocates of the application of the *shari'a* a tremendous victory. Yet the decisions of the Court have had the precise opposite effect; as of this writing, only one law has been struck down primarily on the basis of Article 2. How has the strengthened version of Article 2, interpreted by the Court to bar legislation contravening the *shari'a*, had so little effect?

First, in an early case, the Court ruled that the revised article barred legislation contravening the *shari'a* only if it was passed after the date of the amendment. In other words, the text revised in 1980 contained instructions to the legislature to base its subsequent work on the principles of the Islamic *shari'a*. Preexisting legislation should be reviewed to assure its compatibility with the *shari'a* and amended if necessary, but the amendment did not immediately require the Court to invalidate such laws.[51]

More important in the long run, the Court has endorsed a modernist view of the *shari'a* that distinguishes between two kinds of *shari'a*-based rules: those unambiguously established both in their authenticity and their meaning, and those based on more malleable applications of *shari'a*-based principles. Legislation incompatible with an unalterable principle is invalid. On the other hand, the executive and legislative authorities are given wide latitude where the *shari'a* provides unclear or multiple answers.

The Court has articulated this principle on numerous occasions. In 1996, for instance, a father brought a case to the Court involving an administrative decree issued by the Minister of Education barring female students from wearing the *niqab* [a veil covering the full face in contradistinction to the permitted *hijab*, a veil covering only the hair] in state schools. The proponents of a *shari'a*-based constitutional jurisprudence finally seemed to have a strong case. The challengers could cite not only Article 2, but also personal rights provisions of the constitution. The father claimed that the minister's decree violated both the Islamic *shari'a* and rights of a liberal provenance. The Court rejected the claim, however, laying out once again a view that grants executive and legislative authorities tremendous latitude:

> It is not permitted for a legislative text to contradict those *shari'a* provisions definitive in their certainty and meaning [*qat' al-ithbat wa-l-dalala*]. These rules alone are those for which *ijtihad* is forbidden because they signify the comprehensive principles and fixed roots of the *shari'a*, accepting neither interpretation nor substitution. . . .
>
> The judgments of reason, where there is no text, develop on a practical basis and are more compassionate to humankind and more dedicated to their affairs in their content. [The judgments based on reason] are more protective of humanity's true interests, which the [*shari'a*] provisions are prescribed to realize in terms of what is appropriate for these interests. The underlying factor is that the essence of God's *shari'a* is truth and justice. Being limited by the *shari'a* is better than widespread depravity. For [the *shari'a*] to be closed upon itself is neither acceptable nor necessary. The statements of an expert of *fiqh* on a matter related to the *shari'a* are not granted any sanctity, or placed beyond review or reexamination. Rather they can be replaced by other [such statements]. Opinions based on *ijtihad* in debated questions do not in themselves have any force applying to those who do not hold them. It is not permitted to hold [such opinions] to be firm, settled *shari'a* law that cannot be contravened. To do so would be to end contemplation of and reflection over Almighty God's religion; it would deny the truth that error is possible in all *ijtihad*. . . .
>
> The challenged decree does not contradict . . . the text of Article 2 of the constitution. The ruler has—in debatable questions—the right of *ijtihad* to facilitate the affairs of the people and reflect what is authentic in their customs and traditions, so long as the overarching purposes of their *shari'a* is not abrogated. . . .[52]

Such an argument robs Article 2 of much of its force.[53]

An attempt to use Article 2 as the basis for the application of a *shariʿa*-based law must now overcome one of two hurdles. First, one might resort directly to the Court. Yet by rejecting any claim that is not based on a clear and permanent injunction of the *shariʿa*, the Court has made this barrier formidable indeed. Others have distinguished between unalterable sources of law (the Qurʾan and the *sunna*) on the one hand and those based on human judgment on the other. The Court's view invalidates any *shariʿa* provision based on the latter—and thus much of the body of existing *fiqh*—as a basis for a constitutional claim. Indeed, it might be possible to escape some clear statements from the Qurʾan and the *sunna* if it can be argued that they are obviously of a particular and time-bound rather than general nature (while the Court has never advanced such an argument, some Islamists actually have). It should be no surprise, therefore, that the Court has only been able to rely primarily on Article 2 to strike down legislation only once. (The decision came in a difficult and controversial ruling on rights to housing after a divorce in which the Court found that the personal status law had infringed on the husband's rights under the *shariʿa*. The case took the Court an uncharacteristically long period—ten years—to resolve.)[54] Most remarkable, perhaps, the judgment of whether a rule is a permanent and unalterable principle rests not with scholars of the *shariʿa* but with secularly trained judges. The piety of individual members of the Court, while beyond question, would not compensate for their lack of training in the minds of many *shariʿa* advocates.

A second path toward the implementation of *shariʿa* law flows through the legislative and executive branch. But here the barrier to practical application of the *shariʿa* is equally formidable. The position of the Court is that rulers (meaning the executive and legislative branches) are entirely free when there is no authoritative and binding *shariʿa* principles. The Court does not insist that rulers choose a specific school of law or authority or consult those trained in *fiqh*. Instead it assigns the task of *ijtihad* directly to the rulers themselves. In short, for any question that lacks an incontrovertible and permanent answer in the Islamic *shariʿa*, the rulers have total discretion.

Thus a modernist view of the *shariʿa* is endorsed, but it is one that would frustrate many Islamic constitutionalists. Granting such deference to the existing authorities translates the Islamic *shariʿa* into only the vaguest limit on state authority. Would it be possible to follow a much more ambitious path that would lay responsibility for deriving and applying *shariʿa*-based rules directly in the hands of those trained to do so? This path is the basis of the Iranian constitutional experiment.

Iran

In 1979, a diverse revolutionary coalition overthrew the Iranian monarchy. While there was a widespread consensus rejecting the old political order, it was not immediately clear what sort of political system should replace it. During the first year of the revolution, those who wished to build some form of Islamic republic emerged victorious. Yet the political contours of such a system were unclear even to its proponents. The most authoritative indication came from the published lectures of Ayatollah Khumayni, in which he advanced an argument for a strong governing role for a member of the *'ulama.*[55] Khumayni echoed the claim of earlier Sunni thinkers that sovereignty properly rests with God and that a practical implication of this was the necessity of applying the *shari'a.* While Khumayni's claims in this regard stood out only by their stridency, he introduced a further argument that has little appeal to Sunni thinkers: if Islamic law is to prevail then those most knowledgeable about Islamic law are in the best position to exercise political authority. This idea constituted a radical extension of the doctrine of *wilayat al-faqih* [guardianship of the jurist], which had emerged in Shi'i thought to confer a measure of authority on the legal opinions of religious scholars in the absence of the Imam (the proper holder of political authority for the Shi'a).

Having put forward this argument, Khumayni demonstrated a consistent disinterest in particular constitutional forms and constitutional drafting. While some revolutionaries began work on a new constitution began even before their triumph, the draft initially produced was better described as an attempt to move the 1906–07 basic laws in a republican direction than as a thoroughly Islamicized order. The constitutional architecture more closely resembled France's Fifth Republic than any previous system of government in the Islamic world.[56] Very little institutional basis was given to Khumayni's interpretation of *wilayat al-faqih,* although the Islamic elements of the 1906–07 basic laws were not abandoned. Nevertheless, when presented with the draft, Khumayni indicated his assent. Constitutionalist leaders in Iran viewed constitutions as emanating from the popular will and therefore insisted that the draft, however laudable, be submitted to a constituent assembly. While leaders from the *'ulama* resisted this idea, a compromise was finally agreed in which a smaller body would be elected to edit the draft. That process resulted in radical changes, however. The body elected was dominated by members of the *'ulama* enthusiastic about practical application of the *shari'a* and institutional expression of Khumayni's conception of *wilayat al-faqih.*[57]

The constitution that resulted was the most original such document produced in the Muslim world since the Tunisian Constitution of 1861. While many of its provisions were borrowed, directly or indirectly, from Western Europe, it contained some startling new elements. The document does not stop with a legalistic description of political structure, it goes on to adduce authority (sometimes in the form of Qur'anic verses) for some of its provisions within the text itself. Perhaps of more practical consequence than this innovation was the construction of wholly new institutions designed to give concrete meaning to Iran's new status as an Islamic republic. Alongside a popularly elected parliament and president, the constitution designated a leader (the *faqih*) and transformed the council of senior clergy (established at the beginning of the century) into a greatly strengthened Council of Guardians. The authority of these new institutions was such that Chibli Mallat has described them as forming a second tier of separation of powers, on top of the more traditional separation between the executive, legislative, and judicial powers.[58]

The leader of the Islamic republic was to be selected on the basis of scholarly and political credentials; Khumayni was designated by name as the first occupant of this post. The leader exercises specific authority over key appointments as well as a general supervisory role. The Council of Guardians consists of six specialists in *fiqh* (selected by the leader) and six lay lawyers (nominated by the judiciary and elected by the Assembly) and is entrusted with two critical tasks. First, it is to review all legislation passed by parliament to ensure that it contradicts neither the *shari'a* nor the constitution. Second, it has a supervisory role in elections, which has allowed it to disqualify candidates for public office if it deems them morally or politically unsound.

Perhaps not since the American constitution was a document written more likely to breed competition and struggle among structures with overlapping authority. During its first decade of operation, strong rivalries developed between the president and the parliament (with the first president deposed in the process) and between the Council of Guardians and the Assembly. Extraconstitutional structures (such as revolutionary committees) complicated these struggles even more, especially during the Islamic Republic's early years. Some of these constitutional struggles were referred to Khumayni himself for resolution, though few issues were definitively settled. Khumayni played this oversight role not simply based on his constitutional prerogatives, but also outside of the constitutional order, issuing direct instructions to the parliament, the judiciary, and other officials.[59]

In 1988, rivalries among the various structures and political orientations led Khumayni to issue a series of statements that seemed designed to promote a more permanent resolution of the constitutional conflicts. In the process, he articulated a reinterpretation of his ideas that dismayed constitutionalists and astounded many *shari'a*-minded supporters. The specific occasion was the continuing struggle between the Assembly and the Council of Guardians regarding some legislation as well as a sermon by then President 'Ali Khamene'i emphasizing the need to rule within the bounds of the Islamic *shari'a*—the very essence of Islamic constitutionalism. Khumayni denounced Khamene'i directly and personally, stating that Islamic government itself was an injunction with priority over all other religious commandments, including prayers, fasting, and the pilgrimage. Khumayni even went so far as to appoint a new body that was to resolve disputes between the Assembly and the Council of Guardians. Not only did this body draw its only authority from Khumayni (there was no change in the constitutional text and the members were appointed as individuals rather than by office), but its decisions were to be made according to the public interest (rather than Islamic law) and were binding.[60]

Khumayni's statement represents a stark reversal for Islamic constitutionalism in many ways. Khumayni directly undermined the constitutional text by investing authority in an ad hoc body simply by edict. His statement's underlying rationale cannot be reconciled with Islamic constitutionalism and even seems to repudiate Khumayni's pre-Revolutionary insistence on the *shari'a* as the basis of Islamic governance.[61] Despite this seeming shift, there is an underlying continuity in Khumayni's words and actions. For all his emphasis on the Islamic *shari'a* as the basis of governance, Khumayni displayed a strong personalistic focus throughout his political career. His theoretical writings emphasized not simply Islamic law but also the rule of the jurist. And he showed a consistent disinterest in constitutional texts. Not simply did he fail to develop his own; he offered no objection to a modified version of the 1906–07 constitution, itself modeled on the Belgian constitutional order. When he agreed to have the draft modified, it was his enthusiastic supporters who worked to incorporate *wilayat al-faqih*. Once the constitution was written, Khumayni acted in a general supervisory role, regularly moving outside of the constitutional text. Only at the very end of his life did he move to have evolving practices rendered in constitutional form. His proclamations in 1988, and the claim that Islamic government is the religious obligation that surpasses all others grows out of the same disinterest in constitutional texts and structures.

Resistance to constitutionalism has a long history among the Iranian *'ulama*, though it has hardly been the dominant strain.[63] Khumayni's attitude toward constitutionalism displayed more indifference than opposition, however.

His solution to the problem of implementing Islamic government owed less to legalism and constitutionalism than it did to a faith that pious, well-trained, and expert individuals could be personally entrusted with the task of governance. To his opponents, Khumayni ruled tyranically, propounding an ideology that arrogated all legal authority to himself and even allowed him to move outside of the law that he had a monopoly on interpreting. However, if a tyrant is an unbounded and unjust ruler, then in the view of his supporters Khumayni could not have been less tyrannical. He ruled not according to whim or personal interest but in accordance with his profound understanding of Islam. For his supporters, Khumayni was not chosen at random to lead the country, and his actions were far from arbitrary. He emerged because of his superior scholarship and political skills. As a leader, he was bound not by legal texts but by his own knowledge and nature, which combined an unyielding commitment to Islam with an ability to discern the public interest.

Such an image of a just ruler might be sufficient to differentiate Khumayni's personal authority from that of a tyrant in the minds of his supporters, but it is a deeply anticonstitutional vision. It places faith not in the articulation and implementation of clear principles but in the virtues of an individual. Khumayni's disinterest in constitutional texts betrayed an essential departure from Islamic constitutionalism despite a common starting point in dedication to Islamic legalism. And it was precisely the substitution of personal authority for constitutionalism that has made many of the Sunni constitutionalists extremely wary of the Iranian experiment. Some Sunni thinkers locate their opposition to the Iranian model in the Shi'i nature of the Islamic Republic, noting that Sunni Muslims have been far less willing to accept personalistic religious authority. Muhammad al-'Awwa is more gentle but equally firm in his rejection of the institutionalization of *wilayat al-faqih*. Clearly sympathetic with the Iranian attempt to draft an Islamic constitution, he portrays Khumayni's innovations as a departure from traditional Shi'ism and founded more on revolutionary strategy than on *fiqh*.[63]

While Khumayni's own words and actions may have stemmed from motives inimical to constitutionalism, the Iranian experiment as a whole cannot be dismissed as anticonstitutionalist so quickly. From the very beginning, there was a far more constitutionalist version of *wilayat al-faqih* current among some Shi'i thinkers. Muhammad Baqir al-Sadr, an extremely influential *mujtahid* executed by the Iraqi regime in 1980, wrote a brief presentation of constitutional principles at the time that the Iranian constitution was being drafted.[64] His version more closely resembles that of the Sunni constitutionalists than it does the personalistic vision of Khumayni. Beginning at the starting point of the sovereignty of God, al-Sadr acknowledges that some of the prophets exercised direct political authority. He also notes, however, that some rulers have used the principle of divine sovereignty to monopolize power in their hands. God's sovereignty does not mean that rulers are unaccountable to the people but simply that they must rule in accordance with the *shari'a*. In making these arguments, al-Sadr echoed themes of many Sunni constitutionalists.

Al-Sadr interpreted divine sovereignty in an original way, however, when he argued that while God is the source of political authority, that authority is exercised by the people, who, in turn, are responsible to God. This melding of divine sovereignty with a popular role in governance is given practical expression in a constitutional structure similar to that proposed by Muhammad al-'Awwa or Rashid Ghannushi. In cases in which the *shari'a* is unambiguous, it must be automatically applied. In places in which there is more than one legitimate interpretation, a popularly elected assembly should select which interpretation should be applied. And in cases in which there is no clear indication from the Islamic *shari'a*, then the assembly must develop a rule that accords with the public interest and does not contradict the *shari'a*. In these arguments, al-Sadr was only slightly more restrictive than Egypt's Supreme Constitutional Court.

On top of this structure, however, al-Sadr adds the second tier (to borrow Mallat's conception again) of a leading *mujtahid* who is assisted in his functions by a council he appoints of spiritual intellectuals and at least ten *mujtahidin*.[65] The Sunni constitutionalists would probably be uncomfortable with the degree to which the superior learning of leading members of the *'ulama* translates into political authority in this scheme. Yet in some ways al-Sadr restricts the *'ulama* more than the Sunni constitutionalists do by allowing a popularly elected assembly the right to chose among authoritative interpretations.

This constitutionalist version of *wilayat al-faqih* was very influential in the writing of the Iranian constitution.[66] Of course, Khumayni's own actions considerably exceeded the boundaries anticipated by al-Sadr (and the Iranian constitution itself) and his decisions of 1988 seemed to push Iranian politics in a very different direction. Yet if the more constitutionalist vision of al-Sadr was momentarily submerged under Khumayni, it hardly disappeared. Indeed, soon after dealing such a seeming defeat to constitutionalism, Khumayni appointed a committee to revise the constitution. While there is no evidence that he overcame his ideological indifference to constitutional texts, there is every reason to suspect that he wished to further the institutionalization of the changes he had wrought and therefore saw constitutional amendment as desirable.

The constitutional revisions were completed shortly after Khumayni's death and immediately strengthened the constitutionalist nature of the Iranian experiment. First, the qualifications for the position of leader were downgraded, a step that was necessary in order to find a politically suitable successor to Khumayni. At the same time, this step was based on a recognition that Khumayni's successor would lack his stature, limiting his ability to move outside of constitutional structures. The same motive may have lay behind the decision to add some prerogatives to the position, perhaps to compensate for the loss in moral authority. Second, the structure that Khumayni had ordered into existence to mediate between the Assembly and the Council of Guardians was given a constitutional basis and greatly strengthened. Third, the existing constitutional institutions were centralized and mechanisms were adopted to make cooperation easier. The original constitution had a triple executive—a leader, a president, and a prime minister. The revised constitution eliminated the position of prime minister. It also centralized the judiciary, in order to allow it to act more coherently (and coordinate better with other branches).

It should also be noted that if Khumayni's 1988 decisions were anti-constitutionalist in inspiration, they also had the effect of finally defeating any attempt to transform the Islamic *shari'a* into a comprehensive legal system. By elevating the authority of the state and the importance of the public interest in legislation, Khumayni all but admitted that the *shari'a* was incomplete; much supplementary legislation had to be adopted.[67] This had the effect of strengthening parliamentary and other popularly elected actors (such as the president). Thus, when Khumayni died, the system that was left behind had actually moved closer in both spirit and structure to that originally advocated by al-Sadr. Iranian constitutionalism is very much alive. And a decade after his death, the attempt to move Iran in a constitutionalist direction assumed a central place in Iranian politics. The election of Muhammad Khatami as president essentially pitted the long-submerged constitutionalist spirit of the Islamic revolution against the version emphasizing the leadership of expert and politically sound members of the clergy.

Constitutionalism is far from triumphant, however. The ability of the Council of Guardians to screen candidates for public office—an authority it has expanded and used quite energetically—has allowed political power to be concentrated in a fairly homogenous group. Accountability is not absent, but it is often circular.

Iranian constitutionalism is limited by the failure of the constitution to guarantee robust mechanisms to ensure that political authority is accountable to clearly articulated standards. While Khumayni was alive, political actors were essentially (though hardly constitutionally) ultimately accountable to the leader in a personalistic fashion. With Khumayni's death, the personalistic nature of political authority has diminished but not disappeared. Muhammad Khatami's successful election campaign in 1997 was based on unmistakably and primarily constitutionalist rhetoric.[68] Even with Khatami's victory, it is still not clear if institutions and rules can force political actors to remain within the bounds established by the Islamic *shari'a* and the constitution. The enforced homogeneity of the leadership weakens constitutional guarantees. It does not eliminate them, however, especially as splits among Iran's top leaders (often on constitutional issues) have become increasingly apparent since Khatami's election. As Said Arjomand has observed, the central problem confronting Khatami's constitutionalist project is how to strengthen constitutionalism when critical constitutional structures seek to contain and even undermine his efforts.[69] Perhaps more ominously for Islamic constitutionalism more generally, Khatami's struggle with his clerical opponents leads him to cite his popular election and democratic legitimacy more frequently, implicitly aligning constitutionalism with democracy but not necessarily with Islam.

In the end it seems that would-be constitutionalists in Iran have perhaps been insufficiently alert to some Western lessons. The American constitutional experience in particular is rich in experience with precisely the problem that confronts Iran today: can the political system rely on something other than the virtue of its leaders to ensure that it remains within constitutional bounds? The major lesson of the Iranian experience for Islamic constitutionalists is that they must take the concerns of their critics on the left very seriously. A political system that purports to base itself on the *shari'a* must still address the question of whose interpretation of the *shari'a* is authoritative. Khumayni's answer was based on his personal authority; that solution might have been adequate for many Iranians, but it was hardly constitutional. Post-Khumayni Iran has moved away from that solution but has yet to establish a clear alternative. The ambitious attempt to erect a political system wholly based on the *shari'a* has fallen short without any clear principle articulated to replace it.

Earlier chapters underscored that constitutional texts often preceded constitutionalist practice. A political opening in Iran sufficient to render the existing mechanisms of accountability less circular might be sufficient to bring into being a more complete and very genuine, if often illiberal, constitutionalism.

Conclusion

Islamicizing constitutionalism would seem to be quite possible in theory, especially given the increasing emphasis on the *shari'a* in Islamic writings. Not only is it possible, it has been advocated by an influential group of writers. Even those who criticize these writers often actually affirm many of the key principles of Islamic constitutionalism. But attempts to build constitutional orders based on these ideas have encountered severe problems. The centerpiece of most Western constitutional experiments has been a document that emphasizes procedural aspects of constitutionalism. Even substantive limitations on state authority are often expressed in procedural terms (the American constitution guarantees freedom of the press, for instance, by barring Congress from passing a law abridging it). Islamic constitutionalists portray the Islamic *shari'a* less as a procedural than a substantive limitation on the authority of rulers. The weakness of procedural aspects in Islamic legal thought has not gone unnoticed, and Islamic constitutionalist writers have attempted to address it by elevating the importance of such ideas as consultation. Yet when putting these ideas into practice, the constitutional experiments in Egypt and Iran have encountered the same problem: in both cases, attempts to use the Islamic *shari'a* as the basis of a more authentic constitutionalism resulted in the imposition of few procedural restraints on rulers. In Egypt, the revision of Article 2 of the constitution led the normally bold Supreme Constitutional Court to authorize the executive and legislature to devise and enforce their own interpretations of the *shari'a*. That authority is limited only by clear and unambiguous principles (the likes of which the Court has found violated only rarely). In Iran, the attempt to establish an Islamic constitutional order ultimately came to rely not on written texts or clear principles but on the personal authority of the ruler. In both cases, the authority of the rulers increased through allowing them to establish legally binding interpretations.

A Western constitutionalist would insist that combining the authority to rule with the authority to interpret the *shari'a* is fundamentally nonconstitutional. The two functions must be separated. Many Muslim thinkers have shied away from this conclusion for many reasons. Some are suspicious of attempts to regulate political authority by establishing institutionalized rivalries; such efforts would seem to promote disunity. Others, especially Sunni thinkers, have rejected the idea that any human has the authority to issue authoritative interpretations of Islamic law. If rulers need an authoritative interpretation they are free to adopt one for the moment, but they cannot impose their judgment on any scholar. Authorizing an individual or body to issue binding judgments risks freezing Islamic law and enshrining the views of fallible individuals as definitive.

The Egyptian and the Iranian experiments do not show that Islamic constitutionalism must fail. But they do raise the importance of the skeptical questions suggested by Western constitutionalist practice: How can one apply divinely inspired law without giving authority to human beings? And how can human beings be held accountable to divine standards? The answers to these questions must be given institutional expression. Western constitutionalism has concentrated much effort on analogous procedural questions. In short, Islamic constitutionalists have yet to succeed not because they have borrowed too much from Western constitutionalism but because they have borrowed too little.

CONCLUSION

Lessons from the Arab Constitutional Experience

WHY ARE CONSTITUTIONS written in the Arab world? What purposes are they designed to serve? Constitutions have generally been written to augment political authority; constitutionalism (aimed at restraining political authority) has generally been at most a secondary goal. Even though constitutionalism has been a secondary goal, movement in a constitutionalist direction is more likely than often appears.

Some of those responsible for drafting Arab constitutions have sought to define and limit political authority, but even those constitutionalists who realized modest success in having a text reflect these goals were generally defeated in practice. Arab constitutions have rarely been written to serve primarily constitutionalist purposes.

Instead, it was suggested in Part One that constitutions might serve other purposes. First, they can be symbols of sovereignty. This goal was found to operate in the Arab world (particularly in countries obtaining independence and sometimes in republics anxious to strike antiimperialist poses), but even in these cases Arab constitutions served as far more than merely symbolic declarations of statehood. The second purpose that constitutions might serve—indicating basic policy and ideological orientation—also operated, especially in republics. Earlier constitutions and more recent monarchical ones generally eschewed the opportunity to proclaim ideological principles at length, however. And even in republics, the increasing loquaciousness of constitutions on ideological questions accounts for only a small portion of their content. Most Arab constitutions focus primarily on questions of political structure.

Thus the third purpose adduced for issuing constitutions—augmenting authority through establishing clear structures and chains of command—has generally dominated the constitution-writing process in the Arab world. Early Arab constitutions were written to support ambitious programs of political and fiscal reform; twentieth-century constitutions have been written to establish clear political structures, processes, and succession mechanisms.

Yet augmenting political authority is not necessarily the opposite of limiting it: both goals depend on establishing clear rules and procedures; both similarly depend on defining the difference between legitimate and illegitimate uses of political power. Part Two considered various routes to transforming existing constitutional documents into bases for constitutionalist practice. It did so by departing from the standard emphasis in comparative constitutional analysis on text and composition. Instead, the analysis centered on historical evolution, considering results rather than original intent. Elsewhere, parliaments and courts have sometimes emerged as instruments of the sort of accountability that lies at the center of any constitutionalist vision. Might these structures play a similar role in the Arab world, less by design than by accretion?

The prospects for any full-fledged constitutionalism are not bright, but the prospects for evolution in a constitutionalist direction are much stronger than might be expected.

Arab parliaments are generally left in weak constitutional positions but many retain significant potential for exercising oversight over the executive despite their weaknesses. They are generally prevented from realizing their potential because the electoral and party systems deny them the possibility of establishing any autonomy. The same is true for Arab judiciaries, especially those that are assigned the task of constitutional interpretation. While judicial review has spread throughout most of the Arab world (based on recognition of a need for clear and authoritative interpretation of constitutional texts), most bodies entrusted with the task have failed to establish autonomy from the institutions (especially in the executive) that they are supposed to oversee. Islamic law may provide an alternative basis for the emergence of constitutionalism: most Arab constitutional texts acknowledge its authority and include provisions that would seem to offer the possibility of holding political authorities accountable to a legal, intellectual, and religious framework. The promise of Islamic constitutionalism has not been met, however, because of the poverty of procedural provisions (either in Islamic political thought or in existing Arab constitutional texts): existing arrangements make it possible for Arab regimes to proclaim fealty to Islamic law without restricting their freedom of action.

Constitutionalists might well be justified in finding current Arab political reality quite discouraging. Nevertheless, a clear path to constitutionalist practice has been staked out. Some countries have taken definite steps in a constitutionalist direction. The path involves allowing political structures and processes progressively greater autonomy so that they might hold each other (and, most important, the executive) accountable to constitutional standards.

Egypt, Jordan, Kuwait, and Morocco have allowed limited (and, thus far, quite reversible) autonomy to constitutional structures. If they allow constitutionalism to develop further, it will differ from Western constitutionalism in two principal ways. First, the tentative Arab constitutionalism is based on the balance of autonomous state structures, not on a bargain among competing political forces with strong social bases. Arab constitutionalism—if it emerges—would seem to be based less on a negotiated arrangement between ruler and ruled and more on a set of evolving relationships among different groups of rulers.[1] Western constitutionalism may have emerged less in a transcendental moment of self-definition than many liberals now acknowledge, but it did still arise out of intense political struggles over who could rule and where sovereignty lay. Such issues are less salient in Arab constitutionalism: emerging constitutionalist practice is based primarily on forcing rulers to live by the rules they make for themselves. The prospect of constitutionalism is based primarily on the likelihood that authority to enforce constitutional rules will be partially wrested from their authors and placed in the hands of other state structures. Constitutionalism will continue to progress in some Arab countries most reliably when this path seems to threaten executive authorities less and to offer them the promise of political stability. It is far from naïve to see such gradual movement already occurring in some countries.

To be sure, another path to constitutionalism—more akin to the Western experience—is possible in some Arab polities. Deeply divided societies in which no single faction can impose its view might find an ability to hammer out a series of political compromises in constitutional form. Yemen seemed in the 1990s to be following some version of this path. A second possible Arab candidate at present is Algeria, where the most promising alternative to fratricidal struggle and bloody repression may be a carefully negotiated constitutional solution. Once momentary political compromises outlive the circumstances that brought them into being and transform themselves into ongoing institutional arrangements and processes, constitutionalism has triumphed. Outside of Yemen and Algeria, no other Arab state seems sufficiently vulnerable to opposition or social division, however. The more gradual, state-centric path to constitutionalism seems more likely in the vast majority of Arab states where existing structures of political authority, though stultifying, seem inevitable.

This path to constitutionalism differs from Western constitutionalism in a second respect: it is far more separate from democracy. Western constitutionalism was born in a spirit of skepticism of democracy; constitutionalists feared the self-interested, egalitarian, and unstable nature of democratic politics. Beginning in the United States, constitutionalism began not only to accommodate democracy but also to offer solutions to the perceived excesses of democratic politics. By the mid-twentieth century, constitutionalism and democracy became so closely intertwined that many societies forgot the distinction between them: accountability to the people became synonymous with accountability to the constitutional text. To be sure, constitutionalist and democratic values still can be at odds (such as in the debate over judicial power in the United States), but the underlying tension between constitutionalism and democracy has been forgotten in much public political debate.

Arab constitutionalism (at least in the form explored here) does not share in this ambivalent relationship with democracy. Instead it is centered primarily within the elites and serves to hold them accountable only to their own standards. In some ways, the analysis presented here demonstrates that the path to constitutionalism in the Arab world lies in insulating potentially autonomous state structures from the nominally democratic procedures effectively dominated by the executive. It is true that a more fully constitutional order might eventually transform such nominally democratic procedures into genuine and effective instruments of holding government accountable to the people. At least in its early stages, however, Arab constitutionalism would seem to have much less to do with forcing rulers to follow the people's will, focusing instead on forcing them to follow the constitutional text.

The Arab experience does carry important lessons for political analysis elsewhere. First, the study of constitutional texts can be of interest even in the absence of constitutionalist practices. For over a generation, students of politics have dismissed constitutions in nonconstitutionalist settings and considered a focus on such documents naive. But the Arab experience shows that one can take constitutions seriously and remain a cynic. Constitutions may serve rulers even more than they hold them accountable. Scholars would be better served by taking constitutional texts as seriously as rulers do. Rulers can augment their authority through carefully written constitutional texts; to realize how they do so, scholars must concentrate closely on constitutional procedures and context. Most constitutions are far more accurate (if always incomplete) descriptions of political reality than has been generally acknowledged, and they serve to organize state institutions to serve rulers.

Second, those who write constitutions must pay careful attention to the language they use. A close reading of Arab constitutional texts shows how easy it is to hint at liberal democracy without providing for it and how effectively constitutionalist mechanisms can be undermined by the constitutional text. The necessity of careful phrasing seems obvious, but constitution writers tend to focus on positive rather than negative examples. They are far more likely to adopt language from a political system they like than they are to avoid language of a distant failure. Arab constitutions might serve as a very useful negative example. Would-be democracies building presidential systems often emulate the United States and France; they are less likely to see how similar institutional arrangements have resulted in authoritarian politics in the Arab world. A constitutional council is popular in countries that follow French constitutional development; less attention is given to the ways a constitutional council guts judicial review in the Arab world. Constitutional drafters regularly consult other constitutions in deciding which rights to grant constitutional recognition, yet the Arab experience shows far greater attention should be given to how (and not which) rights are to be guaranteed.

Third, constitutional analysis requires revival of conceptual categories, language, and distinctions that have fallen into desuetude: constitutions are not always constitutionalist; constitutionalism is not democracy; liberal constitutionalism is not the only form of constitutionalism. The conflation of constitutionalism, democracy, and liberalism is based on fairly recent Western experience. While such fuzziness is understandable, it serves us poorly when we try to understand either our own history or the politics of other societies.

Finally, we must be careful not to use an idealized understanding of Western constitutionalism as the only standard for measuring the extent of constitutionalism elsewhere. Western constitutionalism was established slowly and after protracted struggle; it was the outcome of hard political bargains more than altruistic philosophical argument. To expect societies experimenting with constitutionalism to abandon self-interest politics in order to define their timeless values is to set a standard that no country could meet (and that most—including arguably the United States—have not even aspired to, except in retrospect). The Arab experience suggests that the idealized understanding of constitutionalism is not only naïve, it also misses the extent to which constitutionalism can emerge by accident more than design. It is far more likely that Arab polities will become more constitutionalist by the steady but almost

imperceptible growth in autonomy of constitutional structures (especially parliaments and courts). Since these structures are created by rulers they seem
innocuous, but they have already begun to move a few countries—however
modestly—in a constitutionalist direction. It may be that the resulting political
system will be a far cry from a full-fledged constitutionalism, but most inhab-
itants of the Arab world—who see very little political accountability at present—
may well see it as a tremendous step forward.

NOTES

Introduction

1. For instance, Kathleen Thelen and Sven Steinmo describe the "old institutionalism": "This work was often deeply normative, and the little comparative 'analysis' then existing largely entailed juxtaposing descriptions of different institutional configurations in different countries, comparing and contrasting." See "Historical Institutionalism in Comparative Politics," in Sven Steinmo, Kathleen Thelen, and Frank Longstreth (editors), *Structuring Politics: Historical Institutionalism in Comparative Analysis* (Cambridge University Press, 1992), p. 3.

This description is fair, but it hardly distinguishes the "new institutionalism" (or at least its historical variant) from the old—both are highly inductive and deeply normative, at least in the choice of topics (with social democracy and liberal democracy informing most recent scholarship). Newer institutionalism is characterized by greater analytical sophistication, a friendlier attitude toward sociology, somewhat broader definitions of institutions, and more conscious research design. None of these virtues, however, necessarily lead away from constitutional analysis.

2. Herbert J. Spiro, *Government by Constitution: The Political Systems of Democracy* (New York: Random House, 1959), p. 436.

3. Karl Loewenstein, *Political Power and the Governmental Process* (Chicago: University of Chicago Press, 1957), p. 146.

4. Loewenstein, *Political Power*, p. 137.

5. See Yash Ghai's discussion of East Africa, particular Tanzania, in "The Rule of Law, Legitimacy and Governance," *International Journal of the Sociology of Law* 14 (1986): 179–208.

6. Articles 9 and 23, from the text of the constitution in Albert P. Blaustein and Jay A. Sigler (editors), *Constitutions that Made History* (New York: Paragon House, 1988).

7. Igor Grazin, "The Rule of Law: But of Which Law? Natural and Positive Law in Post-Communist Transformation," *John Marshall Law Review* 26 (1993): 719–737.

8. This was a regular feature of Latin American constitutions in the nineteenth century. See Brian Loveman, *The Constitution of Tyranny: Regimes of Exception in Spanish America* (Pittsburgh: University of Pittsburgh Press, 1993).

9. Loewenstein himself was confusing when discussing such situations. On the one hand, he introduced the category of the "semantic constitution" in which "the constitution is fully applied and activated, but its ontological reality is nothing but the formalization of the existing location of political power for the exclusive benefit of the actual power holders in control of the enforcement machinery of the state" (*Political Power*, p. 149). Thus he seemed to advance the view that such constitutions were applied but did not restrict state action. Later, however, he stated that in such constitutions rulers "hardly ever pay more than scant lip service to the letter, let alone the spirit of their constitutions" (*Political Power*, p. 152), implying that the constitutions were not seriously applied.

10. While the description of the judiciary as "the least dangerous branch" in the *Federalist Papers* is occasionally remembered, less quoted is the admonition that in a representative republic "it is against the enterprising ambitions" of the legislature that "the people ought to indulge all their jealousy and exhaust all their precautions." See Federalist 48 in *The Federalist* (New York: Modern Library, n.d.), p. 323.

11. Robert Putnam, *Making Democracy Work* (Princeton: Princeton University Press, 1993); John Elster and Rune Slagstad (editors), *Constitutionalism and Democracy* (Cambridge: Cambridge University Press, 1988); Adam Przeworski, *Democracy and the Market: Political and Economic Reforms in Eastern Europe and Latin America* (New York: Cambridge University Press, 1991); and Stephan Haggard and Robert Kaufman, *The Political Economy of Democratic Transitions* (Princeton: Princeton University Press, 1995).

12. As will become clear, both these definitions reflect current and past usage but remain slightly narrow. Defining "constitution" in this way, for instance, allows for the possibility of a constitution that is not established out of constitutionalist motives. Some scholars have resisted such a definition. See, for instance, Loewenstein, *Political Power*, p. 125. Giovanni Sartori saw it as a modern innovation. (See "Constitutionalism: A preliminary discussion," *American Political Science Review* 56 (1962): 835.) This view has been contested by others. See Harvey Wheeler, "Constitutionalism," in Fred I. Greenstein and Nelson W. Polsby, *Handbook of Political Science* (Reading: AddisonWesley, 1975); and Graham Maddox, "A note on the Meaning of Constitution," *American Political Science Review* 76 (December 1982): 805–809. Since most documents called constitutions in the world today have nonconstitutionalist origins, the definition advanced in this work seems both reasonable and necessary.

The definition of "constitutionalism" used here allows for the possibility of a non-liberal constitution. More demanding definitions have been advanced that would require constitutionalism to be based on liberalism and a faith in government by reason. An example can be found in John Finn's *Constitutions in Crisis: Political Violence and the Rule of Law* (New York: Oxford University Press, 1991). I use the term *liberal constitutionalism* to refer to such ideas; given the oft-adduced religious and feudal roots of Western constitutionalism, the possibility of nonliberal constitutionalism must be admitted. It is examined more concretely in the discussion of Islamic constitutionalism.

13. The first clear constitutional document governing a sovereign entity, the United States constitution, itself can be viewed as an attempt to curb democracy in a constitutionalist spirit. The separation of constitutionalism from democracy continued until fairly recently. In 1939, C. H. McIlwain wrote,"Whatever its form may be, whether monarchical, aristocratic, or democratic, in any state that we may properly call constitutional, the supreme authority must be defined and defined by a law of some kind." See *Constitutionalism and the Changing World* (New York: MacMillan, 1939), p. 244. Carl Friedrich reflected this centuries-old view but admitted that meanings had changed when he wrote, "Constitutionalism may be monarchical or it may be republican, it may be aristocratic or democratic, and it has been all of these. When people in America speak of 'democracy,' they usually mean constitutional democracy." *Constitutional Government and Democracy* (Waltham, MA: Blaisdell, 1968), p. 4. Several of the contributors to Elster and Slagstaad, *Constitutionalism and Democracy* explore older ideas about the opposition between constitutionalism and democracy. The decline of the older tension between constitutionalism and democracy may have originated in the United States where ethnic, racial, and religious minorities joined property elites in seeking constitutional protections (see Ian Shapiro, *Democracy's Place*, Ithaca, NY: Cornell University Press, 1996, pp. 16–17). But it probably owes more to twentieth-century totalitarianism, which convinced most constitutionalists that democratic accountability could provide a check on executive authority.

14. Adam Przeworski, "Democracy as a Contingent Outcome of Conflicts," in Elster and Slagstad, *Constitutionalism and Democracy*, p. 62.

15. Przeworski, "Democracy," p. 60.

16. Stephen Holmes, "Precommitment and the Paradox of Democracy," in Elster and Slagstaad, *Constitutionalism and Democracy*, p. 233.

17. Loewenstein, *Political Power*, pp. 135–136.

18. Said Amir Arjomand, "Constitutions and the Struggle for Political Order: A Study in the Modernization of Political Traditions," *Archives Européenes de Sociologie* 33 (1992), p. 40.

19. Arjomand, "Constitutions," p. 46.

20. See Gary Jeffrey Jacobsohn, *Apple of Gold: Constitutionalism in Israel and the United States* (Princeton: Princeton University Press, 1993).

21. Montesquieu, *The Spirit of the Laws,* edited by David Wallace Carrithers (Berkeley: University of California Press, 1977), Book V, Chapter 14, pp. 145–146.

22. Lovemen, *Constitution of Tyranny.*

23. It might be noted that the power-enhancing nature of tools associated with liberalism have led to ambiguity from the beginning of modern Western political thought. Interpretations of the thought of Jean Bodin, for example, have not only focused on his absolutism but also on his latent constitutionalism—and such diverse interpretations have been extant almost since the time of Bodin's own writings. See J. H. M. Salmon, "The Legacy of Jean Bodin: Absolutism, Populism or Constitutionalism," *History of Political Thought* 17 (4, 1996): 500.

24. Wheeler, citing Mosca, pursues this idea briefly; see "Constitutionalism," p. 4.

25. Loewenstein, *Political Power*, pp. 142–143.

26. Hans Kelsen, *General Theory of Law and State* (translated by Anders Wedberg, Cambridge: Harvard University Press, 1949), pp. 264–265.

Chapter 1. Early Constitutional Documents in the Middle East

1. It is necessary at this point to recall the definition of "constitution" introduced in the Introduction: "the basic legal framework for governing." Certainly there had been previous documents of great political importance in Arab history; the Tunisian constitution of 1861 marked an innovation in that it presented a fundamental underlying political framework.

2. This account on background to the Tunisian constitution of 1861 is based on the following sources: L. Carl Brown, *The Tunisia of Ahmad Bey 1837–1855* (Princeton: Princeton University Press, 1974); Lisa Anderson, *The State and Social Transformation* (Princeton: Princeton University Press, 1987); Theresa Liane Womble, *Early Constitutionalism in Tunisia, 1857–1864: Reform and Revolt* (Ph.D. dissertation, department of Near Eastern Studies, Princeton University, 1997); and Charles Combs Harber, *Reforms in Tunisia 1855–1878*, (Ph.D. dissertation, department of history, Ohio State University, 1970).

3. The most noted incident involved the execution of a Jew accused of insulting Islam in a street dispute. For more details, see Harber, Chapter II.

4. The text of the *'ahd al-iman* can be found in 'Abd al-Fattah 'Umar and Qays Sa'id (editors), *Nusus wa-watha'iq siyasiyya tunisiyya* (Tunis: Markaz al-dirasat wal-buhuth wal-nashr bi-kulliyat al-huquq wa-lil-'ulum al-siyasiyya bi-tunis, 1987).

5. The most complete work on the political circumstances of the composition and operation of the Tunisian constitution is Womble's *Early Constitutionalism in Tunisia*. On the committee's work, see pp. 61–64.

6. The text is in 'Umar and Sa'id, *Nusus wa-watha'iq*.

7. Womble, *Early Constitutionalism*, pp. 105–121.

8. Harber claims that the French consul was convinced that the Tunisian leadership had become too closely aligned with Britain and therefore demanded,

among other things, the dismissal of Khaznadar and the suspension of the constitution. See Harber, *Reforms in Tunisia*, p. 61.

9. Anderson does speculate that the constitution did aggravate conditions for most rural dwellers by substituting new tribunals for direct appeal to the *bey* or a representative. See *State and Social Transformation*, p. 83. See Womble, Chapter Five, on the rebellion and the abandonment of the constitution.

10. Leon Carl Brown, *The Surest Path: The Political Treatise of a Nineteenth-Century Muslim Statesman, A Translation of the Introduction to* The Surest Path To Knowledge Concerning The Condition of Countries *by Khayr al-Din al-Tunisi*, Harvard Middle Eastern Monographs, XVI, Center for Middle Eastern Studies, Harvard University, 1967, pp. 28–29. The passage quoted is from Brown's introduction to his translation of Khayr al-Din's work.

11. Brown, *Surest Path*, p. 84. The clarifying phrases are both Brown's and mine.

12. Scholarly writings on the Ottoman constitution of 1876 are reasonably extensive, but because of the declining interest among scholars in legal and political history, the most comprehensive works tend to be older. The account here depends primarily on such older works, including Robert Devereux, *The First Ottoman Constitutional Period: A Study of the Midhat Constitution and Parliament* (Baltimore: Johns Hopkins Press, 1963); Roderic H. Davison, "The Advent of the Principle of Representation in the Government of the Ottoman Empire," in *Essays in Ottoman and Turkish History, 1774–1923: The Impact of the West* (Austin: University of Texas Press, 1990); Roderic H. Davison, *Reform in the Ottoman Empire 1856-1876*, (Princeton: Princeton University Press, 1963); and Stanford J. Shaw and Ezel Kural Shaw, *History of the Ottoman Empire and Modern Turkey, Volume II: Reform, Revolution, and Republic: The Rise of Modern Turkey, 1808–1975* (Cambridge: Cambridge University Press, 1977).

13. I have relied heavily on Devereux, *First Ottoman Constitutional Period*, for this account of parliamentary period. See especially pp. 238–244.

14. I have transliterated foreign words according to their Arabic pronunciation (even when the original document is Turkish or Persian) only for the sake of comparability and consistency.

15. Devereux, *First Ottoman Constitutional Period*, p. 28.

16. This account of the second constitutional period in Ottoman history is based on Shaw and Shaw, *History of the Ottoman Empire*, Bernard Lewis, *The Emergence of Modern Turkey* (Oxford: Oxford University Press, 1968); and Nader Sohrabi, "Historicizing Revolution: Constitutional Revolutions in the Ottoman Empire, Iran, and Russia, 1905–1908," *American Journal of Sociology* 100 (6, May 1995): 1383–1447.

17. Historical writings on the period up to and including the 1882 'Urabi Revolt in Egypt are extensive. The most thorough political history of this period is Alexander Scholch, *Egypt for the Egyptians! The Socio-political Crisis in Egypt 1878-1882* (London: Ithaca Press, 1981). Two other works are helpful. First, Juan R. I. Cole, *Colonialism and Revolution in the Middle East: Social and Cultural Origins of*

Egypt's 'Urabi Movement (Princeton: Princeton University Press, 1993) covers social and, to a lesser extent, intellectual developments during the period. Byron Cannon's *Politics of Law and the Courts in Nineteenth-Century Egypt* (Salt Lake City: University of Utah Press, 1988) provides the best legal history, though there is surprisingly little coverage of the constitution.

18.   For an analysis of the draft, see Scholch, *Egypt for the Egyptians*, pp. 198–200.

19.   In his analysis of the constitution, Scholch rightly stresses the ambiguity on the issue of ministerial responsibility, but he may miss the importance of this precedent. As is explored in Part Two, it was precisely through such precedents rather than through explicit constitutional texts that the matter of parliamentary responsibility was often resolved in Europe. Scholch also portrays the document as less of a constitution than an organic law for the Assembly. His argument is not without merit, but probably rests partly on implicit comparisons with much more exhaustive twentieth-century European constitutional texts, rather than their more succinct nineteenth-century predecessors.

20.   The text of the document can be found in *Al-dasatir al-misriyya 1805–1971: nusus wa-tahlil* [The Egyptian Constitutions 1805–1971: Texts and Analysis] (Cairo: Markaz al-tanzim wa-l-mikrufilm, 1976).

21.   Cole, *Colonialism and Revolution*, p. 105.

22.   Scholch, *Egypt for the Egyptians*, p. 213.

23.   Eugene Rogan mentions a 1920 "Constitution of the Arab Government of Moab" in *Frontiers of the State in the Late Ottoman Empire* (Cambridge: Cambridge University Press, 1999), p. 251. The constitutional efforts of the Tripoli Republic, partly negotiated with Italy, are treated in Karim Mezran, "Constitutionalism in Libya" in Sohail Hashmi and Houchang Chehabi (editors), *Islam and Constitutionalism* (forthcoming).

24.   The Iranian constitution—and the Constitutional Revolution that produced it—have received much more sustained attention from scholars. Two recent works that deal with it in some detail are Mangol Bayat, *Iran's First Revolution: Shi'ism and the Constitutional Revolution of 1905-1909* (New York: Oxford University Press, 1991); and Said Arjomand, *The Turban for the Crown: The Islamic Revolution in Iran* (New York: Oxford University Press, 1988).

25.   My account of the constitution is based primarily on two sources: Jill Crystal, *Oil and Politics in the Gulf: Rulers and Merchants in Kuwait and Qatar* (Cambridge: Cambridge University Press, 1995); and 'Uthman 'Abd al-Malik al-Salih, *Al-nizam al-dusturi wa-l-mu'assasat al-siyasiyya fi al-kuwayt* [The Constitutional Order and Political Institutions in Kuwait] (Kuwait: Kuwait Times Press, 1989).

26.   The text is included in al-Salih, *Al-nizam al-dusturi*, pp. 107–108.

27.   Brown (in his introduction to *The Surest Path*) notes that in the nineteenth century Middle East, ideological explications generally followed practical attempts. Thus, Khayr al-Din's treatise came after the Tunisian constitution rather than before it.

28.   Details can be found in 'Abd al-Karim Ghalab, *Al-tatawwur al-dusturi wa-l-niyabi bi-l-maghrib 1908–1992* (Casablanca: Matba'at al-najah al-jadida, 1993), pp. 102–126.

Chapter 2. Constitutions and Arab Monarchies

1.   Sidney Low, *Egypt in Transition* (New York: The Macmillan Company, 1914), p. 217.

2.   A succinct description of the authority and composition of the council can be found in Majid Khadduri's section on Egypt in the article on "Dustur" in the *Encyclopedia of Islam*. Another useful summary is found in Kevin Boyle and Adel Omar Sharif, *Human Rights and Democracy: The Role of the Supreme Constitutional Court of Egypt*, London: Kluwer Law International, 1996. The text of the 1883 law, as well as the 1913 amended law, can be found in *Al-dasatir al-misriyya 1805–1971: nusus wa-tahlil* [The Egyptian Constitutions 1805–1971: Texts and Analysis], Cairo: Markaz al-tanzim wa-l-mikrufilm, 1976.

3.   The minutes were published by the Egyptian Senate under the title *Al-dustur: ta'liqat 'ala mawadihi bi-l-a'mal al-tahdiriyya wa-l-munaqashat al-barlamaniyya* [The Constitution: Commentaries on its Articles in the Preparatory Works and Parliamentary Discussions] (Cairo: Matba'at misr, 1940).

4.   For discussions of the work of the drafting committee, see Marius Deeb, *Party Politics in Egypt: The Wafd and its Rivals, 1919–1939* (London: Ithaca Press, 1979), pp. 58–61; and Elie Kedourie, "The Genesis of the Egyptian Constitution of 1923," in P. M. Holt (editor), *Political and Social Change in Modern Egypt* (London: Oxford University Press, 1968).

5.   Article 154 pledged that agreements and customs involving foreigners would not be disturbed. In the discussion of the article, Husayn Rushdi, one of the most prominent and active members of the committee, explicitly cited the need to make the British understand the foreigners were to be protected by the constitution. See the section on article 154 in *Al-dustur*. For the politics surrounding the capitulations more generally, see my article, "The Precarious Life and Slow Death of the Mixed Courts of Egypt," *International Journal of Middle East Studies* 25 (1, 1993): 1.

6.   These arguments are covered not only in the minutes but also in Muhammad Husayn Haykal's *Muzakkirat fi al-siyasa al-misriyya* [Memoirs of Egyptian Politics] (Cairo: Maktab al-nahda al-misriyya), part 1, chapter 3, especially pp. 133–134.

7.   See, for instance, the discussion of freedom of the press in Haykal, *Muzakkirat*, p. 166–167.

8.   Deeb also claims British encouragement for the 1928 suspension of the constitution. See *Party Politics*, pp. 145–146.

9.   One of the most detailed accounts of these constitutional crises is contained in 'Ali al-Din Hilal, *Al-siyasa wa-l-hukm fir misr: al-'ahd al-barlmani 1923–1952* [Poli-

tics and Governance in Egypt: The Parliamentary Age 1923–1952] (Cairo: Maktabat al-sharq, 1977).

10. 'Abd al-Mun'im al-Disuqi. "The Position of Village 'Umdas and Shaykhs in the Sidqi Election of 1931," *Al-majalla al-ta'rikhiyya al-misriyya* 27 (1981): 279.

11. See especially Muhammad Mahir Abu al-'Aynayn, *Al-inhiraf al-tashri'i wa al-riqaba 'ala dusturiyya: dirasa tatbiqiyya fi misr* [Legislative Deviation and Constitutional Review: An Applied Study in Egypt] Cairo: Dar al-nahda al-'arabiyya, 1987, especially pp. 557 ff.

12. I have written elsewhere of the nature of parliamentary elections in rural areas; see *Peasant Politics in Modern Egypt: The Struggle Against the State* (New Haven: Yale University Press, 1990), chapter 6.

13. Colonial Office, *'Iraq. Report on 'Iraq Administration. October, 1920– March, 1922*, London: His Majesty's Stationery Office (republished by Archive Editions), p. 14.

14. The process presented the following form to "representative committees": "We, the undersigned residents of Nahiyah/Mahallah in Qadha/Town of _____, in the Liwa of _____ have heard, understood and fully considered the above Resolution of the Council of State, and it results that _____ express themselves in agreement therewith, and profess their allegiance to Amir Faisal while _____ have signified their dissent." See *ibid.*

15. Nigel G. Davidson, "The Constitution of Iraq" *Journal of Comparative Legislation and International Law* 7 (1925), pp. 44–45.

16. Ahlam Husayn Jamil, *Al-khalifiyya al-siyasiyya wa-l-ijtima'iyya li-l-awda' allati kan yutabbiq fi thulliha dustur 1925 fi al-'iraq* [The Political and Social Background to the Conditions in which the Constitution of 1925 in Iraq Were Applied], Beirut: Al-dar al-'arabiyya li-l-mawsu'at, 1986, pp. 13–14.

17. See the forword by E. M. Drower, adviser to the Ministry of Justice in Iraq in C. A. Hooper, *The Constitutional Law of 'Iraq*, Baghdad: Mackenzie and Mackenzie, 1928, p. vii.

18. Jamil, *Al-khalfiyya al-siyasiyya wa-l-ijtima'iyya*, pp. 17–18.

19. Henry A. Foster, *The Making of Modern Iraq: A Product of World Forces*, Norman: University of Oklahoma Press, 1935, p. 192.

20. Ibid, pp. 194–197 covers the agreements in detail.

21. For the British account of the boycott, see *Report by His Britannic Majesty's Government on the Administration of 'Iraq for the period April, 1923–December 1924*, pp. 5–17.

22. See *Report by His Britannic Majesty's Government on the Administration of 'Iraq for the period April, 1923–December 1924*, pp. 21–23 for the text of the resolution.

23. Jamil, *Al-Khalfiyya al-siyasiyya wa-l-ijtima'iyya*, pp. 22–25.

24. Hooper, *Constitutional Law of Iraq*, pp. 89–91. The Iraqi government argued that the constitutional amendment left the clause on parliamentary recess unaffected; Hooper dismisses that view as baseless.

25.   This is a major theme in Jamil, *Al-Khalfiyya al-siyasiyya wa-l-ijtimaʿiyya.*

26.   The crisis between the British and ʿAbd Allah over "constitutionalism" and finances peaked in 1924; the relevant correspondence is contained in the records of the Colonial Office (CO 733) and the Foreign Office (FO 371/10101). Much of this is reprinted in A. De L. Rush (editor), *Ruling Families of Arabia. Jordan: The Royal Family of al-Hashim, Volume I,* Archive Editions and Jane Priestland (editor), *Records of Jordan 1919–1965. Volume 2: 1923–1926,* Archive Edition, 1996.

27.   See Maʾan Abu Nowar, *The History of the Hashemite Kingdom of Jordan. Volume I. The Creation and Development of Transjordan: 1920–1929,* Oxford: Ithaca Press, 1989. The British documents are contained in FO 371/11476 and 13024, reprinted in Priestland, *Records of Jordan 1991–1965. Volume 3: 1927–1932,* Archive Editions, 1996; and CO 831, reprinted in Rush, *Ruling Families of Arabia. Jordan: The Royal Family of al-Hashim, Volume I,* Archive Editions.

28.   Cox to Storrs, 27 January 1926, FO 371/11476; reprinted in Priestland, *Records of Jordan 1919–1965. Volume 2: 1923–1926,* Archive Edition, 1996

29.   On some of the efforts to adopt a constitution, see Kamel S. Abu Jaber, "The Legislature of the Hashemite Kingdom of Jordan: A Study in Political Development," *The Muslim World* 59 (3, July/October 1969): 220–250.

30.   See Abu Nowar, *History of the Hashemite Kingdom of Jordan,* pp. 273–279 for the text of the law.

31.   Hans Kohn, "The Road to India," *Foreign Affairs,* March 1927, p. 237.

32.   See Abu Nowar, *History of the Hashemite Kingdom of Jordan,* pp. 300–303 for the text.

33.   Abu Jaber, "Legislature of Jordan," pp. 224–225.

34.   See the undated note by Sir A. Kirkbridge, "Constitutional Changes in Jordan", FO 371/98859, for a summary of the changes and the debate surrounding them. The note is reprinted in Priestland, *Records of Jordan 1919–1965. Volume 7: 1950–1953.* I have also relied on the Jordanian daily *Filastin* for accounts of the parliamentary debate.

35.   This discussion of preindependence efforts to write a constitution is based on ʿAbd al-Karim Ghallab, *Al-tatawwur al-dusturi wa-l-niyabi bi-l-maghrib 1908–1992* [Constitutional and Parliamentary Development in Morocco 1908–1992] (Casablanca: matbaʿat al-najah al-jadida, 1993), pp. 102–135.

36.   Ibid., pp. 150–153. For the background to the Moroccan constitution of 1962, see ibid. generally for a constitutionalist account. See also Charles F. Gallagher, "Toward Constitutional Government in Morocco: A Referendum Endorses the Constitution," American Universities Field Staff, North Africa Series, Volume IX, No. 1 (Morocco), 1963; and Willard A. Beling, "Some Implications of the New Constitutional Monarchy in Morocco," *Middle East Journal* 18 (2, Spring 1964): 163–179. Ahmad Majid Binjalun provides a more royalist account in *Al-dustur al-maghribi: mabadiʾihi wa ahkamihi* [The Moroccan Constitution: Its Principles and Its Provisions] (Casablanca: dar al-kitab, 1977), pp. 73–83.

37. See Gallagher, "Towards Constitutional Government."

38. Charles F. Gallagher, "The Moroccan Constitution: Text and Comment," *American Universities Field Staff*, North Africa Series, Volume IX, No. 2 (Morocco), 1963, p. 4.

39. Ghalab, *Al-Tattawur al-dusturi*, pp. 313–317.

40. See Guilain Denoeux and Abdeslam Maghraoui, "King Hassan's Strategy of Political Dualism," *Middle East Policy* 5 (4, June 1998): 104–130.

41. I have written about the writing of the Kuwaiti constitution elsewhere. See *Rule of Law*, chapter 6. That account was based primarily on 'Uthman 'Abd al-Malik al-Salih, *Al-nizam al-dusturi wa-l-mu'assasat al-siyasiyya fi al-kuwayt* [The Constitutional System and Political Institutions in Kuwait] (Kuwait: Kuwait Times Press, 1989); 'Adil al-Tabtaba'i, *Al-nizam al-dusturi fi al-kuwayt* [The Constitutional System in Kuwait] (Kuwait: n.p., 1994); and British Foreign Office records. The treatment here is based on my previous work and some additional research consisting primarily in interviews of the surviving members of the Founding Assembly.

42. See Jill Crystal, *Oil and Politics in the Gulf: Rulers and Merchants in Kuwait and Qatar* (Cambridge: Cambridge University Press, 1995), pp. 85–86.

43. The information on the motives of the members of the Founding Assembly is derived largely from interviews with its members. In December 1997 I interviewed 'Abbas Munawwir and Yusuf al-Mukhlid.

44. For more detail on the controversy surrounding this action, its legal basis, and its constitutional implications, see Brown, *Rule of Law*, chapter 6.

45. The statement at the end of the popular conference on October 1990 was published by the Al-markaz al-a'lami al-kuwayti, Cairo, 1990.

46. Such statements were widely reported, for instance, in the constitutional crisis leading to the dissolution of parliament in 1999.

47. Al-mahmasani, *Al-dustur wa-l-dimuqratiyya*, p. 49.

48. See Salih al-Ashqar, "The Amir of Qatar Changes Clauses of the Basic System of Government, *Al-sharq al-awsat*, 24 October, 1996, p. 1.

49. Taj al-Din 'Abd al-Haqq, "The Constitution of the Emirates Moves from Settled Customs into Permanent Texts," *Al-majalla*, 30 June 1996, p. 33; and "The Emirates Make their Temporary Constitution Permanent," *Al-sharq al-awsat*, 21 May 1996, p. 1.

50. Nikolaus A. Siegfried, "Legislation and Legitimation in Oman: The Basic Law," *Islamic Law and Society* 7 (3 October 2000): 359.

51. Michael Herb, *All in the Family: Absolutism, Revolution, and Democracy in the Middle Eastern Monarchies* (Albany: SUNY Press, 1999). Herb does claim that the ambiguity of succession mechanisms actually enhances their resiliency. I do not share this view, but I do agree with Herb's observation that constitutions have been used to regulate succession. I would go on to observe that peninsular constitutions often do so in a way that clarifies procedures and enhances the position of the ruler without eliminating the role of the royal family (which Herb sees as critical).

52.   On this point generally, see John Finn, *Constitutions in Crisis: Political Violence and the Rule of Law* (New York: Oxford University Press, 1991).

Chapter 3. Republican Constitutions

1.   The text of the document can be found in Yusuf Qazma Khuri, *Al-dasatir fi al-'alim al-'arabi 1839–1987* (Beirut: Dar al-Hamra', 1989).

2.   Interwar politics in Syria is covered in Philip S. Khoury, *Syria and the French Mandate: The Politics of Arab Nationalism, 1920–1945* (Princeton: Princeton University Press, 1987); see also Elizabeth Thompson, *Colonial Citizens: Republican Rights, Paternal Privilege, and Gender in French Syria and Lebanon,* (New York: Columbia University Press, 2000). For constitutional details, see also Majid Khadduri, "Constitutional Development in Syria," *Middle East Journal* 5 (2, Spring 1951), 137–160. Also useful is Subhi Mahmasani, *Al-dustur wa-l-dimuqratiyya* [Constitution and Democracy], Beirut: Dar al-'ilm li-l-malayin, 1952.

3.   The episode is briefly recounted in Steven Heydemann, *Authoritarianism in Syria: Institutions and Social Conflict 1946–1970* (Ithaca: Cornell University Press, 1999), p. 155.

4.   For instance, two constitutional documents providing for union with other Arab countries (in 1963 with Iraq and Egypt and in 1971 with Libya and Egypt) were briefly drafted and forgotten.

5.   The major sources on the Lebanese constitution are Mahmasani, *Al-dustur wa-l-dimuqratiyya* and Ahmad Sirhal, *Dustur al-jumhuriyya al-lubnaniyya* [Constitution of the Lebanese Republic], Beirut: Dar al-bahith, 1991. A comprehensive political history that contains useful constitutional analysis is Meir Zamir's *Lebanon's Quest: The Road to Statehood 1926–1939* (London: I. B. Tauris, 1997).

6.   The Algerian regime's extended disinterest in constitutional texts has spread to the scholarly world. There are few writings on Algeria's constitutional development until the late 1980s when constitutions became far more central to Algerian politics. On Algeria's first two constitutions, it is worth consulting John P. Entelis, *Comparative Politics of North Africa* (Syracuse: Syracuse University Press, 1980), and Said Amir Arjomand, "Constitutions and the struggle for political order: A study in the modernization of political traditions," *Archives Européenes de Sociologie* 33 (1992): 39, which has a particularly rich discussion of the ideology underlying the 1976 constitution.

7.   William B. Quandt, *Revolution and Political Leadership: Algeria, 1954–1968* (Cambridge: MIT Press, 1969), p. 218.

8.   Arjomand, "Constitutions," p. 67.

9.   The political tribulations of Algeria over the past decade have been very well covered in the press; for a review that incorporates some constitutional analysis, see Mona Yacoubian, "Algeria's Struggle for Democracy: Prospects for Incremental Change," Council on Foreign Relation, Studies Department Occasional Paper Series, Number 3, 1997.

10. For one account of the period, see Lisa Anderson, *The State and Social Transformation in Tunisia and Libya, 1830–1980* (Princeton: Princeton University Press, 1986). For basic documents demonstrating the constitutional orientation of these groups, see 'Abd al-Fattah 'Umar and Qays Sa'id (editors), *Nusus wa-watha'iq siyasiyya tunisiyya* [Tunisian Political Texts and Documents] (Tunis: Markaz al-dirasat wa-l-buhuth wa-l-nashr bi kulliyyat al-huquq wa-l-'ulum al-siyasiyya, 1987).

11. Drafts of the assembly's work are included in 'Umar and Sa'id, *Nusus wa-watha'iq.*

12. The history of this debate is extensively covered in an essay by Zuhayr al-Mazfar, the president of the Tunisian Constitutional Council, printed in *7 Nuvimbir: Al-thawra al-hadi'a* [November 7: The Quiet Revolution], Tunis: Mu'assasat 'abd al-karim bin 'abd allah li-l-nashr wa-l-tawsi', 1992.

13. Ben 'Ali's declaration is printed in *ibid.* Only an unspecified medical report is mentioned in support of the argument that Bourguiba was incapable of performing the duties of the presidency. The strongest Arab precedent for such an action was the deposition of Talal in Jordan; that act was taken by the parliament.

14. See the coverage of the Tunisian presidential election in *Al-hayah*, 25 August 1999.

15. I have treated this effort to draft a constitution in *The Rule of Law in the Arab World: Courts in Egypt and the Gulf*, pp. 75–76

16. The text of these can be found in *Al-dasatir al-misriyya 1805–1971* [The Egyptian Constitutions 1805–1971] (Cairo: Markaz al-tanzim wa-l-mikrufilm, 1977).

17. See *ibid.* for the text of the 1956 constitution.

18. The texts of the documents can be found in *Al-dasatir al-misriyya.* For a contemporary political analysis of the circumstances of Egypt's constitutional development during this period, see P. J. Vatikiotis, "Some Political Consequences of the 1952 Revolution in Egypt," in P. M. Holt (editor), *Political and Social Changed in Modern Egypt: Historical Studies from the Ottoman Conquest to the United Arab Republic* (London: Oxford University Press, 1968).

19. Kevin Boyle and Adel Omar Sherif, "The Road to the 1971 Constitution—A Brief Constitutional History of Modern Egypt," in Kevin Boyle and Adel Omar Sherif (editors), *Human Rights and Democracy: The Role of the Supreme Constitutional Court of Egypt* (London: Kluwer Law International, 1996).

20. The discussion here is based on the minutes, copies of which are held in the library of the People's Assembly in Cairo. I am grateful to Bruce Rutherford for bringing the documents to my attention and to Adel Omar Sherif for arranging access. The minutes make Egypt's 1971 constitution easily the best documented Arab constitution.

21. Minutes of the Preparatory Committee for Drafting the Constitution, Committee on the System of Government, meeting of June 29, 1971, p. 7.

22. See Brown, *Rule of Law in the Arab World*, chapters 3 and 4.

23. For an argument that the decline of the ASU necessitated a strengthening of legal and judicial institutions, see James H. Rosberg, *Roads to the Rule of Law: The*

Emergence of an Independent Judiciary in Contemporary Egypt, (Ph.D. dissertation, Department of Political Science, Massachusetts Institute of Technology, 1995).

24.   On the presidential nature of the document, see Muhammad Mahir Abu al-'Aynayn, *Al-inhiraf al-tashri'i wa al-riqaba 'ala dusturiyya: dirasa tatbiqiyya fi misr* Cairo: Dar al-nahda al-'arabiyya, 1987.

25.   The most extended treatment of the subject is Ismail Raghib Khalidi's, *Constitutional Development in Libya* (Beirut: Khayat, 1956). For a shorter but sophisticated and more analytical treatment of Libya's constitutional development, see Karim Mezran, "Constitutionalism in Libya," in Sohail Hashimi and Houchang Chehabi, *Islam and Constitutonalism* (forthcoming).

26.   The text is printed in Khuri, *Al-dasatir.*

27.   An English translation can be found in Albert P. Blaustein and Gisbert H. Flanz (editors), *Constitutions of the World,* Dobbs Ferry: Oceana Publications.

Introduction to Part Two. Constitutions and Constitutionalism

1.   Philip A. Hamburger, "Natural Rights, Natural Law, and American Constitutions," *Yale Law Journal* 102 (1993): 907.

2.   Article V of the 1791 Polish constitution, as in Albert P. Blaustein and Jay A. Sigler (editors). *Constitutions that Made History* (New York: Paragon House, 1988), p. 74.

3.   Montesquieu, *The Spirit of Laws* (edited by David Wallace Carrithers, Berkeley: University of California Press, 1977), Book V, Chapter 11, p. 142.

4.   Holmes, "Precommitment," pp. 227–229.

5.   See John Finn, *Constitutions in Crisis: Political Violence and the Rule of Law* (New York: Oxford University Press, 1991), especially pp. 30–31.

6.   See Bruce Ackerman, *The Future of Liberal Revolution* (New Haven: Yale University Press, 1992).

7.   John Rawls, *The Law of Peoples* (Harvard: Harvard University Press, 1999), p. 140.

8.   For an explanation of forms of European constitutionalism emphasizing historical evolution and sociology rather than ideology and conscious design, see Thomas Ertman, *Birth of the Leviathan: Building States and Regimes in Medieval and Early Modern Europe* (Cambridge: Cambridge University Press, 1997).

9.   The American constitution struck a limited bargain over slavery; that bargain proved inadequate to address the territorial expansion of the United States. In the case of the Weimar constitution, the Nazi government undermined and then repudiated it. The resulting violence was ultimately even more horrific than in the American case.

10.   Ackerman's own political activism may be an example of this point, although it seems almost churlish to point this out. In 1998, he testified before Congress as a

constitutional authority opposed to the impeachment of President Bill Clinton. In his testimony he adduced the argument that impeachment approved by the House of Representatives in 1998 would expire with that body; the new House in January 1999 would have to impeach President Clinton again in order for the matter to be tried in the Senate. While the argument is plausible, one might suspect that Ackerman's constitutional interpretation was influenced primarily by its relevance to the immediate matter at hand.

11.   Jon Elster, Claus Offe, and Ulrich K. Reuss with Frank Boenker, Ulrike Goetting, and Friedbert W. Rueb, *Institutional Design in Post-communist Societies: Rebuilding the Ship at Sea* (Cambridge: Cambridge University Press, 1998).

12.   Article 66 of the 1831 Belgian constitution stated simply that "The King appoints and dismisses ministers." But Article 65 required that all royal decrees be countersigned by a minister who would be responsible for that act. Articles 89 and 90 barred ministers from adducing royal instructions for escaping responsibility and allowed the parliament the right to bring ministers to trial. See the text in Albert P. Blaustein and Jay A. Sigler (editors), *Constitutions that Made History* (New York: Paragon House, 1988). Unambiguous political responsibility of ministers to parliament rather than the monarchy emerged gradually from practice rather than from this text.

13.   Gaetano Mosca, *The Ruling Class* (edited and revised by Arthur Livingston, translated by Hannah D. Kahn, New York: McGraw-Hill, 1939 [originally published 1896]), pp. 261–264.

14.   Federalist 49, in *The Federalist*, p 330.

15.   While the Italian constitution hardly caused Mussolini's downfall, its mechanisms were used to depose him. More recently, the tremendous political changes associated with the downfall of communism in Eastern Europe were sometimes brought about by bringing latent constitutional provisions to life.

16.   See especially Carl J. Friedrich, *Transcendent Justice: The Religious Dimension of Constitutionalism* (Durham: Duke University Press, 1964).

17.   Daniel P. Franklin and Michael J. Baun (editors), *Political Culture and Constitutionalism: A Comparative Approach* (Armonk: M. E. Sharpe, 1995).

18.   See *The Rule of Law in the Arab World: Courts in Egypt and the Gulf* (Cambridge: Cambridge University Press, 1997).

19.   Montesquieu, *Laws*, Book XI, Chapter 6, p. 202.

20.   This is the argument adduced by Mosca. See *Ruling Class*, p. 140.

21.   Friedrich, *Constitutional Government*, p. 16.

22.   Loewenstein, *Political Power*, p. 128.

23.   The analogy between Islamic law and constitutional law is more fully addressed in Chapter Six. The analogy with natural law was more common in the nineteenth century but is still made today; for an example, see Tawfiq al-Shawi, *Siyadat al-shari'a al-islamiyya fi misr* (Mansoura: Al-zahra' li-l-a'lam al-'arabi, 1986), p. 10.

24. See Graham Walker, "The New Mixed Constitutions" in Irena Grudzin-ska Gross (editor), *Constitutionalism and Politics: International Symposium, November 11–14, 1993* (Bratislava: Slovak Committee of the European Cultural Foundation, 1994); and Brad Roth, "Constitutionalism in Eastern Europe: Alternatives to the Liberal Social Contract," *Dickinson Journal of International Law* 11 (2, Winter 1993): 283.

25. This argument is made more gently in Gary Jeffrey Jacobsohn, *Apple of Gold: Constitutionalism in Israel and the United States* (Princeton: Princeton University Press, 1993).

26. This argument is made, for instance, by John O. Haley, "Political Culture and Constitutionalism in Japan," in Franklin and Baun, *Political Culture.*

27. Hamburger, "Natural Rights."

28. See this argument as put forward by Kelsen, *General Theory,* p. 266.

Chapter 4. Parliamentarism and Constitutional Possibilities in the Arab World

1. See "The Jordanian National Assembly is an Independent Legislative Body," *Al-dustur,* 27 May 1998.

2. For a recent and useful exception, see Abdo Baaklini, Guilain Denoeux, and Robert Springborg, *Legislative Politics in the Arab World: The Resurgence of Democratic Institutions* (Boulder and London: Lynne Rienner Publishers, 1999).

3. Nigel G. Davidson, "The Constitution of Iraq" *Journal of Comparative Legislation and International Law* 7 (1925), pp. 46–47.

4. Mindful of this history, a Palestinian constitutional expert unsuccessfully suggested that Palestinian Assembly include a clause in the Basic Law requiring that every presidential decision be countersigned by a minister. Thus the minister would be politically accountable to the parliament even if the president was not. (Personal interview, Ahmad al-Khalidi, February 1997)

5. The practice of going outside the parliament for ministers has been debated most extensively in two countries: Jordan and Kuwait. Interestingly, advocates of parliamentary prerogatives generally take directly contrary positions in the two countries. In Jordan, some parliamentary critics charge that the practice of appointing members of parliament as ministers and deputy ministers saps the parliament of its strength. Ambitious parliamentarians jockey for positions in the frequently reshuffled cabinet by currying favor with the palace and other political leaders. In Kuwait, parliamentarians regularly pressure the prime minister to appoint a large number from their body. The practice of going outside the parliament for most cabinet positions is seen as bypassing the parliament; since several key cabinet positions are monopolized by members of the royal family, only a bold, even defiant, parliament would challenge their appointment.

6. The episode was covered extensively in the Kuwait press, but perhaps the best summary of the affair appeared in *Al-hayah*, 16 February 2000, p. 1.

7. On the institutional capacity of several Arab politics, see Baaklini et al., *Legislative Politics.*

8. The Kuwaiti parliament, one of the most generous, allows each member of parliament a small staff (generally three people), though moves have been made in recent years to increase this support slightly. These staff members provide support to the MP unrelated to drafting legislation (secretarial support and driving are far more common tasks than legal drafting). I did come across one case in which an individual member of parliament had proposed a fairly complex arbitration law. The MP, himself a lawyer, stated that he had turned primarily to outside bodies (such as the Chamber of Commerce) for assistance. (Mishari al-'Usaymi, personal interview, January 1995).

9. In a personal interview in December 1997, the secretary-general (senior administrative official) of the Egyptian People's Assembly, Sami Muharran, affirmed these conclusions, though he was insistent that individual MPs are given the support they need from parliamentary institutions.

10. One of the most notorious uses of agenda manipulation occurred with the presentation of amendments to the press law in Egypt in 1995. The speaker introduced the proposals without advanced warning in an evening session; they were passed as a routine matter at the same session after a superficial discussion. When some journalists had an opportunity to examine the amendments the parliament had passed, they denounced them as draconian and severely inhibiting of freedom of the press. A protracted confrontation between the government and the press syndicate led to passage of a revised law the following year.

11. I have noted this in virtually every parliamentary session I have witnessed. In Kuwait in 1995, the speaker declared a subject closed after a vote was taken. When one member of parliament sought to continue discussion of the matter, the speaker ordered his microphone cut off. In 1985 in a televised session of the Egyptian parliament, a member representing Luxor began a speech calling for a new bridge with references to his district's historical past. The speaker dismissively ordered the member to cease lecturing the parliament on Egyptian history; when the member continued in a very formal tone, the speaker continued to interrupt until the member sheepishly sat down. In 1999, I was present at a meeting of the Palestinian Legislative Council in which a pugnacious parliamentarian demanded to be told why the chair of the Council's budget committee had resigned. The speaker informed him not only that his intervention was out of order but that the matter was "none of your business." In a January 2000 budget debate, the speaker moved for a quick vote once he realized that government supporters momentarily outnumbered opponents in the chamber.

12. Recognizing this, some Western aid agencies and organizations have worked to support parliamentary institutions in recent years. In Morocco, Yemen, Egypt, and the Palestinian Authority, external actors have attempted to build a stronger parliamentary capacity for information gathering and legislative drafting.

13. Indeed, the secretary-general of the Egyptian parliament described the presidential role as the referee among the executive, legislative, and judicial branches. (Personal interview with Sami Muharran, December 1997) Such a role is not based on any constitutional text but on an unspoken—and generally nonconstitutional—image of the head of state as a sovereign actor.

14. James A. Rohr, "French Constitutionalism and the Administrative State: A Comparative Textual Study," *Administration and Society* 24 (2, August 1992), p. 237.

15. On the extent of fraud in the 1995 elections, see Eberhard Kienle, "More than a Response to Islamism: The Political Deliberalization of Egypt in the 1990s," *Middle East Journal* 52 (2, Spring 1998), pp. 219–235.

16. This view was expressed by Makram 'Ubayd, a founder of the Wafd party who later split with the party leadership, accusing it of corruption. See the debate on the issue of parliamentary sovereignty in the drafting committee as reported in *Ruz al-yusuf,* 1 February 1954, p. 10.

17. I have examined the growth of judicial power in *The Rule of Law in the Arab World,* especially chapter 4.

18. The approach of parliamentary elections in 2000 coincided with the arrest of Sa'd al-Din Ibrahim, a prominent intellectual involved in election-monitoring efforts. Security forces also arrested dozens of members of the Muslim Brotherhood, which was threatening to enter its candidates in the elections.

19. The action had the support of the members of the High Judicial Council. Since the judge was the only person involved willing to talk extensively about the move in public, the connection with the press law decision remained unclear. For some of the judge's comments, see "Former justice reiterates charges that judiciary lacks independence," *Jordan Times,* 23 April 1998.

20. The letter was printed in all the Jordanian dailies. See *Jordan Times,* 16 April 1998.

21. See Jill Crystal, *Oil and Politics in the Gulf: Rulers and Merchants in Kuwait and Qatar* (Cambridge: Cambridge University Press, 1995), for elaboration of this theme.

22. Shafeeq Ghabra, "Voluntary Associations in Kuwait: The Foundation of a New System," *Middle East Journal* 45 (2, Spring 1991), p. 205.

23. On the government's motives, see Crystal, *Oil and Politics,* p. 102. On the proposed modifications, see Salah al-Ghazzali, *Al-hayah al-dimuqratiyya fi al-kuwayt* [Democratic Life in Kuwait] (Kuwait: National Union of Kuwaiti Students), pp. 137–144.

24. See Shafeeq Ghabra, "Democratization in a Middle Eastern State: Kuwait, 1993," *Middle East Policy* 3 (1, 1994), p. 103, and Crystal, Oil and Politics, p. 105.

25. The account of post-1992 Kuwaiti parliamentary politics is based primarily on the Kuwaiti press coverage but also on interviews with parliamentarians carried out in 1994 and 1995.

26. Muhammad 'Abd al-Muhsin al-Muqatti', "Ahamiyyat al-ahzab al-siyasiyya li-tatwir al-nizam al-dimuqrati al-kuwayti wa-mashru'iyyatiha al-dusturiyya" [The importance of political parties for the development of the Kuwaiti democratic system and their constitutional legitimacy], unpublished paper presented at the 1997 Cairo Conference on "Democracy and the Rule of Law."

27. I have treated this issue in more detail in "Constituting Palestine: The Effort to Write a Basic Law for the Palestinian Authority," *Middle East Journal* 54 (1, Winter 2000): 24–43. I also hope to treat it in still more detail in *Resuming Arab Palestine* (forthcoming).

28. This information is based on interviews with participants in the process carried out in Gaza, Ramallah, and Nablus in December 1996 and February 1997.

29. This discussion is based primarily on Palestinian press coverage, supplemented by interviews with some of the Council members and legal experts engaged in the effort to draft the basic law. For the public argument between 'Arafat and Quray', see *Al-sharq al-awsat*, 31 July–2 August 1996.

Chapter 5. Judicial Review in Arab Constitutional Systems

1. Alexander Hamilton, John Jay, and James Madison, *The Federalist* (New York: The Modern Library, n.d., originally published 1787), p. 504.

2. Indeed, Cass Sunstein suggests that judicial review is the strongest surviving mechanism to play that role in the American political system; other mechanisms (the electoral college, indirect election of senators) have either declined or disappeared. "Constitutions and Democracies: An Epilogue," in Elster and Slagstad, *Constitutionalism and Democracy*, p. 337.

3. See Nils Stjernquist, "Judicial Review and the Rule of Law: Comparing the United States and Sweden," *Policy Studies Journal* 19 (1, Fall 1990), pp. 106–115.

4. Alec Stone, "The Birth and Development of Abstract Review: Constitutional Courts and Policymaking in Western Europe," *Policy Studies Journal* 19 (1, Fall 1990), p. 84.

5. Mauro Cappelletti, *Judicial Review in the Contemporary World* (Indianapolis: Bobbs-Merrill, 1971), pp. 72–73.

6. Hans Kelsen, the chief architect of the Austrian Constitutional Court, explicitly viewed it as a legislative body distinct from parliament and saw parliamentary appointment as a means of lessening the conflict between the two legislatures. See *General Theory of Law and State* (Cambridge: Harvard University Press, 1949), pp. 268–269. On the Austrian experiment generally, see Kelsen's article "Judicial Review of Legislation: A Comparative Study of the Austrian and the American Constitution," *Journal of Politics* 4 (1942): 183.

7. Robert S. Barker, "Taking Constitutionalism Seriously: Costa Rica's Sala Cuarta," *Florida Journal of International Law* 6 (3, Summer 1991), pp. 349–397.

8. The Indian court essentially held that certain clauses of the constitution took precedence over the rest of the constitution, even over amendments. Amending those clauses themselves easily circumvented the court's rulings, however. See Anthony R. Brunello and Kenneth F. Lehrman III, "Comparative Judicial Politics: Case Studies of the Federal Republic of Germany and the Republic of India," *Comparative Political Studies* 24 (3, October 1991), pp. 267–298.

9. Jon Elster revives the older current when he writes "Constitutionalism refers to limits on majority decisions; more specifically, to limits that are in some sense self-imposed" ("Introduction," in Elster and Slagstad, *Constitutionalism and Democracy*, p. 2). Yet in many recent cases the motivating force behind constitutionalism was to limit state authorities (acting on their own behalf, not on the behalf of the majority).

10. *The Role of the Constitutional Court in the Consolidation of the Rule of Law: Proceedings of the UniDem Seminar Organized in Bucharest on 8–10 June 1994 in Co-operation with the Romanian Constitutional Court with the Support of the Ministry of Foreign Affairs of Romania* (Strasbourg: Council of Europe, 1994), p. 15.

11. The text of the constitution is included in *Al-dasatir fi al-'alim al-'arabi 1839–1987* [Constitutions in the Arab World 1829–1987], prepared and investigated by Yusuf Qazma Khuri (Beirut: Dar al-hamra', 1989).

12. I am indebted to 'Adil al-Tabtaba'i of Kuwait University for pointing out the inclusion of judicial review in the 1925 constitution of Iraq. The Iraqi High Court consisted of nine members, five of whom (including the president) came from the Senate. The other four were senior judges. Thus the judicial role was diluted in a manner then sometimes used in Europe.

13. Abdel Rahman Nosseir, "The Supreme Constitutional Court of Egypt and the Protection of Human Rights," unpublished paper, 1992, p. 1.

14. Enid Hill, "Al-Sanhuri and Islamic Law," *Cairo Papers in Social Science* 10 (1987), pp. 95–96.

15. Interestingly, in two Arab countries—Jordan and Syria—some form of judicial review is mandated in the constitution but the courts themselves have widened the practice. The Jordanian case is discussed in the previous chapter. On Syria, see Nasrat Munla Haydar (president of the Syrian Supreme Constitutional Court), "The Role of the Judiciary in Defending Public Rights and Freedoms," unpublished paper, 1993. The paper was presented at a June 1993 conference on the judiciary and human rights sponsored by the Syrian Ministry of Justice.

16. 'Uthman 'Abd al-Malik al-Salih, *Al-nizam al-dusturi wa-l-mu'assasat al-siyasiyya fi al-kuwayt* [The Constitutional System and Political Institutions in Kuwait], Kuwait: Kuwait Times Press, 1989, pp. 665–67.

17. *Ibid.*, p. 664; 'Adil al-Tabtaba'i, *Al-nizam al-dusturi fi al-kuwayt* [The Constitutional System in Kuwait], Kuwait: n.p., 1994, pp. 885–893.

18. See the text as printed in Khuri, *Al-dasatir*.

19. The text of the 1971 constitution can be found in Albert P. Blaustein and Gisbert H. Flanz (editors), *Constitutions of the World*, Dobbs Ferry: Oceana Publications.

This reference is periodically updated; the UAE constitution is included in the 1973 supplement.

20. On the 1970 Yemeni constitution and the 1973 Sudanese constitution, see Blaustein and Flanz, *Constitutions of the World,* 1971 and 1974. On the 1992 Yemeni constitution, see *Arab Law Quarterly* 7 (1, 1992), p. 70.

21. Blaustein and Flanz, *Constitutions of the World,* 1991.

22. Rafi' ibn 'Ashur, "The Question of Constitutional Review of Laws and its Development in the End of 1987," *Al-majalla al-qanuniyya al-tunisiyya,* 1988, p. 9.

23. On Algeria, see Kahlula Muhammad, "Constitutional Review in Algeria in the Framework of the work of the Constitutional Council," *Al-majalla al-jaza-'iriyya li-l-'ulum al-qanuniyya wal-iqtisadiyya wa-l-siyasiyya* 28 (3, September 1990), p. 666. For the text of the 1989 constitution establishing the council, see *Arab Law Quarterly* 9 (1/1994), p. 107. On the Lebanese constitutional council, see Chibli Mallat, "Constitutional law in the Middle East: The emergence of judicial power," SOAS Law Department, working paper no. 3, February 1993, SOAS, University of London, p. 31.

24. The matter has been discussed at great length in the Kuwait. Two legal analyses of the issues involved are 'Adil al-Tabtaba'i, "The Extent of the Jurisdiction of the National Assembly in Examining Decree-Laws Issued in the Case of Dissolution," 1994 Arabic manuscript [a subsequent version was to be published in the Kuwaiti *al-Muhamah*], and Ibrahim Muhammad al-Humud, "The Effects Resulting from the Parliament's Refusal of Law Number 35/1990, Issued in the Period of the Suspension of Parliamentary Life," *Majallat al-huquq* 18 (3/September 1994), p. 560.

25. See Mallat, "Constitutional Law in the Middle East," and "A Concentration on More Modest Tasks from the Heights of Supreme Policies," *Al-hayah,* 10 November 1993.

26. Kahlula Muhammad, "Constitutional Review."

27. Kamal Abu al-Majd, personal interview, November 1995. Abu al-Majd is a leading intellectual and constitutional scholar with close ties to the regime.

28. Interviews with Kuwaiti legal scholars and parliamentarians, April 1994 and January 1995.

29. It is possible that the Jordanian High Court will carve out a role for itself based not on abstract review but in connection with concrete cases. Its ruling on the press law constitutes a possible precedent here, though the Court has been publicly warned by the King not to repeat such rulings. See chapter 4 for more details.

30. Indeed, I first heard the constitutional argument against transferring civilian cases to military courts during a personal interview with a member of the Supreme Constitutional Court in 1991.

31. Administrative courts have jurisdiction in all cases in which an official actor is a party. In November 1995, lawyers for some Muslim Brotherhood leaders being tried in military courts resorted to the administrative courts to challenge the president's order transferring their case to the military courts. The military courts refused to sus-

pend the case as they would normally be required to do and convicted most of those charged. As of this writing the Supreme Constitutional Court has yet to rule on the constitutional issue. The Court did rule on another aspect of the issue several years ago, however. The law establishing the Court also allows specific officials to refer questions of law to it for clarification. The minister of justice therefore asked the Court in 1993 if the referrals were legal under the law governing the military courts. While the Court upheld the government's interpretation of the law, it did not speak to the constitutional issue. Yet the military courts interpreted the Supreme Constitutional Court's ruling as a constitutional one. In 1995 I asked the president of the military courts in a private meeting if any civilian defendant had ever challenged the constitutionality of the military court's jurisdiction. He responded (incorrectly) that the Supreme Constitutional Court had ruled definitively on the issue.

32. 'Adil al-Tabtaba'i, personal communication, February 1995.

33. The situation is not unique to the Arab world. Brazil's Supreme Federal Tribunal refused to overturn a presidential decree that prevented it from issuing preliminary injunctions or provisional proceedings against President Collor's freeze of Brazilian bank accounts. While a cogent constitutional challenge could have been made to the freeze, the freeze would have expired by the time it would have reached the Tribunal through normal channels. See Keith S. Rosenn, "Brazil's New Constitution: An Exercise in Transient Constitutionalism for a Transitional Society," *American Journal of Comparative Law* 38 (1990), pp. 792–793.

34. In interviews with Qatari judges and lawyers in 1994, all expressed the opinion to me that there had never been a constitutional claim made in a Qatari court.

35. Elizabeth Thompson, *Colonial Citizens* (New York: Columbia University Press, 2000), p. 53.

36. For a defense of this view, see al-Humud, "Parliament's Rejection of Law."

37. For a more comprehensive treatment of the subject of constitutionalism and emergency powers, see John E. Finn, *Constitutions in Crisis: Political Violence and the Rule of Law* (New York: Oxford University Press, 1991).

38. Many Arab judges regard the "acts of sovereignty" with a strong measure of embarrassment. In 1996, I presented a critique of the doctrine at a seminar at the Jordanian judicial training academy. One judge responded (to general approval) that the doctrine was a "black page in the history of the Arab judiciary."

39. The information on Syria is based on Haydar, "Role of the Judiciary."

40. Nosseir, "The Supreme Constitutional Court," p. 12.

41. The record of the deliberations of the committee that drafted the 1971 constitution are available but are not regularly consulted by members of the court. Personal interview, Adel Omar Sherif, Commissioners Body of the Supreme Constitutional Court, May 1995.

42. This is the clear implication of the presentation of the issue by 'Awad El-Morr, "The Supreme Constitutional Court," p. 256.

43. This passage is based on Nosseir, "The Supreme Constitutional Court," pp. 45–50. If the Court continues along this path, the political implications may be significant. In Austria, the adoption of the European Convention on Human Rights on a constitutional level transformed the Constitutional Court from a passive into an activist body. Rudolf Machacek, *Austrian Contributions to the Rule of Law* (Kehl: N. P. Engel, 1994), p. 16.

Chapter 6. Islamic Constitutionalism

1. For an older expression of this consensus, see Hamilton Gibb, "Constitutional Organization," in Majid Khadduri and Herbert J. Liebesny (editors), *Law in the Middle East. Volume I. Origin and Development of Islamic Law* (Washington: Middle East Institute, 1955).

2. Hamid Enayat, *Modern Islamic Political Thought* (Austin: University of Texas Press, 1982), p. 131.

3. Ibn Taymiyya is often cited by modern writers in this regard. See Emmanuel Sivan, *Radical Islam* (New Haven: Yale University Press, 1990). See also Sherman A. Jackson, "From Prophetic Actions to Constitutional Theory: A Novel Chapter in Medieval Muslim Jurisprudence," *International Journal of Middle East Studies* 25 (1, 1993): 71–90.

4. The argument in these two paragraphs is based on my article "Shari'a and State in the Modern Middle East," *International Journal of Middle East Studies* 29 (1997): 359–376.

5. In the following paragraphs I concentrate primarily on those writers who have gained less attention in the English-language literature (such as Muhammad al-'Awwa and 'Abd al-Qadir 'Awda).

6. For examples of scholarship on Islamic law that concentrate on its dynamic rather than rigid nature, see Brinkley Messick, *The Calligraphic State: Textual Domination and History in a Muslim Society* (Berkeley: University of California Press, 1993); and Wael B. Hallaq, *Law and Legal Theory in Classical and Medieval Islam* (Aldershot: Valiorum, 1994). To be fair, al-Sanhuri questioned the view that the *shari'a* was incapable of development. But he did see the *'ulama* as relying excessively on *taqlid* [imitation, or acceptance of past opinions as authoritative] and insufficiently on *ijtihad* [independent reasoning]. See his essay, "On What Basis Will the Egyptian Civil Code be Improved," *Al-kitab al-dhahabi li-l-mahakim al-ahliyya* [The Golden Book of the National Courts] (Cairo: Al-matba'a al-amiriyya bi-bulaq, 1937), pp. 118–121.

7. For an English-language treatment of Rashid Rida's ideas on an Islamic state, see Enayat, *Modern Islamic Political Thought*, chapter 3.

8. For direct and succinct expressions of al-Sanhuri's views, see "Our Legal Duty after the Treaty," *Al-ahram*, 1 January 1937; and "On What Basis Will the

Egyptian Civil Code be Improved." See also Enid Hill, "Al-Sanhuri and Islamic Law," *Cairo Papers in Social Science* 10 (1, 1987): 1; and Brown, *The Rule of Law in the Arab World*. Also of interest in Shwikar Ibrahim Elwan, *Constitutional Democracy and Islam: A Comparative Study*, Ph.D. dissertation, Emory University, 1971.

9. 'Abd al-Qadir 'Awda, *Al-islam wa-awda'na al-qanuniyya* [Islam and Our Legal Situation] (Beirut: Mu'assasat al-risala, 1985; originally published 1951), pp. 14 and 17.

10. Ibid., p. 61.

11. Ibid., pp. 14–18.

12. See, for instance, his *Al-nizam al-ijtima'i fi al-islam* [Social Order in Islam] (Jerusalem: Hizb al-Tahrir, 1953)

13. The testimony came in the trial of the accused killer of Egyptian secularist Faraj Fawda. Al-Ghazzali argued that the ruler of the community was required to take action in such a case. If the ruler did not take action, the offense would not be cancelled but individuals who took it upon themselves to punish the offense would be operating outside of the law. See "Al-Ghazzali: No Punishment in Islam for Anyone Who Kills an Apostate," *Al-hayah*, 23 June 1993.

14. Sayyid Qutb, *Milestones* (Cedar Rapids: Mother Mosque Foundation, N.C., originally published 1966), pp. 10–11.

15. See Sivan *Radical Islam*; see also Rudolph Peters (editor), *Jihad in Classical and Modern Islam : A Reader* (Princeton: Markus Wiener, 1996).

16. See Leonard Binder, *Islamic Liberalism: A Critique of Development Ideologies* (Chicago: University of Chicago Press, 1988), Chapter Five for a comparison of Mawdudi and Qutb along these lines.

17. Qutb, *Signposts*, pp. 20–21.

18. Ahmad Kamal Abu al-Majd, "Nazarat hawla al-fiqh al-dusturi fi al-islam," lecture delivered January 9, 1962 (Cairo: Matba'at al-azhar); Rashid Ghannushi, *Al-hurriyyat al-'amma fi al-islam* [Public Freedoms in Islam] (Beirut: Markaz dirasat al-wihda al-'arabiyya, 1993); Muhammad Salim al-'Awwa, *Fi al-nizam al-siyasi li-l-dawla al-islamiyya* (Cairo: Al-maktab al-misri al-hadith, 1983); see also the translation of an earlier and shorter edition, Mohamed S. El-Awa, *On the Political System of the Islamic State* (Indianapolis: American Trust Publications, 1980); and Tawfiq Shawi, *Fiqh al-shura wa-l-istishara* (Mansura: Dar al-wafa', 1992).

19. El-Awa, *Political System of the Islamic State*, p. i.

20. Both the modern Arabic term *siyada* and the term coined by Mawdudi, *hakimiyya* are used, generally interchangeably, to refer to sovereignty.

21. Ghannushi, *Al-huriyyat al-'amma*, p. 105.

22. Tawfiq Shawi, *Siyadat al-shari'a al-islamiyya fi misr*, (al-Mansura: Al-zahra' li-l-a'lam al-'arabi, 1986), p. 8.

23. Shawi, *Fiqh al-shura wa-l-istishara*, pp. 168–170.

24. I have expanded on this idea in Brown, "Shari'a and State."

25.   Lawyers Committee for Human Rights, *Islam and Justice* (New York: Lawyers Committee for Human Rights, 1997), p. 115. Ghannushi's statement came in the context of a discussion with human rights activists.

26.   Shawi, *Fiqh al-shura wa-l-istishara*, pp. 195–196.

27.   Al-'Awwa, *Political System*, p. 86.

28.   El-Awa, *Political System*, p. 27.

29.   Ghannushi, *Al-hurriyyat al-'amma.* See also Ann Elizabeth Mayer, *Islam and Human Rights* (Boulder: Westview Press, 1995).

30.   Abu al-Majd, "Nazarat hawla al-fiqh al-dusturi."

31.   These attitudes come out clearly in the discussion recorded in Lawyers Committee, *Islam and Justice.*

32.   For a version of the argument in English, see M. Sa'id al-'Ashmawi, "Shari'a in the Discussion on Secularism and Democracy," in Christopher Tell and Jakop Skovgaard-Petersen (editors), *Law and the Islamic World: Past and Present* (Copenhagen: Royal Danish Academy of Sciences and Letters, 1995). For an exposition of al-'Ashmawi's views, see William E. Shepard, "Muhammad Sa'id al-'Ashmawi and the Application of the Shari'a in Egypt," *International Journal of Middle East Studies* 28 (1, February 1996): 39.

33.   Abdullah Ahmed An-Na'im, "Constitutionalism and Islamization in the Sudan," *Africa Today* 36 (3/4, 1989), pp. 11–12.

34.   In an extended debate in the Egyptian press in the late 1980s, various interpretations were offered of the *hadith* in which the Prophet instructed those confronting evil to change it with their hands; those who are unable to use their hands should use their tongues; and those unable to use their tongues should use their hearts. The view advanced by radical Islamists was that the *hadith* legitimated direct action (use of the hand) against rulers who refused to enforce the *shari'a.* The view of more establishment figures was that direct action was a community rather than individual obligation and as such could only be undertaken under the leadership of the ruler.

35.   In his celebrated testimony in the trial of the accused assassins of Faraj Fawda, for instance, Muhammad al-Ghazzali effectively declared those who oppose application of the *shari'a* as apostates. This position frightened the more secular minded. Yet al-Ghazzali went on to say that punitive action should be undertaken by the ruler and that those who acted on their own were vigilantes.

36.   *Majmu'at rasa'il al-imam al-shahid Hasan al-Banna*, (Beirut: Dar al-Shihab, 1993), pp. 170–174.

37.   Charles F. Gallagher, "Toward Constitutional Government in Morocco: A Referendum Endorses the Constitution," American Universities Field Staff reports, Volume IX, No. 1 (Morocco), 1963.

38.   See the political *fatwas* [religious responsa] in Yusuf al-Qardawi, *Fatawi mu'asira, al-juz' al-thani* [Contemporary Fatwas, Part Two], Mansura: Dar al-wafa' li-l-taba'a wa-l-nashr wa-l-tawzi', 1993.

39.   For the constitution and an analysis, see Sa'id al-Hasan, *The Concept of the Rules of Public Order in the Political Thought of Hizb al-Tahrir*, M.A. thesis, Department of economics and political science, American University in Cairo, October 1989.

40.   Ghannushi, *Al-hurriyyat al-'amma*, p. 116.

41.   Rashid Ghannushi and Kamal Abu al-Majd come closer to this pole.

42.   Tawfiq Shawi and 'Abd al-Qadir 'Awda probably lean toward this pole, though al-Shawi seems more willing to engage in creative and original approaches.

43.   See Introduction to Part Two, note 24, above.

44.   Montesquieu, *The Spirit of Laws* (edited by David Wallace Carrithers, Berkeley: University of California Press, 1977), p. 200.

45.   The discussions of the drafting committee for the 1923 constitution were published by Egypt's Senate: Majlis al-shuyukh, *Al-dustur: ta'liqat 'ala mawadihi bi-l-a'mal al-tahdiriyya wa-l-munaqashat al-barlamaniyya* [The Constitution: Commentaries on its Provisions in the Preparatory Efforts and the Parliamentary Discussions], Cairo: Matba'at misr, 1940.

46.   See *Majmu'at rasa'il al-imam al-shahid Hasan al-Banna*, pp. 170–174 and 215–218.

47.   The minutes of the drafting committee are kept in the Majlis al-Sha'b library in Cairo. See also Joseph P. O'Kane, "Islam in the New Egyptian Constitution: Some Discussions in *al-Ahram*," *Middle East Journal* 26 (2, 1972): 137–148, for an excellent coverage of the debate in the press. A leading legal authority and influential writer on the topic, Jamal al-'Utayfi, gathered some of his articles in *Ara' fi al-shari'a wa-fi al-hurriyya* [Opinions on Shari'a and Freedom], Cairo: Al-hay'a al-misriyya al-'amma li-l-kitab, 1980. Al-'Utayfi's articles are especially worth studying because they represent fairly authoritative presentations of the views that ultimately prevailed; they are also fairly accurate indications of how Article 2 would eventually be interpreted.

48.   It is not clear why the final version referred to *tashri'* rather than *taqnin*. The first term is more commonly used for the legislative process, but it is derived from the word *shari'a*. The second word is more commonly used for codification of law, but it is derived from the word *qanun*, which has come to indicate positive law.

49.   For some of the debate over the role for the Islamic *shari'a* during this period, see Bernard Botiveau, "Contemporary Reinterpretations of Islamic Law: The Case of Egypt," in Chibli Mallat, *Islam and Public Law* (London: Graham and Troutman, 1993).

50.   The Court's rulings have been examined by several scholars, especially at two conferences sponsored by the Court in Cairo in 1996 and 1997. The contributions are being published; the Court's rulings on Article 2 were examined in 1996 by Baber Johansen and in 1997 by Frank Vogel, John Murray and Mohamed El-Molla, and Nathan Brown. See also Hatem Aly Labib Gabr, "The Interpretation of Article 2 of the Constitution: Islamic Sharia Principles as a Source of Law," in Kevin Boyle and Adel Omar Sherif, *Human Rights and Democracy: The Role of the Supreme Constitutional Court of Egypt* (London: Kluwer, 1996).

51. This ruling is discussed by Gabr, "Interpretation of Article 2."

52. Case 8, Judicial Year 17, issued by the Supreme Constitutional Court 18 May 1996.

53. The idea that Islamic jurisprudence has been influenced not only by divine guidance but also by prevailing ideas and conditions (which are far more subject to change) is not new. Some in the past have been willing to go so far as to argue that the founders of Islamic jurisprudence were influenced by social practice as much as text. See, for example, Haim Gerber's presentation of the argument by Muhammad Amin ibn 'Abdin, a Damascus-based mufti of the late eighteenth and early nineteenth centuries. (*Islamic Law and Culture 1600–1840*, Leiden: Brill, 1999, Chapter 6). When this argument is made in the context of an attempt to bring positive legislation in line with Islamic jurisprudence, however, the effects are far-reaching and effectively liberate rulers considerably.

54. Case number 5; Judicial year 8 (submitted in 1986; decided in 1996).

55. Khumayni, *Islamic Government*. Khumayni's ideas have been covered extensively in the Western scholarly literature. For a particularly accessible English-language account, see Roy Mottahadeh, *The Mantle of the Prophet*, (New York: Pantheon, 1985).

56. See Said Amir Arjomand, "Authority in Shi'ism and Constitutional Developments in the Islamic Republic of Iran," in W. Ende and R. Brunner (editors), *The Twelver Shia in Modern Times: Religious Culture and Political History* (Leiden: Brill, 2000).

57. This account is based primarily on Arjomand, "Authority in Shi'ism;" Shaul Bakhash, *The Reign of the Ayatollahs*, (New York: Basic Books, 1984); Said Arjomand, *The Turban for the Crown* (New York: Oxford University Press, 1988); and Asghar Schirazi, *The Constitution of Iran: Politics and the State in the Islamic Republic* (London: I. B. Tauris, 1997). The interpretation here follows Arjomand's in spirit most closely. Schirazi's account is by far the most comprehensive and in addition is quite sophisticated in its analysis and very thoroughly researched, and I have relied on it fairly heavily elsewhere in this chapter. However, on the drafting of the constitution he implies an implausible level of consistent duplicity (rather than initial disinterest in constitutional drafting) on the part of Khumayni and other members of the *'ulama*. See also the comments of Ayatollah Montazeri in "Re-Thinking the Islamic Republic: A 'Conversation' with Ayatollah Hossein 'Ali Montazeri," *Middle East Journal* 55 (1, Winter 2001): 15.

58. Chibli Mallat, *The Renewal of Islamic Law* (Cambridge: Cambridge University Press, 1993), chapters 2 and 3.

59. Khumayni's extraconstitutional actions are best described by Schirazi, *Constitution of Iran*, and Arojomand, "Authority in Shi'ism."

60. See Mallat, *The Renewal of Islamic Law*, Chapter Three; Schirazi, *Constitution of Iran*, "Khomeyni Expands Government's Powers, Boosts Radicals' Agenda," *Foreign Broadcast Information Service Trends* 27 January 1988; and "Khomeyni-

Created Arbitration Body Undercuts Conservatives," Foreign Broadcast Information Service *Trends* 24 February 1988.

61. This interpretation is favored by Schirazi, *Constitution of Iran*, and Arjomand, *Turban for the Crown*, pp. 71–80.

62. For a comprehensive treatment of attitudes toward constitutionalism among the Iranian *'ulama* in the twentieth century, see Abdul-Hadi Hairi, *Shi'ism and Constitutionalism in Iran: A Study of the Role Played by the Persian Residents of Iraq in Iranian Politics*, Leiden, E. J. Brill, 1977.

63. Al-'Awwa makes these views clear in an appendix on the Iranian constitution in *Fi al-nizam al-siyasi*.

64. Muhammad Baqir al-Sadr, *Lamha fiqhiyya tamhidiyya 'an mashru' dustur al-jumhuriyya al-islamiyya fi iran* [A Preparatory Jurisprudential Glimpse of the Draft Constitution of the Islamic Republic of Iran] (n.p., 1399 A.H.). For a much more extensive treatment of al-Sadr's political views, see Mallat, *Renewal of Islamic Law*, especially chapter 2.

65. Al-Sadr speaks here of the "*marja'*" apparently referring to a single individual who is a "source of imitation" or leading *mujtahid* and the "*marja'iyya*" which is the council through which much (though not all) of this authority is exercised.

66. See Mallat, *Renewal of Islamic Law*, chapters 2 and 3.

67. This struggle over the relationship between the Islamic *shari'a* and parliamentary legislation is best traced by Schirazi, *Constitution of Iran*, Parts Three and Four.

68. See Stephen C. Fairbanks, "Theocracy versus Democracy: Iran Considers Political Parties," *Middle East Journal* 52 (1, Winter 1998): 17–31 for an analysis of the political circumstances of Khatami's election focusing on the problem of political parties in the Islamic Republic.

69. Said Amir Arjomand, "Civil Society and the Rule of Law in the Constitutional Politics of Iran under President Khatami," *Social Research* 76 (2, 2000): 1–20.

Conclusion: Lessons from the Arab Constitutional Experience

1. For an account of political liberalization in Jordan—albeit one that stresses bargains among elite individuals rather than institutions—see Malik Mufti, "Elite Bargains and the Onset of Political Liberalization in Jordan," *Comparative Political Studies* 32 (1, February 1999): 100–129.

BIBLIOGRAPHY

Interviews

Mishari al-'Usaymi, Kuwaiti member of parliament, Kuwait, April 1994 and January 1995

'Abbas al-Munawwir, member of Kuwaiti Founding Assembly, Kuwait, December 1997

Yusuf al-Mukhlid, member of Kuwaiti Founding Assembly, Kuwait, December 1997

Haydar 'Abd al-Shafi, member, Palestinian Legislative Council, Gaza, February 1997

Ahmad al-Khalidi, Palestinian legal and constitutional scholar, Nablus, February 1997

Camille Mansur, Palestinian legal and constitutional scholar, Bir Zayt, February 1997

Raji al-Surani, Palestinian human rights activitst, Gaza, February 1997

Kamal Abu al-Majd, Egyptian legal and constitutional scholar, Cairo, November 1994

Sharhabil al-Za'im, Palestinian lawyer, Gaza, February 1997

Sami Muharran, Secretary-General, Egyptian People's Assembly, Cairo, December 1997

Newspapers and magazines

Al-ahram, Cairo, daily
Al-ayyam, Jerusalem, daily
Al-dustur, Jordan, daily
Al-haya, London, daily
Al-majalla, London, weekly
Al-qabas, Kuwait, daily

229

Al-sharq al-awsat, London, daily
Al-watan, Kuwait, daily
Filastin, Jordan, daily
Jordan Times, Jordan, daily
Ruz al-yusuf, Cairo, weekly

Archives

British foreign office records
Minutes of the Preparatory Committee for Drafting the Constitution, [for the Arab
    Republic of Egypt, 1971] (held in the library of the Majlis al-Shaʻb, Cairo)

Books and articles

Abdo, Geneive. "Re-Thinking the Islamic Republic: A 'Conversation' with Ayatollah
    Hossein ʻAli Montazeri," *Middle East Journal* 55 (1, Winter 2001): 9–24.
Abu al-ʻAynayn, Muhammad Mahir. *Al-inhiraf al-tashriʻi wa al-riqaba ʻala dusturiyya:
    dirasa tatbiqiyya fi misr* [Legislative Deviation and Constitutional Review: An
    Applied Study in Egypt] (Cairo: Dar al-nahda al-ʻarabiyya, 1987).
Abu Jaber, Kamel S. "The Legislature of the Hashemite Kingdom of Jordan: A Study
    in Political Development," *The Muslim World* 59 (3, July/October 1969):
    220–250.
Abu Nowar, Maʼan. *The History of the Hashemite Kingdom of Jordan. Volume I. The
    Creation and Development of Transjordan: 1920–1929* (Oxford: Ithaca Press,
    1989).
Abu al-Majd, Ahmad Kamal. "Nazara hawla al-fiqh al-dusturi fi al-islam" [A View
    Concerning Constitutional Jurisprudence in Islam], lecture delivered January
    9, 1962 (Cairo: Matbaʻat al-azhar).
Ackerman, Bruce. *The Future of Liberal Revolution* (New Haven: Yale University Press,
    1992).
Al-dasatir al-misriyya 1805–1971: nusus wa-tahlil [The Egyptian Constitutions 1805–
    1971: Texts and Analysis] (Cairo: Markaz al-tanzim wa-l-mikrufilm, 1976).
Ahamidah, Khalifah. *Constitutional Court of Kuwait: A Comparative Study,* Ll.M.
    paper, Harvard University, Harvard Law School, 1996-1997.
Al-kitab al-dhahabi li-l-mahakim al-ahliyya [The Golden Book of the National Courts]
    (Cairo: Al-matbaʻa al-amiriyya bi-bulaq, 1937).
An-Naʻim, Abdullah Ahmed. "Constitutionalism and Islamization in the Sudan,"
    Africa Today 36 (3/4, 1989): 11–28.
Anderson, Lisa. *The State and Social Transformation* (Princeton: Princeton University
    Press, 1986).

Arjomand, Said Amir. "Authority in Shi'ism and Constitutional Developments in the Islamic Republic of Iran," in W. Ende and R. Brunner (editors), *The Twelver Shia in Modern Times: Religious Culture and Political History* (Leiden: Brill, 2000).

———. "Civil Society and the Rule of Law in the Constitutional Politics of Iran under President Khatami," *Social Research* 76 (2, 2000): 1-20.

———. "Constitutions and the struggle for political order: A study in the modernization of political traditions," *Archives Européennes de Sociologie* 33 (4, 1992): 39–82.

———. *The Turban for the Crown* (New York: Oxford University Press, 1988).

'Awda, 'Abd al-Qadir. *Al-Islam wa-awda'na al-qanuniyya* [Islam and Our Legal Situation] (Beirut: Mu'assasat al-risala, 1985).

'Awwa, Muhammad Salim al-. *Fi al-nizam al-siyasi li-l-dawla al-islamiyya* (Cairo: Al-maktab al-misri al-hadith, 1983).

——— [Mohamed S. El-Awa]. *On the Political System of the Islamic State* (Indianapolis: American Trust Publications, 1980).

Baaklini, Abdo, Guilain Denoeux, and Robert Springborg, *Legislative Politics in the Arab World: The Resurgence of Democratic Institutions* (Boulder and London: Lynne Rienner Publishers, 1999).

Bakhash, Shaul. *The Reign of the Ayatollahs*, (New York: Basic Books, 1984).

Barker, Robert S. "Taking Constitutionalism Seriously: Costa Rica's Sala Cuarta," *Florida Journal of International Law* 6 (Summer 1991, number 3): 349–397.

Bayat, Mangol. *Iran's First Revolution: Shi'ism and the Constitutional Revolution of 1905–1909* (New York: Oxford University Press,1991).

Binder, Leonard. *Islamic Liberalism: A Critique of Development Ideologies* (Chicago: University of Chicago Press, 1988).

Binjalun, Ahmad Majid. *Al-dustur al-maghribi: mabadi'ihi wa ahkamihi* [The Moroccan Constitution: Its Principles and Its Provisions] (Casablanca: Dar al-kitab, 1977).

Blaustein, Albert P. and Gisbert H. Flanz (editors). *Constitutions of the World* (Dobbs Ferry: Oceana Publications, various years).

Blaustein, Albert P., and Jay A. Sigler (editors). *Constitutions that Made History* (New York: Paragon House, 1988).

Beling, Willard A. "Some Implications of the New Constitutional Monarchy in Morocco," *Middle East Journal* 18 (2, Spring 1964): 163–179.

Boyle, Kevin, and Adel Omar Sharif, *Human Rights and Democracy: The Role of the Supreme Constitutional Court of Egypt* (London: Kluwer Law International, 1996).

Brown, Leon Carl. *The Surest Path: The Political Treatise of a Nineteenth-Century Muslim Statesman, A Translation of the Introduction to* The Surest Path To Knowledge Concerning The Condition of Countries *by Khayr al-Din al-Tunisi*, Harvard Middle Eastern Monographs, XVI, Center for Middle Eastern Studies, Harvard University, 1967.

————. *The Tunisia of Ahmad Bey 1837–1855* (Princeton: Princeton University Press, 1974).

Brown, Nathan J. "Constituting Palestine: The Effort to Write a Basic Law for the Palestinian Authority," *Middle East Journal* 54 (1, Winter 2000): 24–43.

————. *Peasant Politics in Modern Egypt: The Struggle Against the State* (New Haven: Yale University Press, 1990).

————. "The Precarious Life and Slow Death of the Mixed Courts of Egypt," *International Journal of Middle East Studies* 25 (1, 1993): 1.

————. *Resuming Arab Palestine* (forthcoming).

————. *The Rule of Law in the Arab World: Courts in Egypt and the Gulf* (Cambridge: Cambridge University Press, 1997).

————. "Shari'a and State in the Modern Middle East," *International Journal of Middle East Studies* 29 (3, 1997): 359–376.

Brunello, Anthony R., and Kenneth F. Lehrman III. "Comparative Judicial Politics: Case Studies of the Federal Republic of Germany and the Republic of India," *Comparative Political Studies* 24 (3, October 1991): 267–298.

Cannon, Byron. *Politics of Law and the Courts in Nineteenth-Century Egypt* (Salt Lake City: University of Utah Press, 1988).

Cappelletti, Mauro. *Judicial Review in the Contemporary World* (Indianapolis: Bobbs-Merrill, 1971).

Cole, Juan R. I. *Colonialism and Revolution in the Middle East: Social and Cultural Origins of Egypt's 'Urabi Movement* (Princeton: Princeton University Press, 1993).

Crystal, Jill. *Oil and Politics in the Gulf: Rulers and Merchants in Kuwait and Qatar* (Cambridge: Cambridge University Press, 1995).

Davidson, Nigel G. "The Constitution of Iraq" *Journal of Comparative Legislation and International Law* 7 (Fall 1925): 41–52

Davison, Roderic H. *Essays in Ottoman and Turkish History, 1774–1923: The Impact of the West* (Austin: University of Texas Press, 1990).

————. *Reform in the Ottoman Empire 1856-1876,* (Princeton: Princeton University Press, 1963).

Deeb, Marius. *Party Politics in Egypt: The Wafd and its Rivals, 1919–1939* (London: Ithaca Press, 1979).

Denoeux, Guilain, and Abdeslam Maghraoui. "King Hassan's Strategy of Political Dualism," *Middle East Policy* 5 (4, June 1998): 104–130.

Devereux, Robert. *The First Ottoman Constitutional Period: A Study of the Midhat Constitution and Parliament* (Baltimore: Johns Hopkins Press, 1963).

Disuqi, 'Abd al-Mun'im al-. "The Position of Village 'Umdas and Shaykhs in the Sidqi Election of 1931," *Al-majalla al-ta'rikhiyya al-misriyya* 27 (1981): 279.

"Dustur," *Encyclopedia of Islam* (Leiden: E. J. Brill, 1965).

Egypt. Majlis al-shuyukh. *Al-dustur: ta'liqat 'ala mawadihi bi-l-a'mal al-tahdiriyya wa-l-munaqashat al-barlamaniyya* [The Constitution: Commentaries on its Articles in the Preparatory Works and Parliamentary Discussions] (Cairo: Matba'at misr, 1940).

Egypt. Supreme Constitutional Court. *Al-ahkam* [Judgments] (Cairo: Supreme Constitutional Court, published annually).

Elster, Jon, Claus Offe, and Ulrich K. Reuss with Frank Boenker, Ulrike Goetting, and Friedbert W. Rueb, *Institutional Design in Post-communist Societies: Rebuilding the Ship at Sea* (Cambridge: Cambridge University Press, 1998).

Elster, John and Rune Slagstad (editors), *Constitutionalism and Democracy* (Cambridge: Cambridge University Press, 1988).

Elwan, Shwikar Ibrahim. *Constitutional Democracy and Islam: A Comparative Study*, Ph. D. dissertation, Emory University, 1971.

Enayat, Hamid. *Modern Islamic Political Thought* (Austin: University of Texas Press, 1982).

Entelis, John P. *Comparative Politics of North Africa* (Syracuse: Syracuse University Press, 1980).

Ertman, Thomas. *Birth of the Leviathan: Building States and Regimes in Medieval and Early Modern Europe* (Cambridge: Cambridge University Press, 1997).

Fairbanks, Stephen C. "Theocracy versus Democracy: Iran Considers Political Parties," *Middle East Journal* 52 (1, Winter 1998): 17–31.

Finn, John. *Constitutions in Crisis: Political Violence and the Rule of Law* (New York: Oxford University Press, 1991).

Foreign Broadcast Information Service. "Khomeyni-Created Arbitration Body Undercuts Conservatives," *Trends* 24 February 1988.

———. "Khomeyni Expands Government's Powers, Boosts Radicals' Agenda," *Trends* 27 January 1988.

Foster, Henry A. *The Making of Modern Iraq: A Product of World Forces* (Norman: University of Oklahoma Press, 1935).

Franklin, Daniel P., and Michael J. Baun (editors), *Political Culture and Constitutionalism: A Comparative Approach* (Armonk: M. E. Sharpe, 1995).

Friedrich, Carl. *Constitutional Government and Democracy* (Waltham: Blaisdell, 1968).

———. *Transcendent Justice: The Religious Dimension of Constitutionalism* (Durham: Duke University Press, 1964).

Gallagher, Charles F. "The Moroccan Constitution: Text and Comment," American Universities Field Staff, North Africa Series, Volume IX, No. 2 (Morocco), 1963.

———. "Toward Constitutional Government in Morocco: A Referendum Endorses the Constitution," American Universities Field Staff, North Africa Series, Volume IX, No. 1 (Morocco), 1963.

Gerber, Haim. *Islamic Law and Culture 1600–1840* (Leiden: Brill, 1999).

Ghabra, Shafeeq. "Democratization in a Middle Eastern State: Kuwait, 1993," *Middle East Policy* 3 (1, 1994): 102–119.

———. "Voluntary Associations in Kuwait: The Foundation of a New System," *Middle East Journal* 45 (2, Spring 1991): 199–215.

Ghai, Yash. "The Rule of Law, Legitimacy and Governance," *International Journal of the Sociology of Law* 14 (1986): 179–208.

Ghalab, 'Abd al-Karim. *Al-tatawwur al-dusturi wa-l-niyabi bi-l-maghrib 1908–1992* (Casablanca: Matba'at al-najah al-jadida, 1993), pp. 102–126.

Ghannushi, Rashid. *Al-hurriyyat al-'amma fi al-islam* [Public Freedoms in islam] (Beirut: Markaz dirasat al-wihda al-'arabiyya, 1993).

Ghazzali, Salah al-. *Al-hayah al-dimuqratiyya fi al-kuwayt* [Democratic Life in Kuwait] (Kuwait: National Union of Kuwaiti Students, 1985).

Grazin, Igor. "The Rule of Law: But of Which Law? Natural and Positive Law in Post-Communist Transformation," *John Marshall Law Review* 26 (1993): 719–737.

Gross, Irena Grudzinska (editor), *Constitutionalism and Politics: International Symposium, Bratislava, November 11–14 1993* (Bratislava: Slovak Committee of the European Cultural Foundation, 1994).

Haggard, Stephan, and Robert Kaufman, *The Political Economy of Democratic Transitions* (Princeton: Princeton University Press, 1995).

Hairi, Abdul-Hadi. *Shi'ism and Constitutionalism in Iran: A Study of the Role Played by the Persian Residents of Iraq in Iranian Politics* (Leiden, E. J. Brill, 1977).

Hallaq, Wael B. *Law and Legal Theory in Classical and Medieval Islam* (Aldershot: Valiorum, 1994).

Hamburger, Philip A. "Natural Rights, Natural Law, and American Constitutions," *Yale Law Journal* 102 (4, 1993): 907–960.

Harber, Charles Combs. *Reforms in Tunisia 1855–1878*, Ph.D. dissertation, Ohio State University, 1970.

Hasan, Sa'id al-. *The Concept of the Rules of Public Order in the Political Thought of Hizb al-Tahrir*, M.A. thesis, Department of economics and Political Science, American University in Cairo, October 1989.

Hashmi, Sohail, and Houchang Chehabi (editors), *Islam and Constitutionalism* (forthcoming).

Haydar, Nasrat Munla. "The Role of the Judiciary in Defending Public Rights and Freedoms," unpublished paper, 1993.

Haykal, Muhammad Husayn. *Muzakkirat fi al-siyasa al-misriyya* [Memoirs of Egyptian Politics] (Cairo: Dar al-Ma'arif, 1978).

Herb, Michael. *All in the Family: Absolutism, Revolution, and Democracy in the Middle Eastern Monarchies* (Albany: SUNY Press, 1999).

Heydemann, Steven. *Authoritarianism in Syria: Institutions and Social Conflict 1946–1970* (Ithaca: Cornell University Press, 1999).

Hilal, 'Ali al-Din. *Al-siyasa wa-l-hukm fir misr: al-'ahd al-barlmani 1923–1952* [Politics and Governance in Egypt: The Parliamentary Age 1923-1952] (Cairo: Maktabat al-sharq, 1977).

Hill, Enid. "Al-Sanhuri and Islamic Law," *Cairo Papers in Social Science* 10 (1, 1987): 1–140.

Holt, P. M. (editor). *Political and Social Change in Modern Egypt* (London: Oxford University Press, 1968).

Hooper, C. A. *The Constitutional Law of 'Iraq,* (Baghdad: Mackenzie and Mackenzie, 1928).

Humud, Ibrahim Muhammad al-. "The Effects Resulting from the Parliament's Refusal of Law Number 35/1990, Issued in the Period of the Suspension of Parliamentary Life," *Majallat al-huquq* 18 (3, September 1994): 551–597.

ibn 'Ashur, Rafi'. "The Question of Constitutional Review of Laws and its Development in the End of 1987," *Al-majalla al-qanuniyya al-tunisiyya*, 1988: 9–23

Jackson, Sherman A. "From Prophetic Actions to Constitutional Theory: A Novel Chapter in Medieval Muslim Jurisprudence," *International Journal of Middle East Studies* 25 (1, 1993): 71–90.

Jacobsohn, Gary Jeffrey. *Apple of Gold: Constitutionalism in Israel and the United States* (Princeton: Princeton University Press, 1993).

Jamil, Ahlam Husayn. *Al-khalifyya al-siyasiyya wa-l-ijtima'iyya li-l-awda' allati kan yutabbiq fi thulliha dustur 1925 fi al-'iraq* [The Politial and Social Background to the Conditions in which the Constitution of 1925 in Iraq Were Applied] (Beirut: Al-dar al-'arabiyya li-l-mawsu'at, 1986).

Jerusalem Media and Communication Centre, *The Palestinian Council* (Jerusalem: JMCC, 1996).

Kelsen, Hans. *General Theory of Law and State* (translated by Anders Wedberg, Cambridge: Harvard University Press, 1949).

———. "Judicial Review of Legislation: A Comparative Study of the Austrian and the American Constitution," *Journal of Politics* 4 (May 1942): 183–200.

Khadduri, Majid. "Constitutional Development in Syria," *Middle East Journal* 5 (2, Spring 1951): 137–160.

———, and Herbert J. Liebesny (editors). *Law in the Middle East* (Washington: Middle East Institute, 1955).

Khalidi, Ismail Raghib. *Constitutional Development in Libya* (Beirut: Khayat, 1956).

Khoury, Philip S. *Syria and the French Mandate: The Politics of Arab Nationalism, 1920–1945* (Princeton: Princeton University Press, 1987).

Khuri, Yusuf Qazma. *Al-dasatir fi al-'alim al-'arabi 1839–1987* (Beirut: Dar al-Hamra', 1989).

Kienle, Eberhard. "More than a Response to Islamism: The Political Deliberalization of Egypt in the 1990s," *Middle East Journal* 52 (2, Spring 1998): 219–235.

Kohn, Hans. "The Road to India," *Foreign Affairs* 20 (March 1927): 237.

Lawyers Committee for Human Rights, *Islam and Justice* (New York: Lawyers Committee for Human Rights, 1997).

Lewis, Bernard. *The Emergence of Modern Turkey* (Oxford: Oxford University Press, 1968).

Loewenstein, Karl. *Political Power and the Governmental Process* (Chicago: University of Chicago Press, 1957).

Loveman, Brian. *The Constitution of Tyranny: Regimes of Exception in Spanish America* (Pittsburgh: University of Pittsburgh Press, 1993).

Low, Sidney. *Egypt in Transition* (New York: The Macmillan Company, 1914).

Machacek, Rudolf. *Austrian Contributions to the Rule of Law* (Kehl: N. P. Engel, 1994).

Maddox, Graham. "A Note on the Meaning of Constitution," *American Political Science Review* 76 (December 1982): 805–809.

Mahmasani, Subhi. *Al-dustur wa-l-dimuqratiyya* [Constitution and Democracy], (Beirut: Dar al-'ilm li-l-malayin, 1952).

Majmu'at rasa'il al-imam al-shahid Hasan al-Banna [Collection of Epistles of the Martyred Leader Hasan al-Banna], (Beirut: Dar al-Shihab, 1993).

Mallat, Chibli. "Constitutional Law in the Middle East: The Emergence of Judicial Power," SOAS Law Department, working paper no. 3, February 1993, SOAS, University of London.

———. (editor). *Islam and Public Law* (London: Graham and Troutman, 1993).

———. *The Renewal of Islamic Law* (Cambridge: Cambridge University Press, 1993).

Mayer, Ann Elizabeth. *Islam and Human Rights* (Boulder: Westview Press, 1995).

McIlwain, C. H. *Constitutionalism and the Changing World* (New York: MacMillan, 1939).

Messick, Brinkley. *The Calligraphic State: Textual Domination and History in a Muslim Society* (Berkeley: University of California Press, 1993).

Montesquieu. *The Spirit of the Laws,* edited by David Wallace Carrithers (Berkeley: University of California Press, 1977).

Mosca, Gaetano. *The Ruling Class* (edited and revised by Arthur Livingston, translated by Hannah D. Kahn, New York: McGraw Hill, 1939).

Mottahadeh, Roy. *The Mantle of the Prophet,* (New York: Pantheon, 1985).

Mufti, Malik. "Elite Bargains and the Onset of Political Liberalization in Jordan," *Comparative Political Studies* 32 (1, February 1999): 100–129.

Muhammad, Kahlula. "Constitutional Review in Algeria in the Framework of the Work of the Constitutional Council," *Al-majalla al-jaza'iriyya li-l-'ulum al-qanuniyya wal-iqtisadiyya wa-l-siyasiyya* 28 (3, September 1990): 666.

Muqatti', Muhammad 'Abd al-Muhsin al-. "Ahamiyyat al-ahzab al-siyasiyya li-tatwir al-nizam al-dimuqrati al-kuwayti wa-mashru'iyyatiha al-dusturiyya" [The importance of political parties for the development of the Kuwaiti democratic system and their constitutional legitimacy], unpublished paper presented at the 1997 Cairo Conference on "Democracy and the Rule of Law."

Nabahani, Taqi al-Din. *Al-Nizam al-ijtima'i fi al-islam* [Social Order in Islam] (Jerusalem: Hizb al-Tahrir, 1953).

Nosseir, Abdel Rahman. "The Supreme Constitutional Court of Egypt and the Protection of Human Rights," unpublished paper, 1992.

O'Kane, Joseph P. "Islam in the New Egyptian Constitution: Some Discussions in al-Ahram," *Middle East Journal* 26 (2, 1972): 137–148.

Peters, Rudolph (editor). *Jihad in Classical and Modern Islam : A Reader* (Princeton: Markus Wiener, 1996).

Priestland, Jane (editor). *Records of Jordan 1919–1965* (Slough: Archive Edition, 1996).

Przeworski, Adam. *Democracy and the Market: Political and Economic Reforms in Eastern Europe and Latin America* (New York: Cambridge University Press, 1991).

Publius [Alexander Hamilton, John Jay, and James Madison]. *The Federalist* (New York: Modern Library, n.d.).

Putnam, Robert. *Making Democracy Work* (Princeton: Princeton University Press, 1993).

Qardawi, Yusuf al-. *Fatawi mu'asira, al-juz' al-thani* [Contemporary Fatwas, Part Two], (Mansura: Dar al-wafa' li-l-taba'a wa-l-nashr wa-l-tawzi', 1993).

Quandt, William B. *Revolution and Political Leadership: Algeria, 1954–1968* (Cambridge: MIT Press, 1969).

Qutb, Sayyid. *Milestones* (Cedar Rapids: Mother Mosque Foundation, 1981).

Rawls, John. *The Law of Peoples* (Harvard: Harvard University Press, 1999).

Rohr, John A. "French Constitutionalism and the Administrative State: A Comparative Textual Study," *Administration and Society* 24 (2, August 1992): 224–258.

Rosberg, James H. *Roads to the Rule of Law: The Emergence of an Independent Judiciary in Contemporary Egypt*, Ph.D. dissertation, Department of Political Science, Massachusetts Institute of Technology, 1995.

Rosenn, Keith S. "Brazil's New Constitution: An Exercise in Transient Constitutionalism for a Transitional Society," *American Journal of Comparative Law* 38 (1990): 773–802.

Roth, Brad R. "Constitutionalism in Eastern Europe: Alternatives to the Liberal Social Contract," *Dickinson Journal of International Law* 11 (2, Winter 1993): 283–324.

Rush, A. De L. (editor). *Ruling Families of Arabia. Jordan: The Royal Family of al-Hashim* (Farnham Common: Archive Editions, 1991).

Sadr, Muhammad Baqir al-. *Lamha fiqhiyya tamhidiyya 'an mashru' dustur al-jumhuriyya al-islamiyya fi iran* [A Preparatory Jurisprudential Glimpse of the Draft Constitution of the Islamic Republic of Iran] (n.p., 1399 A.H.).

Salih, 'Uthman 'Abd al-Malik al-. *Al-nizam al-dusturi wa-l-mu'assasat al-siyasiyya fi al-kuwayt* [The Constitutional Order and Political Institutions in Kuwait] (Kuwait: Kuwait Times Press, 1989).

Salmon, J. H. M. "The Legacy of Jean Bodin: Absolutism, Populism or Constitutionalism," *History of Political Thought* 17 (4, 1996): 500–522.

Sartori, Giovanni. "Constitutionalism: A Preliminary Discussion," *American Political Science Review* 56 (4, 1962): 853–864.

Schirazi, Asghar. *The Constitution of Iran: Politics and the State in the Islamic Republic* (London: I. B. Tauris, 1997).

Scholch, Alexander. *Egypt for the Egyptians! The Socio-political Crisis in Egypt 1878–1882* (London: Ithaca Press, 1981).

7 Nuvimbir: Al-thawra al-hadi'a [November 7: The Quiet Revolution], Tunis: Mu'asas-
sat 'abd al-karim bin 'abd allah li-l-nashr wa-l-tawsi', 1992.

Shapiro, Ian. *Democracy's Place* (Ithaca: Cornell University Press, 1996).

Shaw, Stanford J, and Ezel Kural Shaw, *History of the Ottoman Empire and Modern
Turkey, Volume II: Reform, Revolution, and Republic: The Rise of Modern
Turkey, 1808–1975* (Cambridge: Cambridge University Press, 1977).

Shawi, Tawfiq. *Fiqh al-shura wa-l-istishara* [The Jurisprudence of Consultation and
Seeking Advice] (Mansura: Dar al-wafa', 1992).

———. *Siyadat al-shari'a al-islamiyya fi misr* [The Sovereignty of the Islamic Shari'a
in Egypt] (Cairo: Al-zahra' li-l-a'lam al-'arabi, 1986).

Shepard, William E. "Muhammad Sa'id al-'Ashmawi and the Application of the
Shari'a in Egypt," *International Journal of Middle East Studies* 28 (1, February
1996): 39–58.

Siegfried, Nikolaus A. "Legislation and Legitimation in Oman: The Basic Law," *Islamic
Law and Society* 7 (3, October 2000): 359–397.

Sirhal, Ahmad. *Dustur al-jumhuriyya al-lubnaniyya* [Constitution of the Lebanese
Republic], Beirut: Dar al-bahith, 1991.

Sivan, Emmanuel. *Radical Islam* (New Haven: Yale University Press, 1990).

Sohrabi, Nader. "Historicizing Revolution: Constitutional Revolutions in the Ottoman
Empire, Iran, and Russia, 1905–1908," *American Journal of Sociology* 100 (6,
May 1995): 1383–1447.

Spiro, Herbert J. *Government by Constitution: The Political Systems of Democracy* (New
York: Random House, 1959).

Steinmo, Sven Kathleen Thelen, and Frank Longstreth (editors), *Structuring Politics:
Historical Institutionalism in Comparative Analysis* (Cambridge University Press,
1992).

Stjernquist, Nils. "Judicial Review and the Rule of Law: Comparing the United
States and Sweden," Policy Studies Journal 19 (1, Fall 1990): 106–115.

Stone, Alec. "The Birth and Development of Abstract Review: Constitutional Courts
and Policymaking in Western Europe," *Policy Studies Journal 19* (1, Fall 1990):
81–95.

Tabataba'i, 'Adil al-. *Al-nizam al-dusturi fi al-kuwayt* [The Constitutional System in
Kuwait] (Kuwait: n.p., 1994).

———. "The Extent of the Jurisdiction of the National Assembly in Examining
Decree-Laws Issued in the Case of Dissolution", 1994 manuscript [a subsequent version was to be published in the Kuwaiti *Al-muhamah*],

Tell, Christopher, and Jakop Skovgaard-Petersen (editors), *Law and the Islamic World:
Past and Present* (Copenhagen: Royal Danish Academy of Sciences and Letters,
1995).

*The Role of the Constitutional Court in the Consolidation of the Rule of Law: Proceedings
of the UniDem Seminar Organized in Bucharest on 8–10 June 1994 in Co-*

operation with the Romanian Constitutional Court with the Support of the Ministry of Foreign Affairs of Romania (Strasbourg: Council of Europe, 1994).

Thompson, Elizabeth. *Colonial Citizens: Republican Rights, Paternal Privilege, and Gender in French Syria and Lebanon* (New York: Columbia University Press, 2000).

'Umar, 'Abd al-Fattah Qays Sa'id (editors). *Nusus wa-watha'iq siyasiyya tunisiyya* (Tunis: Markaz al-dirasat wal-buhuth wal-nashr bi-kulliyat al-huquq wa-lil-'ulum al-siyasiyya bi-tunis, 1987).

United Kingdom. Colonial Office. *Report by His Britannic Majesty's Government on the Administration of 'Iraq for the Period April, 1923–December 1924* (London: His Majesty's Stationery Office; republished by Archive Editions).

———. *'Iraq. Report on 'Iraq Administration. October, 1920–March, 1922*, (London: His Majesty's Stationery Office; republished by Archive Editions).

'Utayfi, Jamal al-. *Ara' fi al-shari'a wa-fi al-hurriyya* [Opinions on Shari'a and Freedom] (Cairo: Al-hay'a al-misriyya al-'amma li-l-kitab, 1980).

Wheeler, Harvey. "Constitutionalism," in Fred I. Greenstein and Nelson W. Polsby, *Handbook of Political Science* (Reading: AddisonWesley, 1975).

Womble, Theresa Liane. *Early Constitutionalism in Tunisia, 1857–1864: Reform and Revolt*, Ph.D. dissertation, Department of Near Eastern Studies, Princeton University, 1997.

Yacoubian, Mona. "Algeria's Struggle for Democracy: Prospects for Incremental Change," Council on Foreign Relation, Studies Department Occasional Paper Series, Number 3, 1997.

Zamir, Meir. *Lebanon's Quest: The Road to Statehood 1926–1939* (London: I. B. Tauris, 1997).

INDEX

241